It begins here for me on this road. How the whole mess happened, I don't know. But I know it couldn't happen again in a million years. Maybe I could have stopped it early. But once **the trouble was on its way,** I was just going with it. Mostly, I remember the girl. I can't explain it— sad chick like that. But something changed in me. **She got to me.** But that's later, anyway. **This is where it begins for me, right on this road. . . .**

—*The Wild One*, 1953

Get there on a –
HARLEY-
DAVIDSON

HARLEY-DAVIDSON
for 1940

The 80 TWIN shown with 5.00 x 16 tires

'59
HARLEY-DAVIDSON
DUO-GLIDES

finest for you ...
comfort for two

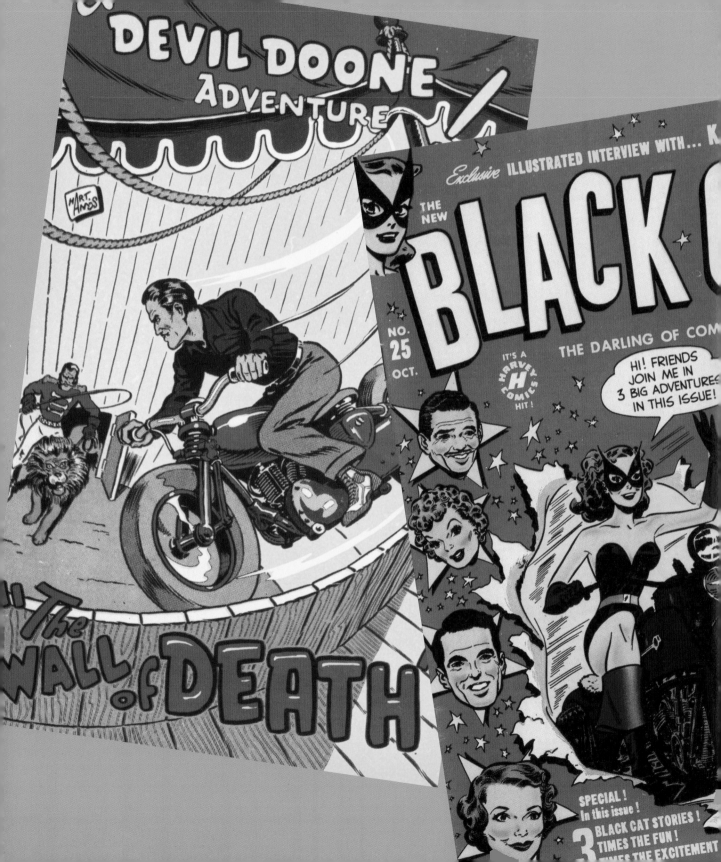

Je n'ai pas besoin personne au Harley-Davidson.

—Brigitte Bardot, "Harley-Davidson"

I'd rather be busted into the wind like a meteorite than just become dust. God made us to live, not just exist. I'm ready.

—Evel Knievel before the Snake River Canyon jump

We seemed to breathe more freely, a lighter air, an air of adventure.

—Che Guevara, *The Motorcycle Diaries*

I pity the poor people who don't ride motorcycles.

—Malcolm Smith

The Lawyer: "They're not scared of you. They're scared of what you represent to them."

Billy: "Hey man, all we represent to them, man, is someone who needs a haircut."

The Lawyer: "Oh no, what you represent to them is freedom."

Billy: "What the hell's wrong with freedom? Man, that's what it's all about."

The Lawyer: "Oh yeah, that's right, that's what it's all about all right. But talking about it and doing it, that's two different things. I mean, it's real hard to be free when you are bought and sold in the marketplace. But don't ever tell anybody that they're not free because then they gonna get real busy killing and maiming to prove to you that they are. Oh yeah, they gonna talk to you and talk to you and talk to you about individual freedom, but when they see a free individual, it's gonna scare 'em."

—*Easy Rider*, 1969

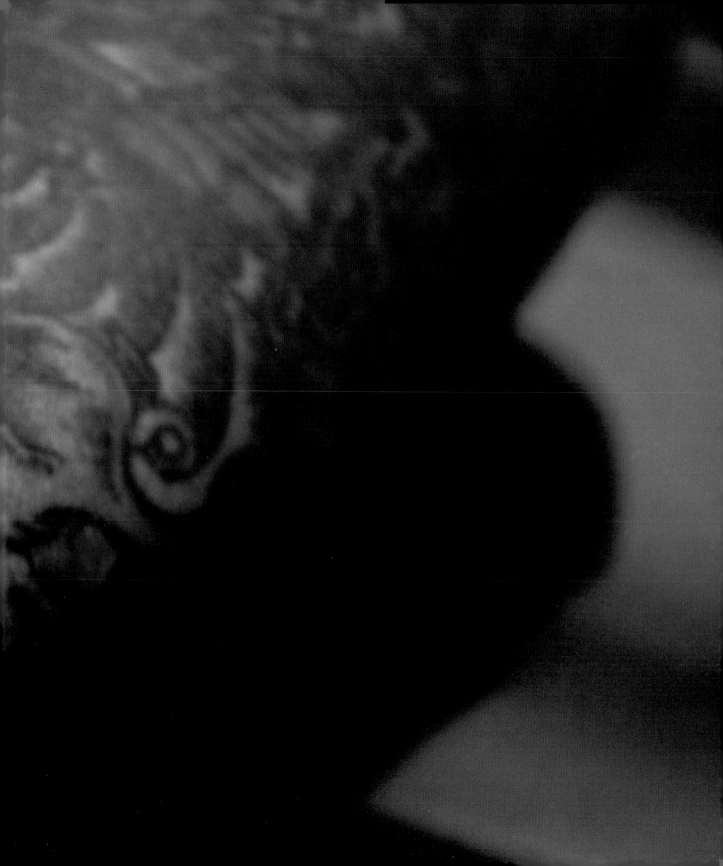

THE
HARLEY-DAVIDSON
READER

Foreword by Jean Davidson
granddaughter of founder Walter Davidson

with
**Hunter S. Thompson, Sonny Barger, Evel Knievel,
Arlen Ness, Peter Egan, Brock Yates, and more**

whitecap

First published in 2006 by Motorbooks, an imprint of MBI Publishing Company, Galtier Plaza, Suite 200, 380 Jackson Street, St. Paul, MN 55101-3885 USA

Published in Canada in 2006 by Whitecap Books Ltd. For more information, contact Whitecap Books Ltd., 351 Lynn Avenue, North Vancouver, British Columbia, Canada V7J 2C4. Visit our website at www.whitecap.ca.

MBI Publishing Company titles are also available at discounts in bulk quantity for industrial or sales-promotional use. For details write to Special Sales Manager at MBI Publishing Company, Galtier Plaza, Suite 200, 380 Jackson Street, St. Paul, MN 55101-3885 USA

ISBN 1-55285-747-6 and ISBN 978-1-55285-747-2

Designer: Maria A. Friedrich

Printed in China

On page 2: Early Harley-Davidson V-twin waiting at ramshackle farm.

On page 3: Enthusiastic Harley-Davidson pilot, circa 1930s.

On pages 4 and 5: Early Harley-Davidson advertising posters. *Courtesy Harley-Davidson*

On pages 6 and 7: Harley-Davidson aces at work. *Photograph © Douglas Craig*

On pages 8 and 9: Comic images of motorcycles through time.

On pages 12 and 13: The Harley-Davidson arm. *Photograph © Russ Bryant.*

On the title pages: The stylish Harley-Davidson rider, circa 1950s.

On page 17: Harley-Davidson as Christmas tree.

On the contents pages: Happy Harley-Davidson owners from the 1910s through the 1950s..

Contents

Foreword

The Harley-Davidson Reader

By Jean Davidson

Throughout time, owning and riding a Harley-Davidson motorcycle has meant different things to the people who love them. It doesn't matter if you are building them, racing them, customizing them, jumping them, or whatever you can think of doing with your Harley-Davidson, each person has his or her own reasons for loving their bike. *The Harley-Davidson Reader* is a collection of writings by some of these people explaining the love affair.

Why does someone get a Harley-Davidson in the first place? This question has been asked over and over. There is not any one answer. After writing my books—*Growing Up Harley-Davidson* and *Jean Davidson's Harley-Davidson Family Album*—I have been traveling around the world and everyone has a different answer. Most of the riders I have talked with tell me there is a wonderful feeling of freedom when they hop on their Harley and go for a ride. They forget the cares of the day and fall into the rhythm of the ride. Pretty soon their worries—whatever they might be—seem to fade into the background of their mind. They can think more clearly. Everything seems so much easier.

People always ask me what the fascination is with owning and riding a Harley. I always answer the same way: Have you ever taken one and gone for a ride? Feeling the wind and the sun on your face makes you feel a part of the environment. Even riding in the rain and snow gives you a feeling of control. You are breaking away from the everyday structure of your job and your responsibilities to do something for yourself. You can choose to ride alone and feel the Zen of riding or you can ride in a group, giving you a feeling of being with friends doing what you all love.

For many, riding a Harley is about making a statement. It is an extension of who you are and what you love. You can customize your bike in anyway you choose, showing the world your own uniqueness. All the choices are your own. It is all about freedom...

The Harley-Davidson Reader is also a collection of writings that explore the many different aspects of what people call the "Harley-Davidson legend." The legend for me is one of pride. I am the granddaughter of Walter Davidson, who was one of the founders and the first president of the Harley-Davidson Motor Company. Every time I see the name Harley-Davidson on anything from a motorcycle to a tattoo, I smile, remembering how it all started in my great-grandparents' basement.

My grandfather, Watlter, his brothers Arthur and William and their best friend William Harley were young boys whose parents were immigrants from Scotland and England. When not in school, their favorite pastime was to go fishing. They rode their bicycles, but it was a long way to the lake. They thought if they could put a motor on a bicycle they wouldn't have to pedal so hard—and have some fun along the way. It all started out so simply. Their friendship and ethics grew their small company into what is now beloved the world over. The main reason for this is that the Harley and Davidson founders and their children were devoted to making quality motorcycles.

The legend started way back at the beginning, and its been building ever since. Even in the tough years, they tried to keep everyone together and the business growing. My father was Gordon Davidson, vice president of manufacturing, and I never found it strange to come home and find motorcycle racers in our kitchen. Later on, getting to know Evel Knievel and hearing about Elvis and his love of the Harley-Davidson seemed like everyday happenings.

I am often asked what the founders would think about today's growth of the legend and how many ways their motorcycle have enhanced people's lives. I know they would be proud of the quality and the love people have for their bikes. I don't think much is different than the early years, for the people back then loved their motorcycles just as much. One of the fastest growing groups of riders is women of all ages. Being a woman myself and growing up when few women rode; I am thrilled to see this new side of independence.

Enjoy this book with the many different aspects of riding a Harley-Davidson, and let me know your own experience.

Rat bike meets the law of the land, from a 1935 magazine cover.

Chapter 1

First
Contact

Don't you know
you can get the same
sensations by
tying
firecrackers
to your legs and sitting
over an oil heater?

—*Collier's* magazine, 1913

Outlaw Machine

By Brock Yates

Brock Yates is himself a legend. His résumé reads at times like a rap sheet, as he was the brains—no, the mad scientist—behind the infamous Cannonball Sea-to-Shining-Sea Memorial Trophy Dash as well as the author of numerous articles and books chronicling his love affair with automobiles and motorcycles.

Brock is an editor at large for *Car and Driver* and has also written for magazines as diverse as *Playboy* and *American Heritage*, *Sports Illustrated*, *Life*, and *Reader's Digest*. His books include *Cannonball! World's Greatest Outlaw Road Race* and *The Hot Rod: Resurrection of a Legend*, both published by Motorbooks International.

Yet it was in his 1999 book *Outlaw Machine: Harley-Davidson and the Search for the American Soul* that Brock put his finger on the pulse of all things Harley. This excerpt mirrors many people's first contact with the legend.

The noise. The god-awful death rattle issuing from the bowels of his infernal machine. He had been a quiet kid, one of those bashful back-markers in elementary school, a pasty-faced runt lost in the playground stampedes and the adolescent classroom chatter. Now, suddenly, as a junior in high school, he had reinvented himself, a transmogrification of quasi-lethal intensity.

Among the brush-cut and bobby-soxed hierarchy of 1950s teenage life, he cut a wide swath, swooping among the Goody Twoshoes aboard his black-and-chrome monster. Wrapped in a wide-collared leather jacket studded with chrome, he was someone to be reckoned with, a stern-faced stud on a bad-ass motorcycle.

His classmates watched him in a confused state of part scorn, part envy, from the vantage point of establishment tools: teenagers operating in the mainstream of conventional lusts over fast cars and faster women. But the notion of a motorcycle—no, make that a Harley-Davidson motorcycle—was beyond the pale, drifting into the lurid red-light districts occupied by the devil drug, marijuana, and the white-slave trade. Other guys tried the zooter gig, fashioning themselves in duck's-ass haircuts and peg pants in open defiance of the conventions of khaki and gray flannel—the Fonzie-like prototypes later to be immortalized in *Grease* and other fifties flashbacks. But the over-the-top gesture, the ultimate fuck-you to the straight arrows and suck-ups of the day was that motherhumper Harley from hell.

"Wheels" of any kind beyond a Schwinn was the ultimate guy fantasy. Decades would pass before the booming middle class could afford to outfit its high-schoolers with automobiles, much less anything as exotic as motorcycles. The periodicals of the early 1950s swooned over the alleged menace of "hot-rodders," a California manifestation involving youths aboard chopped and channeled flathead Fords who engaged in such sociopathic madness as "drag racing" and death-defying games of "chicken." These exotic little home-built machines, hacksawed out of prewar Fords, were viewed as a motorized expression of the newly discovered teenage species known as "juvenile delinquents." This alleged rabble, sporting T-shirts with Camel packs rolled into the sleeves, represented a new surge of Visigoths marauding through the nation's streets. The dreaded hot rods (a contraction of "hot roadster") would be chronicled in countless hysterical magazine and newspaper stories of the day, culminating in the 1955 cult film *Rebel Without a Cause*, starring that paradigm of 1950s punkdom, James Dean. Drag racing, as portrayed in the film's deadly duel, shook moms and pops out of their Barcaloungers from coast to coast. Images of every kid in America behind the wheel of a hopped-up Ford or, God forbid, a thundering Harley slashing through the suburbs at suicidal speeds, seared their suburbanite brains. Hot rods. Motorcycles. Leather jackets, and in the distance the fearsome tribal drumbeats of rock 'n' roll. The fall of Rome was upon them.

Among the foot-sloggers, the kid on the Harley-Davidson enjoyed an automatic status reserved for those with "wheels" of all types, but in his case they belonged to a mysterious, exotic and faintly ominous, flame-belching motorcycle. A scrubbed classmate from the suburbs was also among the anointed, but purely as a midget leaguer. Somehow he had talked his father into letting him buy a used, clapped-out motor scooter, a lumpy Cushman powered by a one-lung lawnmower engine. On days when he rode it to school, he parked it near the Harley, a dinghy moored in the shadow of that battleship, unworthy of notice by the ship's owner.

Early
Harley-Davidson
V-twin packed
for shipping.

The Harley guy would leave class, cloaked in his leather armor on even the warmest days, and stride past the Cushman in total disdain. Legging over the Harley, he fiddled briefly with the fuel valve and the choke before commencing his ritual attack on the kick starter, leaping and cursing as his booted foot rocked up and down on the chromium lever. The monster would fart and grumble, fitfully barking in protest against the intrusion by its master. Finally, after minutes of refusal, the mighty engine would awaken, spewing clouds of raw gas and fire from its twin pipes, rattling windows and sending decent folk scurrying,

their ears covered against the din. Once satisfied that the beast was awake, he would settle into its saddle and, rolling his gloved right hand on the handlebar throttle, rev the engine until the plugs cleared and the last living creature within earshot had been intimidated. Then, with his left hand he would reach for the shifter, jam the thing into gear, and roar away, weaving and yawing in a shower of gravel. To the witless squares who knew no such power, it was like witnessing a moon shot almost twenty years hence.

Properly costumed, he had become a member of a tiny, exclusive clique headquartered in a grease-stained

A pioneer Harley-Davidson dealer shows of his wares.

warren on the edge of town. There a strange, lanky man ran a dealership for Harley-Davidson motorcycles. It was off-limits to decent folk, a corral for outriders and bandits, bikers and weirdos who rode motorcycles, more a collection of shacks than a real building. The floors were soaked black with motor oil and littered with shards of piston rings, broken chains, shattered cylinder heads, and bent forks—the effluvia of a thousand haphazard repairs. Outside leaned a rabble of old motorcycles, bare-boned frames, piles of shredded tires, and broken engines, a graveyard of outlaw machinery tended by the gaunt man who knew all and was all regarding motorcycles—the high priest in the smoky Harley temple.

One day the suburbanite ventured into the forbidden place, naively searching for a part for his Cushman. This was akin to asking the gunnery officer on the USS *Missouri* for a box of BBs. A Cushman motor scooter in a Harley-Davidson store? Send in the clowns! What's that pie-faced twit doing intruding with that puny, gutless slug among real men's machines? The dealer slouched inside, appearing nearly as filthy as the soot-stained walls. He grunted a response to the kid's question, barely deigning to deal with

Classic biker "literature" from the 1910s through the 1970s.

35c

CHARLES RUNYON

Behind them a murdered man. Ahead of them
a lot of loving, lying, speeding and spending.

GOLD
MEDAL
s1268

THE
DEATH CYCLE

NEW ENGLISH LIBRARY

THE BIKE
FROM HELL

By Alex R. Stuart
author of "The Devil's Rider".

NEW ENGLISH LIBRARY

THE DEVIL'S
RIDER

By Alex R. Stuart

THE BLACK LEATHER
BARBARIANS

50c

A SIGNET BOOK • D3277

BY PAT STADLEY
"A ROUGH, REVEALING NOVEL
OF YOUTHFUL CALIFORNIA
MOTORCYCLISTS AND WHAT
MAKES THEM ROAR."
—SAN FRANCISCO CRONICLE

a noncultist. Other men lurked against the workbenches. They wore grimy denims and sported heavy engineer's boots gleaming with caked motor oil. They smoked heavily, filling the morbid room with gray clouds that mingled with the belching and backfiring of the Harley they were attempting to tune with large screwdrivers. The outlander had clearly stifled conversation, and it would remain so until he departed, leaving them to stand in silent witness to the rattle-bone thud of the big machine under the dealer's crude ministrations. The kid never returned. Nor did anyone he knew who was considered a member of decent society ever enter those dreaded precincts.

Who were those men? The term "biker" would not become part of the national slang for another decade, and they were therefore nameless outriders—supplicants to a small but true faith centered around a brutish machine that fit between their legs. Most rode Harley-Davidsons, but others traveled on giant Indians—a similar large American-made motorcycle that remained a steadfast rival, albeit with sagging sales and loyalties. While hard-edged motorcycle gangs were at the time forming in California, the notion of outlaw organizations coalescing around Harleys and Indians in dinky cities was unthinkable. Motorcycle gangs might exist in sybaritic California, where debauched movie stars and other bohemians played their evil games, but not in the great heartland, where motorcycles sputtered on the dark and mysterious perimeter. For most Americans banditry as defined by such strange and frightful cults as the Hell's Angels was still beyond their ken in the early 1950s.

The men who hung around the little motorcycle shop were for the most part lost souls: disoriented and disillusioned WWII veterans, functioning alcoholics, unemployed factory workers, and a few rebellious teenagers, all of whom found solace in the radiated strength of the big bikes. Power was available at the kick of the leg and the flick of the wrist. Equality came at the end of an exhaust pipe, and every Buick-driving Babbitt better know it. Still, the riders were marginalized, meaningless and essentially ignored, crackpots who dressed strangely and hung out in sleazy bars and rode noisy motorcycles. Fringe players in the grand American scheme whose sullen expressions of independence seemed harmless and irrelevant. Beyond the noise and bluster of their blowsy motorcycles, who cared about them, save for a few addled teenagers who retained a fearful fascination for their monster machines?

The suburbanite fitfully tried to keep up with his Harley-rider classmate, wrestling as he could against middle-class conventions but lacking the money, much less the social chutzpah, to make the leap aboard a Harley—which, truth be known, he and his peers viewed with a combination of fear and lurid fascination. He managed to marshal sufficient funds by selling the Cushman to obtain a tiny Czechoslovakian CZ-125, with a cylinder barely as large as a Harley carburetor but still a legitimate motorcycle. It would be a source of considerable pride for him to later learn that in fact James Dean himself had entered the world of bikes on a sister unit, rising then into fast British twins before killing himself behind the wheel of a Porsche 550 Spyder sports-racing car. Still, it was not enough. The Harley-Davidsons—with their seventy-four-cubic-inch "Knucklehead" engines—larger than the sixty-seven-cubic-inch power plants of the Volkswagen Beetles that were beginning to arrive on these shores—remained alone; the baddest, grumpiest, surliest motorcycles on earth.

So what if any number of Brit bikes, BSAs, Triumphs, Nortons, et al., could wax a Harley in a head-to-head race? So what if Harleys leaked oil like sieves and burned valves and warped their cylinder heads? So what if their tub-thumping exhausts infuriated proper folk? So what if only the lower orders rode and coveted them? So what if Harley-Davidson was not a nice machine? So what if the people who rode them scared the wee-wee out of the good burghers? Wasn't that the point?

His CZ-125 was eventually traded for a collection of used sports cars and the rigors of family raising and career chasing. So too for his classmate on the Harley, who gave up his leathers for white perma-press shirts—complete with plastic mechanical pencil holders—and an engineering career in that paradigm of establishmentarianism, General Motors.

His short-lived rebellion was over, and his old Harley had no doubt ended up on the rubble pile behind the shop, now long since demolished and replaced by a miniature golf course and driving range. But his statement had been made, and it would play a minuscule role in the expanding legend of Harley-Davidson, which was about to become one of those precious few machines elevated beyond mere function to the apotheosis of a globe-spanning lifestyle. Its role is a curious one, a duality of good and evil, of raffish innocence and snarling pugnacity. No other icon of the machine age, be it a Ferrari or a Porsche automobile, a rare World War II fighter plane, or a megapriced, English-built Vincent Black Shadow motorcycle, possesses this ambiguity of purpose.

Harley-Davidson prospers worldwide, thanks to its lofty status. It has a patina of history and tradition that cannot be created even by the canniest and most creative of advertising wizards. It is hardly the most technologically advanced or best performing of its breed. Quite to the contrary. The current Harley-Davidson is in essence an antique. Its basic design dates back to 1936 and, in a broad engineering sense, to a French twin-cylinder concept developed at the end of the nineteenth century. It is the perfect flintlock rifle. The world's most refined sundial. But with that antiquity comes tradition and a storied continuity that defies imitation. The Japanese—long masters of the art of creating high-performance engines and capable of making vastly superior motorcycles of all kinds—are frantically dumbing down their product lines in slavish attempts to build faux Harley-Davidsons. The results are perfect replications of the venerable Milwaukee original, but hopeless and hollow gestures. They bring nothing to the table to counter Harley's near century-old aura.

Within that essentially hundred-year saga lies a series of stops and starts and the elements of both success and failure. Contradictions abound, and in a broad sense this grand old machine's persona broadly represents that of the nation that created it—and that radiates its personality around the globe. Rooted in Milwaukee, Harley-Davidson symbolizes the best and the worst of a nation whose growth has been fitful, rebellious, disjointed, and cursed by raging crosscurrents and blurred imagery. If perception equals reality, the source of the Harley mystique begins not with the founding of the company in 1903 by the brothers Davidson, Arthur, William, and Walter, and their friend William Harley, but rather in a steamy farming town in Northern California on Independence Day, 1947.

Early Harley-Davidson dealership, with bicycles pushed to the side and neat rows of new V-twins awaiting buyers.

First Harley

By Peter Egan

Peter Egan has become a sort of garage prophet of motorcyclists. He is equal parts sage and common man, imparting wisdom from the school of hard knocks and relating tales of motorcycling culture chock full of universal truths.

As a columnist and writer for *Cycle World* magazine, Peter Egan boasts one of the best deals going: He actually gets paid to ride motorcycles. In fact, Peter's columns for both Cycle World and Road & Track are the favorite reads of many two- and four-wheel enthusiasts, at times garnering more mail to both magazines than the rest of the editorial content combined.

From Triumphs to Ducatis, BMWs to Vincents, Peter is enamoured with a wide array of makes and models of cycles beyond Harley-Davidson. In this reminiscence, however, he chronicles the circumstances that led him to the Milwaukee fold.

My first Harley? Well, I confess that I did not buy a Harley-Davidson from an actual dealer until 1990, when the product had been made safe from catastrophic mechanical failure by the arrival of the Evolution engine and a decade of hard work by Harley engineers, who strove earnestly to improve quality.

I bought a 1990 883 Sportster, brand new, from a local dealer, then moved up to a 1994 Electra-Glide Sport, which got bartered into an emerald-green 1998 Road King. So I am a latecomer to H-D ownership, but not to Harley exposure.

In truth, the first motorcycles I ever saw, rode upon, and *tried* to buy were all Harleys, right from the early fifties onward. Let me explain.

When my parents moved our family from St. Paul, Minnesota, to the small Wisconsin town of Elroy (pop. 1,503) in 1952, we temporarily rented the upstairs of a house from a widow and her son, Buford. Buford had just returned, unscathed, from the Korean War and belonged to that slightly sullen, restless, pre–rock 'n' roll generation of rebels who felt something was not quite right in their lives, but didn't know what. Maybe it was the H-bomb threat, or the inexplicable cancer of world Communism and the bleak, unromantic police work needed to contain it.

In any case, Buford had a Harley-Davidson, which he parked just outside our back stairs. I was only four at the time and didn't know one motorcycle from another, but this one was no doubt a full-boat Panhead, which I remember as having leather saddlebags and a large, sprung buddy seat, all with more conchos than the Cisco Kid's saddle and gunbelt put together. It also had a full windshield with a Vicks-bottle blue lower half, a tank-shift knob, and tires as big as something off a car.

Buford and his mother used to argue a lot about his motorcycle, the late hours he kept, and his bad friends. When this happened, Buford would slam the back door, climb on the motorcycle, give it a mighty kick, set his black sea-captain's hat just so on his head, light a cigarette, and bellow off down the street, with the cigarette sparkling like a firecracker fuse. His mother would stand on the back stoop, shouting until he was out of sight.

When he returned in the wee hours of the morning, she would reappear on the back stoop like a mechanical *glockenspiel* figure and resume shouting where she'd left off.

Sometimes Buford's mother visited our upstairs apartment and complained about her son to my mother. She would turn her head to one side, scuff her hands off one another like someone playing the cymbals, and moan, "Ohhh, Buford and them *motor*-sickles!"

I was naturally drawn to the excitement of the big Harley (and the miracle of human balance it required), and I spent a lot of time gazing at the bike and watching Buford work on it in his dungarees, engineer boots, and white T-shirt.

One day while I was doing this, I told Buford I really liked his motorcycle. He nodded, and then—as if suddenly struck by a terrible thought—he crouched down, grabbed me by the shoulders, and looked into my face. He squinted at me with one eye (the other one forced closed by smoke streaming upward from his ever-present Lucky Strike) and said fiercely, "Don't ever buy an Indian! Buy a Harley."

I assured him I wouldn't.

As it turned out, the Indian factory went out of business the next year, when I was five years old, so the temptation never materialized.

In fact, I managed to get through the entire decade without so much as a ride on a motorcycle—or a two-wheeled vehicle of any kind. But in 1961 my luck finally changed.

At thirteen, I had become a certified car nut and used to spend my Saturdays hitch-hiking to junkyards all over the county so I could sit in old cars and look at them and assess their street-rod and stock-car potential. I was doing this one fine autumn weekend, standing by the side of Highway 80 between Elroy and New Lisbon, Wisconsin, with my thumb out, trying to bum a ride to a New Lisbon wrecking yard.

Suddenly, a couple of full-dress Harleys roared by and, to my amazement, immediately pulled over and stopped. Or at least one of them did. The other guy took longer to slow down and stop. He wasn't sure it was such a good idea.

"What are you doing?" he said, looking back at his buddy with a pained expression.

"Come on," his pal said, "let's give the kid a ride."

Both guys lit cigarettes (which at that time virtually everyone did during any brief moment of pause) and the friendly one slid forward on his fringed buddy seat and said, "Hop on, kid." He tilted his cap just right, gunned the big Panhead a few times, and we were off.

On the way to New Lisbon I looked over his shoulder, with tears streaming from my eyes in the wind, and saw we were doing an indicated 80 mph on the big round speedometer in the middle of his gas tank. I looked around myself at the passing landscape as we sped down the road and thought, *This is the finest moment of my life; the best thing I've ever done.*

By the time we got to New Lisbon, I was a goner. If these two guys had told me they were going to Denver or California, I would have said "That's exactly where I'm going," and faced the consequences later. (Hi, Mom? Is this you? I'm at a phone booth in North Platte. Listen, I just had to *ride . . . .*")

Fortunately, they were only going to the Harley dealer in New Lisbon, a small shop at the south edge of town. By the time we got there, I didn't want to go to the junkyard any more; I just wanted to be in a shop where motorcycles could be found. Some idling gear in my brain had rotated into position and positively engaged the concept of owning my own motorcycle, the sooner the better.

I spent the rest of the afternoon hanging around in the shadows of the dark, greasy shop as inconspicuously as possible, listening to the talk, looking at bikes, absorbing information, checking out piles of dusty parts, and watching half-disassembled gearboxes and engines drool 60-weight oil into cakepans and sawdust.

It was a whole new world, discovering the engine room of your ship, whose massive crankshaft and pistons made it possible to ply the open seas and travel anywhere on earth. One was immediately connected to the other and they couldn't be separated. Not at that time, anyway. Motorcyclists were mechanics.

This would change when Japanese bikes began to arrive in some numbers a few years later, but in 1961 I was visiting the last of the old-time motorcycle shops, undisturbed by progress, "the nicest people," or my own generation's coming of age.

I visited the shop many times after that, and in 1963 I saw an old Harley for sale at a gas station in the nearby village of Union Center. It was a battered 45-inch flathead, a WLA war surplus Army bike that had been repainted in a kind of dull primer red. Everything was

Happy Harley-Davidson riders of all ages on all styles of machines.

The Silent Gray Fellows: Father and son Harley-Davidson riders, circa 1910s.

red—wheels, spokes, tank, even the sidewalls of the tires. A sloppy spray-can job. But it was a real Harley, and it ran. Or so I was told. The gas station owner wanted $100 for it.

He started it up and I took my first ever motorcycle ride. I was too young (fifteen) to take it on the highway, so I rode down a gravel farm road and did a big lap around a nearby cow pasture. Surprisingly, I was able to operate the foot clutch, hand throttle and tank shift okay (hours and hours of imaginary practice), but had a moment of hesitation with the brakes and ran into a couple of empty oil drums behind the gas station and fell over on the bike's crashbars.

No damage was done and I got the Harley back on its wheels just as the owner—who was building a stock car—came running around the corner with a welding mask tipped up on his head. "What was all that noise?"

"Nothing. I just bumped into an oil drum."

He glared at me uneasily.

I told him I'd buy the bike, and went home to get my meager savings out of the bank and then to sell my .410 shotgun and the Briggs & Stratton–powered mini bike I'd built. Within a couple of weeks, I had the hundred dollars and returned to the gas station.

"I've changed my mind," the man said, without looking up from his work. "I'm going to keep the Harley."

And that was the end of attempted Harley ownership for another twenty-seven years. Instead of the Harley 45, I bought a little Bridgestone 50 Sport, brand new, from the local hardware store. From 45 cubic inches (750 cc) to 50 cc displacement, in one fell swoop. After that, I worked my way upward through a series of Hondas, Triumphs, Nortons, Ducatis, etc.

A friend once said to me, "Your life might have been quite different if you'd bought that Harley instead of the Bridgestone 50. You might have had different experiences, a different outlook, completely different friends . . ."

I don't know how much of that is true. Our friends are our friends. But the open road might have been a lot more inviting—at least in my imagination—on a big Harley than it was on that Bridgestone 50 with its shoulder-hugging top speed of 37 mph. I might have gone to Denver, or even California instead of just buzzing around town and visiting my pals on nearby farms. Maybe the difference between Jack Kerouac and the rest of us was only a sense of scale, or picking the right first bike.

The Old Bike in the Barn, or, What My Folks Didn't Know, Didn't Hurt . . . Me

By Allan Girdler

Allan Girdler has probably logged more miles on a Harley XR-750 than just about anyone. Although Jay Springsteen might beat him around a half-mile dirttrack and Ricky Graham probably has more race jewelry on display in his den, Allan has vintage-raced his own iron XR-750 for years—and even toured on it for goodness sakes.

Allan is a former editor of Car Life and Cycle World as well as an executive editor of Road & Track magazines. He is also the author of an eclectic blend of books on motoring history, from his well-known Harley-Davidson: The American Motorcycle, Harley Racers, The Harley-Davidson and Indian Wars, Illustrated Harley-Davidson Buyer's Guide, and Harley-Davidson XR-750 to tomes on NASCAR and sports-racing specials.

His fascination with motorcycles had humble beginnings, however, as he relates in this classic tale of a bike found in a barn.

When I first sat down to recount—better make that confess—how I got my first motorcycle, taught myself to ride, and didn't tell my folks what I was up to, I thought, Gee, maybe I'd better put in something along the lines of "Kids, don't try this at home."

And then I thought, Naw, history tells us that Gottleib Daimler, builder of the first gas-powered motorcycle, waited until his wife was away before that machine's first test, proving to me at least that if we waited for parental permission or approval, there wouldn't be any motorcycles.

So, kids of all ages, I'm not telling you to try this at home, all I'm saying is I did it, I got away with it, my life has never been the same, and I'm glad I did it.

What I did began the summer I was seventeen, with a call from my best friend, also seventeen and also lacking in common sense. Our mutual interest was in finding derelict Fords, hauling them home and souping them up.

He'd been reading the classifieds and found an ad for a 1934 Harley-Davidson and he wanted me to come help him look at it.

I'd admired motorcycles from a distance and once crashed my cousin's motor scooter into a hedge when I swerved to avoid a passing police car, but my motorcycle knowledge totaled zero, same as his. Seemed to me that two times nothing is nothing, as the song says, but I was game to look and learn.

The seller was a couple of years older than us and vastly experienced. He gave us a short tour, as in "That's the clutch, that's the gearshift, that's the front brake, and that's the throttle," and he clearly figured that was all we needed to know.

We figured the same. When I say now that the 1934 Harley-Davidson had a foot clutch and hand shift, it sounds odd if not impossible. But Harleys, and Indians, used the system until after World War II and although new bikes had hand clutches and foot shifts when we paid this visit, we didn't know that 'cause we didn't know anything about motorcycles.

How little? My pal swung a leg over the bike, unfolded the kick lever, reared up in the air, and gave a mighty heave down.

It hadn't occurred to him that the bike might be in gear, which of course it was. And for the only time in our acquaintance, the old Harley fired on the first kick.

It had been parked in the garage, facing in, and when the engine caught the bike leaped forward, climbed the garage's back wall, and described a perfect half gainer, straight up, then arcing gracefully over and down.

My pal had thoughtfully placed himself between the falling motorcycle and the garage floor, so the bike wasn't damaged.

He was bruised, scraped, and completely uninterested in learning any more about motorcycles.

I was enthralled. I thought this motorcycle was the most wonderful device I'd ever seen, so I anted up the asking price of $50—oh, wait a bit.

Might be useful here to pause for another explanation. When people hear I bought a classic old antique Harley-Davidson for pocket change, they assume that I was smarter than other people, getting this wonderful classic for next to nothing, and they usually wonder, do I regret not having kept it?

No. I didn't buy a collectible antique. What I bought was a clapped-out piece of old iron that nobody else wanted, which is why it was so cheap.

This occurred so long ago, 1954 if you need to know, that not only was nostalgia not as good then as it is now, nostalgia hadn't been invented yet.

What we've done since is shift our focus, so nowadays the folks with too much money are buying old Harleys and the kids with no money are buying obsolete motocross bikes for $50 and learning the hard way how they work.

Which is exactly what I did back then, wobbling home on a motorcycle older than me, stalling the engine and grinding gears until I learned how to coordinate the controls.

That was the easy part.

The part I really had trouble with was, I didn't have to ask to know what mom and dad would say to a motorcycle. My folks came of age in hard times. They were not, as we say now, risk-takers. They didn't have to know even as much as I did to know there were reasons people spoke of murdercycles.

(Years and years later, my dad admitted that his uncle Pat—the family daredevil and, I surmised, ne'er-do-well—rode an Indian. But this wasn't something said in public or when children were present.)

But by happy chance one of my brothers hoped to ride rodeo and he kept his cutting horse in a remote barn up the road, so that's where I put the Harley. There was enough space for me and my brothers to practice starts and stops and riding in circles: One of my treasured childhood images is my younger brother rising into the air above the machine, describing a graceful arc and landing, head-first, in front of the front wheel. The old 74 had quite a kick when you neglected, as my brother had, to retard the spark before leaping on the start lever.

And I ventured out on the open road. I did have a driver's license and I sort of think now there was no motorcycle requirement in my home state then. And the Harley was registered, albeit not to me: I was a minor, after all. Nor did the thought of insurance trouble me. I simply didn't have any.

Oh, one reason I never found out about the legal concerns was that I never got stopped, and I never got stopped I think now because I wasn't wearing a helmet—kids, don't pay attention to this part—and I didn't get stopped because all the cops in that part of the state knew me, because when I was sixteen I looked twelve and when I first got my license I was stopped thirty times in the first thirty-one days I went public with my old Ford, which had lots of carburetors, exhaust pipes sticking out the side, no hood, no top, and no fenders. The police must have figured it was just that loopy kid doing another dumb thing, which of course I was doing. They simply didn't know the degree of dumb, is all.

I had two partners in this foolishness. One was the errant son of an old-money family, whose name you'd recognize if I gave it, which I won't because ratting on pals isn't done in my circle. He had an Indian older than my Harley. The second bike nut was a kid from the docks, who'd quit school and made enough to buy a new Harley-Davidson, the sports model, painted bright red.

Thank goodness.

The thanks are because there I was, rumbling down the only road through our little town when I passed . . . Grandma.

Gulp. As it happened, Grandma was cool, I mean she drove a Barracuda, no kidding. But she was still Grandma and she looked at me and I waved—put on a bold face, I told myself—and she waved back.

She got home before I did, which I know because Mom was at the door.

"Grandma says you passed her, on a big, red motorcycle."

"Oh yeah," I said as the perfect fib occurred to me, "I was on Rocky's bike. I wanted to learn how."

Rocky was a member of the Fix Or Repair Daily Club, so Mom had seen his motorcycle, which was undeniably red, so she delivered Safety Lecture #4, and that was that.

And anyway, I did want to learn how, which I did. Tipped over some but didn't crash, I think now because I was so intimated I didn't take the chances that lead to disaster.

When the registration expired, though, the fun stopped. I knew that would be noticed and I'd be stopped and my goose would be Christmas dinner. I gave the old Harley, still working well, to another pal and what happened to the machine after that, I don't know.

Years and years later I had occasion to ride an Indian from the era of my first Harley, as in foot clutch, hand shift, brakes engineered to not stop you without a lot of warning first, and I thought, This is impossible.

How lucky I was to not have known how tough it was, back then, 'cause if I'd known it was this difficult, I wouldn't have tried it.

And I would have missed the best part.

"Oh yeah," I said as the perfect fib occurred to me, "I was on Rocky's bike. I wanted to learn how."

Rocky was a member of the Fix Or Repair Daily Club, so Mom had seen his motorcycle, which was undeniably red, so she delivered Safety Lecture #4, and that was that.

And anyway, I did want to learn how, which I did. Tipped over some but didn't crash, I think now because I was so intimated I didn't take the chances that lead to disaster.

When the registration expired, though, the fun stopped. I knew that would be noticed and I'd be stopped and my goose would be Christmas dinner. I gave the old

The Harley-Davidson faithful line up in front of their local dealership.

Harley, still working well, to another pal and what happened to the machine after that, I don't know.

Years and years later I had occasion to ride an Indian from the era of my first Harley, as in foot clutch, hand shift, brakes engineered to not stop you without a lot of warning first, and I thought, This is impossible.

How lucky I was to not have known how tough it was, back then, 'cause if I'd known it was this difficult, I wouldn't have tried it.

And I would have missed the best part.

Chapter 2

Birth of the Legend

These bike riders are not the daredevil, death-defying citizens that they appear to be. They are quiet, unassuming men, who go to extremes of care and safety. . . . Motorcyclists eat and sleep and talk like other folks, but at times they can't help feeling that they haven't as long to live as the ordinary man. And they are right.

They are a **fearless** lot, **brave enough to wear their lives on their sleeves,** and have nerves as unimpressionable as flint.

—*The New York Times*, 1913

Cracking the Harley Code:

Myth and Mystery of the First Harley-Davidson Motorcycle, 1901–1905

By Herbert Wagner

Herbert Wagner is equal parts Harley-Davidson scholar and sleuth—a necessary combination for tracing the long road traveled by the world's most famous motorcycle.

Herbert is one of the preeminent experts on early Harley-Davidsons. The author of several books on H-D history, his most famous—or infamous, depending on how you look at it—work is *At the Creation: Myth, Reality, and the Origins of the Harley-Davidson Motorcycle 1901–1909*.

Here, Herbert summarizes the fantastic tale of the creation of the first Harley-Davidson motorcycles.

Grandfather and the Davidson brothers were always forging ahead and rarely looked back. Compiling the company's history was left for others to do, sometimes leading to **unpredictable** and **dubious** results.

—John E. Harley, Jr.

We like to think we're sharp today. That we don't swallow all the advertising hype that motorcycle companies dish out. Not in this age of phony gas tanks and chopper branding plastered on toys, perfume bottles, and video games. We know that marketing honchos bend reality and truth like stage magicians in order to sell their products.

But have you ever wondered how far back the Harley-Davidson Motor Company has used myth and exaggeration to help sell its products?

The answer to that question makes a very good story, although a touchy one. Because already in the first decade of Harley's existence we find a glaring example of such illusionary marketing techniques. In fact, the traditional "Built Three Motorcycles in 1903" origin story that we all know by heart is actually an early episode of adver-

tising hype. All of us, including generations of Harley historians, have been snookered by a myth.

These findings are the result of a decade worth of research and fully documented in my 2003 book on early Harley-Davidson, *At the Creation.* To relate that story in a nut-shell we need first revisit the *official* origin account quoted from the current (2005) Motor Company website.

The year is "1901" and William S. Harley "completes a blueprint drawing of an engine designed to fit into a bicycle." Amazingly, this July 1901–dated bicycle motor blueprint still exists in the Harley family archives today. It depicts a very small engine of 7-cubic-inch piston displacement (116cc) with tiny 4-inch flywheels. This would be a suitably sized engine for a hefty chainsaw, but hardly adequate for a motorcycle.

Fast forward twenty-four months later to "1903" in this *official* version of events. By then, young Bill Harley

This 10x15-foot shed with no electrical service was an unlikely place to build motorcycles from scratch and probably another "1903" myth. The name on the door may be the work of a commercial artist who retouched the photograph around 1909 for advertising purposes. *Bruce Linsday*

and his pal Art Davidson have completely designed, machined, fabricated, assembled, and now "make available to the public the first production Harley-Davidson® motorcycle."

But wait a second before you sing hosannas in the direction of Milwaukee, Wisconsin. This supposed "1903" product that bursts in full creation on the marketplace now has a heavy-duty loop-frame and a big lugging engine "with 3-1/8 inch bore and 3-1/2 inch stroke" yielding some 27-cubic-inches (440cc). Its 9-3/4 inch flywheels alone weighed 28 pounds. No little bicycle motor here. The original 7-cubic-inch engine has inexplicably vanished for another powerplant far too big and heavy for installation in a pedal bicycle frame, and appears instead with an advanced loop-frame chassis. This transformation is as miraculous as it is complete, although no explanation is given. Maybe we're not supposed to notice or ask.

Not only does the *official* story claim that the boys turned out one such advanced motorcycle in "1903" but that they managed to build two more that same year. All this by three young guys (Walter having joined them, but Bill Davidson had not) with no previous experience and no capital backing them. There is no mention of ordering engines or frames out of catalogs, but apparently everything was built from scratch in "a 10 x 15-foot wooden shed" without electrical service or machine tools that was located in Pa Davidson's backyard. Yet this supposed "1903" product was so superior to any motorcycle then built in America that the Harley-Davidson brand was an instant hit. Such a quick success, we are told, that the boys were able to procure a dealer in Chicago that same year who sold one of those "1903" bikes.

Such a scenario is indeed fabulous when you consider that today it took a team of experts and $500,000 just to design the V-Rod's headlight. If this weren't Harley-David-son, we might even consider it a fairy tale. Such superhuman feats of invention and manufacturing genius strain credibility unless you believe in Milwaukee leprechauns or that the humble woodshed opened up into a bustling multi-departmental shop once you passed through its magical door.

All along, a few old collectors and enthusiasts were suspicious that something wasn't right. They could produce old original Motor Company advertisements and literature claiming that the Harley-Davidson motorcycle had first appeared on the market in any of the following years: 1901, 1902, 1903, 1904, or 1905.

Clearly, all those first year claims could not be right when even the 1903 claim reeks of the superhuman. H-D had long ceased to speak about its own origin as seen in this 1942 pronouncement, "Just how the first Harley-Davidson motorcycle was conceived is somewhat of a mystery even to its parents."

There are other contradictions in today's *official* origin story. Let's go back for a moment and examine the claim for "1903" that states "the first Harley-Davidson Dealer, C.H. Lang of Chicago, Ill., opens for business and sells one of the first three production Harley-Davidson motorcycles ever made."

Harley's first dealer was indeed Carl Herman Lang of Chicago. But was Lang actually a Harley dealer in 1903? Did he really sell a motorcycle that year? A "1903" model that according to later company accounts had racked up "100,000 miles" by 1913 and was still going strong?

In 1914, Mr. Lang himself gave a much different version of events. This came during courtroom testimony in a patent infringement lawsuit when Lang stated *under sworn oath* that he first had "become familiar" with the

Old Harley-Davidson enthusiasts and collectors have long known that early ads and other material place Harley-Davidson's market introduction in every year between 1901 and 1905. This ad from 1910 claims that 1902 was the year of introduction. Original evidence shows that 1905 was actually Harley-Davidson's first production year. *MotorCycling*

Around the time in 1903 the boys were finishing up their little motorized bicycle experiment, the innovative loop-frame Merkel motorcycle was just hitting the market. The 1904 prototype and 1905 first-model Harleys are such dead ringers for the Merkel that it appears young Bill Harley was inspired by this earlier Milwaukee-built product. While the Merkel brand would fade away in time, the look-alike Harley-Davidson would go on to achieve immortality. *Cycle and Automobile Trade Journal*

Harley-Davidson motorcycle "in the fall of 1904" and "started to handle the Harley-Davidson motorcycle as a dealer beginning in 1905." The year 1903 wasn't even on Lang's radar screen when testifying in a court of law. One critic has described the discrepancies between such damning evidence and the *official* history as not passing the smell test.

True enough, but where does that leave the origin of the Harley-Davidson motorcycle? If the traditional version of events contains contradictions and falsehoods then what is the truth of the matter?

The original sequence of events as I uncovered them during that decade of hard-won research is both logical and simple. In this revised chronology the actual first motorized vehicle that Harley and Davidson finished in 1903 was *not* the design trotted out today for celebrations and instantly identified by its superior loop-frame and big engine.

Rather, what Harley and Davidson accomplished in 1903 was completing and then attaching the small 7-cubic-inch motor to an ordinary bicycle. That power-cycle of 1903 was *not* a success. For one thing it could not climb Milwaukee's modest hills. For another, it was instantly made obsolete by better designs just appearing on the market that the boys would have seen whizzing down Milwaukee streets. Shrewdly, Harley and Davidson condemned that first motorized bicycle as unworthy of their name. It was not made available to the public in 1903 or in any other year. In fact, no Harley-Davidson motorcycle was available or sold in 1903 because the boys had not yet developed anything suitable to ride, let alone sell.

It would take Harley and the Davidsons another two years to place a motorcycle on the market. The year of introduction was 1905. That machine was a totally different design from the unsuccessful power-cycle of 1901–1903. The new pattern would have the much larger 27-cubic-inch engine and the advanced loop-frame. That vehicle was the first *real* Harley-Davidson motorcycle, a prototype being in existence by late 1904.

That date is verified by a September 1904 article that I discovered in the *Milwaukee Journal* newspaper. There a "Harley-Davidson" is named as an entry in a local motorcycle race. Although the Harley did not win, its presence signals the first documented appearance of a Harley-Davidson motorcycle in the historical record.

The next actual evidence comes from January of 1905 when a small advertisement for Harley-Davidson engines appeared in *Cycle and Automobile Trade Journal.* Not

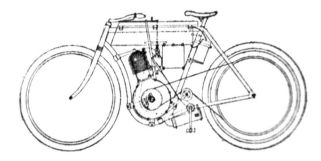

The 1904 Harley prototype may have been configured much like this line drawing published in early 1905 and almost certainly the work of Bill Harley himself. With low handlebar, small seat, and lack of fenders, this oldest known visual representation of a Harley-Davidson motorcycle suggests a racing machine. *Cycle and Automobile Trade Journal*

When my **mood** gets too hot and I find myself wandering beyond control I pull out my motor-bike and **hurl it top-speed** through these unfit roads for hour after hour. My nerves are jaded and gone near dead, so that nothing less than **hours of voluntary danger will prick them into life. . . .**

—T. E. Lawrence, a.k.a. Lawrence of Arabia

The early appeal of the Harley-Davidson is evident in this 1906 photograph. Mailman Pete Olson's bike (left) is an early 1905 model and may have been the third Harley ever built. With those baskets it was probably the first "custom" Harley in existence, too. Arthur Davidson (right) is on a new 1906 model that he had just ridden out from Milwaukee. George Dykesten (rear) impatiently waits for the photo session to end so he can take possession of his new machine. *John E. Harley Family*

complete bikes mind you, just bare engines. Come spring of 1905, the first *production* Harley-Davidson motorcycles trickled out and that appearance was also documented in the press. During 1905, some five to seven or possibly "eight or ten" Harley-Davidsons were built.

Unlike the unsuccessful power-cycle experiment, Harley-Davidson's first production model of 1905 was a powerful, dependable, and good-looking mount. Riders instantly fell in love with it, and that love affair has existed ever since.

At this point you might be wondering how the Motor Company today has gained two full years when claiming its product first hit the market—from 1905 back to 1903. And how did the actual events of Harley's birth get so messed up in the first place?

That too is easy to explain if you go back like I did and examine the original evidence. Recall that we started this account on the premise of corporate branding, marketing hijinks, and advertising guys stretching the truth. Thus we need only return to Harley-D's early marketing department and the person whom I believe instigated this mischief in the first place: the company's first advertising manager, S. Lacy Crolius.

When one examines H-D advertisements and literature from 1905 onwards, it quickly becomes evident that in early 1908 Crolius began to rework the previous record of events for greater impact on the advertising page. Using a sleight-of-hand marketing technique, Harley's advertising writer purposely obscured the identity and dates of the failed power-cycle experiment and substituted in its place the first real Harley-Davidson motorcycle. Through the magic of deceptive advertising, the big-motor 1904–1905 machine would became a 1901–1903 model. Yet the experimental power-cycle was never banished from

This is Harley's first known advertisement and dates from January 1905. Notice that only bare engines were offered at that time. The first complete bikes were available for sale beginning in April 1905. *Cycle and Automobile Trade Journal*

sight completely, and would remain both to confuse but also to provide the necessary clue for constructing an accurate chronology of Harley-D's beginnings.

One finds, therefore, in Harley-Davidson advertisements and articles published between 1908 and 1919 imaginative but conflicting statements. These range from wildly impossible claims of superior Harley-Davidson motorcycles already being sold in 1901—a year that original blueprints prove that Bill Harley had just started to draw a little 7-cubic-inch bicycle motor.

Nor does it take an Einstein to figure out why ad man Crolius falsified Harley history. Back in 1908, Milwaukee was in a bare-knuckle fight with Indian and other early brands for market share. At his desk in the spanking new yellow brick factory, a cocksure young Crolius felt no constraint to tell the truth, but only to create effective advertising. His strategy was to woo new customers with claims that the Harley had been on the market years before it actually was, thereby convincing them that the Harley was inherently superior to the popular but more bicycle-like Indian. Because what really was excellent in

Compared to much of its competition, the 1905 Harley-Davidson had the advantage of being a second-generation motorcycle of advanced design. Loop frame, powerful engine, flexible belt drive, good looks, and durable construction were key elements of its success. *Richard Morsher*

the first model year of 1905 would have been a dream-machine in 1903, and around-the-curve genius if backed up into 1902 or 1901 when motorcycles were little more than wheezy engines strapped onto pedal bicycles. If these grandiose but phony advertisements were effective, Harley would gain new customers, production would increase, and profits soar!

For whatever reason the Motor Company didn't stick with the extreme claims of 1901 or 1902 as the year of its motorcycle's birth but did latch onto the 1903 fiction. That is either one or two years off the true mark: one year by a running prototype (1904), or two years by first production model (1905). As the years passed it apparently became more difficult to sort out myth from reality and the Milwaukee firm grew reluctant to discuss its own origin except for one glorious burst of integrity in 1954 when the Motor Company chose that year to celebrate the 50th anniversary model.

Although now you and I understand why the family-owned and -managed Motor Company in 1954 looked back to 1904 as its motorcycle's origin year of existence, the current crop of *official* historians gaze into their crystal balls and claim that they can't figure it out. One wonders how the current firm's management will handle this "1903" conundrum in the $60-million Harley-Davidson museum slated to open in Milwaukee in 2008.

Early marketing hype, myth-making, and modern fibbing aside, that 1905 Harley really was good. It may have been the best all-around American motorcycle on the market. Of course it had the advantage of being a second-generation design inspired by cutting-edge bikes like the 1903 loop-frame Merkel. In 1909, even Indian threw in the towel and adopted a loop-frame. The boys also had help from their more-experienced friends like Ole

Evinrude. Yet Bill Harley took a giant step forward when he adopted a big-motor philosophy at a time when most builders (again led by Indian) thought that motorcycles should be small and light enough to be pushed or carried over rough spots in the road. Push a Harley-Davidson? Like hell! Along with a few other big-bore bikes of the day like Racine's "Mile-a-Minute" Mitchell, the Harley would *mote* under its own power or not mote at all.

Little wonder that by mid-1905, with a few Harleys on the road, things begin jumping.

While nearly all the history books claim that H-D didn't start speed racing until the teens, that's another fairy tale. As previously mentioned, the first historical note of a running Harley comes from a 1904 race. The spring of 1905 would see the boys out racing again.

We know that from a June 1905 article and photo that I dug out of an old Milwaukee newspaper. This

Compared to the Harley-Davidson of 1905, the established Indian motorcycle was more bicycle-like and obsolescent with a design that dated back to 1901. Little wonder that the heavier, more powerful, and up-to-date Harley achieved rapid popularity and instant cult-like status among early riders. *Bicycling World and Motorcycle Review*

shows H-D's first employee, Perry E. Mack (later a great motorcycle-engine designer himself), with a first-year Harley after setting a speed record on Milwaukee's State Fair Park horse track.

On the heels of this triumph, Perry Mack and Walter Davidson entered Chicago's big July 4th races. In the 15-mile event for heavyweights (bikes over 110 pounds), Mack took first place and Walter second. In the 10-mile race, Walter took first while poor Perry hit a dog that had wandered onto the racetrack. The mishap ended Mack's racing career and showed the boys from Milwaukee that the *motor-sickle* was not a toy as some imagined, but a fast and dangerous device. Yet young Harley-Davidson had reason to feel proud, and from a surviving 1905 letter we hear Arthur Davidson crow, "Up to the present time we have entered four races this season and have secured first in all of them. . . ."

A good design and racing success would boost Harley-Davidson beyond all expectation. Production jumped to around 50 in 1906, to 150 in 1907, and to 450 in 1908. Already in 1907, Harley-Davidson was claiming there were copy-cat imitations of its bike on the market. The greatest early success came in 1908 when Walter Davidson gave such a sterling performance in the National Endurance Contest through New York's Catskill Mountains that he was awarded the diamond medal and a better-than-perfect score of "1,000 plus 5" points.

Bear in mind that this early fame was won by bikes of the original 1904–1905 single-cylinder pattern. A design so good that between 1905 and 1908 the only noticeable addition was a spring fork in 1907. Curiously, Harley-Davidson would shun the V-twin engine for several seasons on the belief that one cylinder was all that riders needed. Not until 1911 would Harley

successfully market a "double," although there is historical and photographic evidence that the firm had been displaying V-twins at motorcycle shows and advertising twin-cylinder models since 1907.

The excellence of those first Harley singles was demonstrated as recently as 2003 during the 100th anniversary celebration in Milwaukee, and you might have been one of the lucky few who witnessed it.

On August 27, 2003, modern history was made when a small group of antique Harleys rolled up to the historic red brick factory on Juneau Avenue. Leading the way was a 1905 model Harley-Davidson nicknamed "Tommy" owned and ridden by Bruce Linsday. This world's oldest running and ridden Harley had just completed the 462½-mile trip from Lindsay's home in Ohio to Milwaukee under its own power. Tommy was seen outside the Juneau Avenue factory and woodshed replica that day and the next. Occasionally Bruce would fire up the 1905 and zip up the street to much acclaim. The old bike also visited the gravesite of its creator, William S. Harley.

Ninety-eight years after the birth of this first year Harley-Davidson you could still feel the magic that it must have evoked in 1905. A magic evident when Bruce gave the pedals a spin like a bicycle, the flywheels turned, and the engine fired and effortlessly off they went. Of the thousands of bikes at the 100th event it was the coolest one of all.

So you see, the goodness of the early Harley-Davidson is no myth. The early Harley could "take it" when other bikes failed. That too was later used for advertising purposes and thereby hangs the greatest unsolved mystery of H-D's beginnings: the fate of the first large-motor, loop-frame Harley, the 1904 prototype.

In 1912–1913, this first Harley-Davidson motorcycle ever built was subject to a colorful advertising campaign.

The early false claims about Harley's first year on the market apparently came from H-D's first ad manager, S. Lacy Crolius, shown here on an early twin. His well-intended but inaccurate claims have fooled generations of Harley historians. *Motorcycle Illustrated*

HOLDS STATE MOTOR CYCLE RECORD

This newspaper clipping and photo from June 1905 is the first known action shot of a Harley-Davidson motorcycle in the real world making good. Rider is Perry E. Mack, shown after setting a speed record on Milwaukee's State Fair Park horse track. *Milwaukee Journal*

By that time the bike had passed through several owners beginning with Henry Meyer and ending with Steven Sparough. Still headed by Crolius, the Motor Company's marketing department cranked out ads and media releases until one in *Factory Facts* claimed that the Meyer–Sparough bike had run "more than 100,000 miles without a single replacement of any motor parts."

While that claim was probably more highfalutin humbug, the bike was real enough. And surrounding it is as much treasure hunt as history because after 1916 that unique and priceless motorcycle went missing!

No matter what anyone may claim today, that first 1904 prototype Harley is not known to exist in any current antique motorcycle collection, including a collection owned by a world-famous Milwaukee firm.

We know this fact from a photograph of the 1904 prototype ("Negative 599") that I discovered at the Milwaukee County Historical Society. Using that photograph, antique Harley experts were able to spot unique features on that bike's engine and frame that differentiate it from all other early Harleys seen in old photos and on surviving collection bikes.

But if this unique and most valuable of all antique motorcycles is not present in anyone's collection today, then what became of it?

We know that around 1913, pioneer dealer C. H. Lang purchased the 1904 prototype back from its final private owner, Steven Sparough. We also know that Lang put the bike in his Chicago showroom window where it remained as an attraction until at least 1916 as described in a magazine article that year. After that time, however, the 1904 prototype fades from sight like a ghostly mirage.

How could that motorcycle, as famous back then as an Elvis bike today, vanish without a trace?

Here are some vague legends along with my own thoughts that might give a modern Sherlock Holmes the necessary clue to crack this greatest unsolved mystery of Harley-Davidson.

In 1926, Lang's dealership was purchased by Kemper. Was the 1904 prototype a part of that deal? Or did Lang transfer the bike to someone between 1916 and 1926? Was it possibly scrapped, stolen, or somehow destroyed? Is there any old rider in the Chicago area who remembers?

One vague legend tells that when the pioneer dealer retired he took a "very old" motorcycle with him. A bike that was supposed to go back to the factory but never did. Lang had retirement homes in both Florida and Michigan. Did the 1904 prototype end up in one of those states?

Or did Lang return the bike after all? In the 1920s, a young test rider named Squibby Henrich was told by early (1907) Harley employee Sherbie Becker that a very old belt-drive job had been walled up in the Juneau Avenue factory. Shortly after that confession Sherbie was hit by a truck and killed on his motorcycle northwest of Milwaukee near Mayville. Did a premonition warn him to pass along the secret that the 1904 prototype had been quietly walled-up as a time capsule? As Henrich told me, "Old Sherbie wasn't fooling."

Those clues aren't much, but they're all we have.

Then consider the vast sentimental and historical value of this first Harley-Davidson motorcycle if it were located. Maybe it's out there still being ridden by some ghost rider in the boondocks of Florida or Upper Michigan running on those same original engine parts!

One thing is certain. While Harley-Davidson made a mess of its first motorcycle's birth-date, Harley-Davidson certainly got that first motorcycle *right*.

Oil-spattered but still game for more after its 462½-mile trip from Ohio, Bruce Linsday's 1905 Harley motor was among the first dozen or so ever built. Its long ride home 98 years later demonstrated that early Harley-David-son reliability was no myth. *Photograph © Herbert Wagner*

Bruce Linsday astride his 1905 Harley (nicknamed Tommy) after riding it from Ohio to Milwaukee in 2003. Photo was taken outside the Juneau Avenue plant during the one hundredth celebration as John Harley Jr. (left) and the author's brother Tom Wagner look on. *Photograph © Herbert Wagner*

The Harley-Davidson– Indian Wars

By Michael Dregni

Michael Dregni is the author of several obscure books on a variety of esoteric subjects. Among others, he has authored an engineering history of Ferrari automobiles, *Inside Ferrari*; several pop-culture histories of motor scooters including *The Scooter Bible*; and two motorcycling histories, *The Spirit of the Motorcycle* (re-released as *Motorcycle Legends*) and *Harley-Davidson Collectibles*.

This essay, adapted from *The Spirit of the Motorcycle*, looks at the friendship and rivalry at the very heart of American motorcycling history.

The day the tide turned in the three-decades-long war between Harley-Davidson and Indian was a time for celebration. The battle between the two dominant motorcycle makers had been the central theme behind American motorcycling. Now, with the debut of Harley's forthcoming Model 61 OHV, the Milwaukee faithful had a new secret weapon.

Harley-Davidson dealers were enraptured. At their banquet after the first unveiling of the new machine at Milwaukee's Schroeder Hotel on November 25, 1935, the celebration quickly went over the top. "Cactus" Bill Kennedy, a cowboy Harley dealer from the wild west of Phoenix, Arizona, was so elated that he pulled his revolver in the middle of the dining hall and "he [drew] a bead on the crystal chandelier, let out a blood-curdling yip-eee . . . and emptie[d] his six-gun," enthused *The Enthusiast*, Harley's house magazine. The more sedate dealers merely passed out after imbibing one toast too many of Milwaukee's finest brews.

It was a day that would go down in Harley history.

At the time, the arrival of the long-awaited overhead-valve motorcycle seemed like a fine tool to win back flagging sales from Harley's arch-rival amidst the Great Depression. And to the men of the orange and black, that was reason enough to drink Milwaukee dry and gun down an innocent chandelier.

In hindsight, however, the event marked the turning point that would make the Milwaukee company the victor after battling for years on the racetracks, sales floors, and drawing boards of American motorcycling.

In January 1901, George M. Hendee of Springfield, Massachusetts, scrawled out a contract on the back of an old envelope putting his faith in his new-found acquaintance, Oscar Hedstrom, to build the future in the form of a motorized bicycle. Hendee and Hedstrom had one thing in common: They were both former bicycle racers who foresaw that future not in pedal power but in mechanical power.

From there, they were very different men. In the late 1880s, Hendee retired from racing and established the Hendee Manufacturing Company in Springfield to build his Silver King bicycles during the booming years of the bicycle craze. Springfield was also home to the Duryea brothers, builders of one of the first automobiles. Hendee was the money man; he had deep pockets that could make things happen.

Hedstrom was the ideas man. In 1899, he was at New York City's Madison Square Garden when Frenchman Henri Fournier's motorized tandem bicycle paced a bicycle race. By the end of the year, Hedstrom had schooled himself in the newfangled gas-powered internal-combustion engine and crafted his own motorized pacer. In 1900, Hendee witnessed Hedstrom and his pacer at work, and an idea was born.

With the ink still drying on their contract written on the old envelope, Hedstrom rented space at the Worcester Bicycle Manufacturing Company in Middletown, Connecticut, and got down to work. Armed with a full machine shop, bicycles and bicycle components, and photographs and drawings of original ideas and other machines he had seen, Hedstrom crafted a motorized bicycle that could be sold to the public. Fifteen months later in May 1901, Hedstrom wired Hendee that the prototype for what would become the Indian "motocycle" was ready.

The first Indians of 1901 and 1902 were for all practical purposes motorized bicycles. They were built on a modified bicycle chassis of a diamond-shaped frame with

A lineup of faithful steeds at Daytona Bike Week 2004. *Photograph © Russ Bryant*

the motor bolted onto the seat tube. Chain drive ran from the engine's output shaft to the bicycle's front chain ring, which retained crank arms and pedals for starting.

The engine was a solid and reliable 15.85 cubic inch (260cc) F-head single that dutifully pumped out 1.75 horsepower. A gas tank was added atop the rear fender and lubricating oil arrived via a drip feed. The machine weighed in at 75 pounds. The engine could be throttled back to a walking speed of 3 mph or up to a startling full-out speed of more than 30 mph—a heady speed in those days.

It was a simple yet solid machine, and the Indian soon became one of the best known, most prolific, and most influential motorcycles anywhere.

The story of the creation of the Harley-Davidson in a shed behind the Davidson family's Milwaukee home has become legend, akin to that of the birth of a certain baby in a manger some 2,000 years ago. Twenty-one-year-old William S. Harley and his childhood pal, 20-year-old Arthur Davidson, were enamored by the newfangled motorcycle. They worked at a Milwaukee manufacturing firm, where Harley was an apprentice draftsman and Davidson a pattern maker. The duo met a German draftsman at work who regaled them with tales of the pioneering European motor bicycles. With his help, they drafted plans for a single-cylinder gas-fueled engine that followed the style set by Count de Dion. In the evenings starting in 1901, they worked in their home basement, building a small 7-cubic-inch engine that they attached to a bicycle frame. Still, the puny power-cycle was not enough to climb even the modest hills of Milwaukee.

It was back to the proverbial drawing board. By 1904, the duo had crafted the prototype for a new machine powered by a grand 27-cubic-inch (440cc) single-cylinder motor.

But the two were struggling with their creation. They had pooled their less-than-ideal engineering knowledge to build the machine: Harley had previously crafted his own bicycle in his spare time and Davidson's pattern-making skills came in handy. What they needed was a mechanic.

So, Arthur wrote his brother Walter, who was a top-notch machinist and worked in the tool room for a Kansas railroad. Arthur painted a glowing picture of their motorcycle and offered Walter a ride on the new machine when he was home in Milwaukee for the wedding of a third Davidson brother, William. As Walter later remembered, "Imagine my chagrin to find that the moto bicycle in question had reached the stage of blueprints, and before I could have the promised ride, I had to help finish the machine." Still, he was intrigued and saw promise in the duo's design. He quit his railroad job, rolled up his shirtsleeves, and got down to work. After his wedding, William, a toolmaker, also joined in.

As legend quaintly has it, the first engine was fed by a carburetor reportedly fashioned from a recycled tomato can. But the engine did not produce enough power, so the tomato-can carburetor was set aside and a friend by the name of Ole Evinrude, who would later find fame building outboard motors, helped craft a carb.

For a frame, they tried first a typical bicycle diamond frame as Oscar Hedstrom was using. But this could not hold the engine's power, so they crafted a loop frame, a design that would be a Harley-Davidson staple for decades.

With their prototype now running, Walter finally took his long-promised ride. He pronounced it a sound machine.

Now that they had a running prototype, the friends decided to enter production. The Davidsons' father, William C., was a cabinetmaker by trade, and inspired by his son's machine, he constructed a 10x15-foot shed in the family's backyard that would become their first "factory." The friends painted their new name on the door: "Harley-Davidson Motor Co." Bill Harley received top billing as he had engineered the first prototype.

The battle in the early years was simply for survival, and at first, Indian and Harley-Davidson did not view themselves as true competitors. The "motocycle" was a newfangled invention and not everyone cottoned to it. The two firms focused on establishing themselves.

Harley was quietly building a reputation for stoic reliability. The fledgling company did not support racing throughout its first decade, choosing instead to prove its machine on the road. In 1913, Harley-Davidson proudly advertised—or hyped, as the facts may be—that the first machine the firm ever built now had more than 100,000 miles under its belt.

Harley also was a staunch defender of quiet motorcycles. It campaigned to muffle the roar of motorcycle exhaust, pointing out in its ads that it fixed large mufflers to its machines so they would not scare horses or the unsuspecting pedestrian. From this "quiet pipes save lives" campaign, the early Harleys won the name Silent Gray Fellow as they were quiet and usually painted in gray. The "Fellow" part of the nickname originated from Harley's promoting its motorcycle as reliable companion on the lonesome road. (Some also claim the moniker mirrored the machine's "father," Bill Harley, who was known as the Silent Gray Fellow.) Either way, then as now, Harley-Davidson was concerned about its image.

Indian, meanwhile, was attacking all markets—perhaps because it didn't have a clear idea in those days of where a motorcycle fit in, so the firm saw it fitting everywhere in the brave new world. At country fair horse-racing tracks and on the boardtrack motordromes, Indians were duking it out with Excelsiors, Flying Merkels, and Reading Standards in bloody battles for race trophies.

On the salesroom floors of the nation, however, Indian's main competition was itself—or at least a shadow of itself. As the Indian was the most influential motorcycle in North America, it naturally inspired copies.

From 1902 to 1907, Indian contracted the Aurora Manufacturing Company of Aurora, Illinois, to build its engines as Indian did not have the manufacturing capacity needed. As part of the deal, Aurora could use or sell any excess engines Indian did not require, so it launched its own motorcycle, the Thor, using not only the same engine as the Indian but an exact duplicate design in all other respects as well.

Other firms also bought the Aurora-built engine and soon launched their own Indian clones, including the Light, Light Thor-Bred, and Thor-Bred motorcycles from the Light Manufacturing & Foundry Company of Pottstown, Pennsylvania, forerunner of the Merkel firm; the DeLong from the Industrial Machine Company of Phoenix, New York; the America from the Great Western Manufacturing Company of LaPorte, Indiana; the Warwick Motor Cycle; the Apache from Brown & Beck of Denver, Colorado; and the Manson from the Fowler-Sherman-Manson Cycle Company of Chicago. There were undoubtedly more.

These Indian copies were a common woe in the pioneering days of motorcycles. Some machines were blatant duplicates of original machines made without the approval of the maker. Sometimes this copying was in the form of "inspiration": An original engine design provided the concept, and perhaps the micrometer measurements, for another engineer. Some makers applied for patents on their creations, but the granting of a patent often took years. And even if the design was patented, actual patent protection was another matter altogether.

At other times, the copying was more obvious. News traveled slowly in the 1900s, and product distribution was often even slower. This created an environment where inventors such as Harley and the Davidsons could release its copy of an engine originally built by Count de Dion in France—and the original maker might never even hear of the copycat machine and attempt to put on the legal brakes.

More common was the creation of "clone" motorcycles, as with Indian. Many original makers sold their machines either assembled or unassembled to budding entrepreneurs. These farsighted individuals might not have had the engineering know-how to design their own motorcycles but they did have deep pockets to finance assembling, distribution, and sales of machines. Indian fought its rival—yet legal—cousins at every step. As one Indian ad read, "There may be motor bicycles that look like the Indian, but looks are deceitful; they are not the equals of the 'Hedstrommed' Indian. . . . When you buy, buy the 'real thing'—the genuine Indian."

But Indian was not completely pure, either. Premier Indian historian Jerry Hatfield believes that Hedstrom based his "original" Indian engine design on a motor created in 1901 by fellow American Emil Hafelfinger, who indeed noted in an advertisement that "Four of the leading Motorcycle Motors are copies of this Motor. . . ."

In 1914, Harley-Davidson decided to go racing, and the war with Indian began in earnest. The Milwaukee factory had adamantly refused to sponsor racing throughout its first decade—although it had proudly championed in its ads race victories won by Harley-mounted privateers, including none other than Walter Davidson himself. But racing had become a big deal, and Harley-Davidson wanted its share of the trophies.

At the major July 4, 1914, race in Dodge City, Kansas, Harley lined up a team of six V-twins to do battle with the Indians and other marques over a 300-mile course. The Indians quickly outpaced the Harleys, and only two of the Milwaukee machines even finished, albeit far back in the dust.

Undaunted, the Harley team continued to challenge Indian's supremacy on the racetracks throughout the year, eventually taking home the trophy for a National Championship race in Birmingham, Alabama.

In 1915, Harley was back. At the Milwaukee factory, new racing machines had been built, including a batch of F-head V-twins. During the year, Harley riders raced to victory in twenty-six major events as well as countless smaller venues. Indian and Excelsior had to grudgingly sit up and take notice of the upstart. Harley's race team, nicknamed the Wrecking Crew, was duking it out with Indians, Excelsiors, Merkels, and Cyclones on board tracks and flat tracks, and at the national races sponsored by the Federation of American Motorcyclists.

Over the next two decades, Indian and Harley remained gentleman competitors on the surface. But at the racetracks, they traded insults, raced until their engines burst, and fought tooth and nail for every trophy and every kiss from the trophy girl.

Throughout the 1920s and 1930s, the battle between Harley and Indian naturally spilled over onto the salesroom floors. This competition between the two dominant makers not only characterized the culture of American motorcycling but also shaped—for better or worse—the technical development of American motorcycles, a heritage that continues to this day.

Although Indian and Harley-Davidson's laurels rest primarily on their V-twins, both makers began with singles and staked their reputations on one-cylinder machines for much of their first decade of production.

In 1907, Indian introduced its first V-twin, the engine still mounted in a diamond bicycle frame similar to its premier model. The 42-degree V-twin displaced 39 cubic inches (639cc), although these were soon followed in 1909 by a larger twin of 60.32 cubic inches (988 cc) mounted in a loop-framed chassis.

Indian's V-twin may have been developed in response to the Curtiss V-twin of 1905. Starting in 1903, Glen Curtiss was Indian's chief threat on the racetrack, winning his share of trophies before the Indian could reach the checkered flag. Curtiss also held many a speed record that Indian coveted for its own. The G. H. Curtiss Manufacturing Company of Hammondsport, New York, offered its V-twin as a 42-cubic-inch (688cc) F-head machine.

Harley was quick to follow the trend. The first notice of Milwaukee's prototype V-twin appeared in *The Bicycling World and Motorcycle Review* in April 1908, describing a 6-horsepower, 53-cubic-inch (868cc) machine under development. In August 1908, the magazine told of a 61-cubic-inch (1,000cc) Harley V-twin.

Harley's V-twin was first introduced as a 1909 model. The cylinders were canted at 45 degrees and measured 3.00x3.50 inches (75x87.50mm) bore and stroke, displacing 49.48 cubic inches (811cc). The engine was rated at 7 horsepower, promising a top speed of 65 mph.

Harley's pride was absent from the 1910 line, only to re-appear in 1911 in two sizes, 49.48 and 60.32 cubic inches (811 and 988cc), both with advanced mechanically operated inlet valves.

Sensing the tide of American motorcycling, the Reading-Standard Company of Reading, Pennsylvania, followed the trend in 1908 with an F-head V-twin. Thor was building Indian's V-twin engines under license, so it offered its own V-twin in 1909 and sold engines to the Minneapolis Motor Company of Minneapolis to build its 1909 machine. Excelsior followed suit in 1910 with its 50-cubic-inch (819cc) V-twins boasting mechanically operated inlet valves. The Merkel-Light V-twin also arrived in 1910, followed in 1912 by Colonel Albert Pope's Pope Manufacturing Company of Hartford, Connecticut.

The competition between Harley and Indian—as well as the rest of the smaller firms—became so intense that Springfield and Milwaukee seemed to be playing Follow-the-Leader. When Indian deviated from the norm to launch an opposed-twin in 1917, Harley rushed its own version into production by 1919. Springfield's side-valve Model O displaced 15.7 cubic inches (257cc), so Milwaukee's Sport upped the ante to 35.6 cubic inches (583cc). At the same time Harley's machine made it to market, Indian decided to discontinue its opposed twin as the engine layout may have been too novel for the market-place. The Harley Sport soldiered on only until 1923.

When Indian feinted, Harley flinched; when Harley bluffed, Indian blinked. When Harley increased engine displacement, Indian quickly bored out its cylinders. Indian had its Chief, Harley had its 61- and 74-cubic-inch (1,000 and 1,212cc) Big Twins. Indian had its Scout, Harley had its 45-cubic-inch (750cc) middleweight twins. Harley had its three-wheeled Servi-Car, Indian had its Dispatch Tow. Even optional equipment, accessories, and clothing items mirrored the other's. One of the few fronts on which the two did not do battle was Indian's Four. Harley never offered its own four-cylinder—although it tried, experimenting with 80- and 90-cubic-inch (1,310 and 1,474cc) V-fours in 1928. But then again, the Indian Four did not last, exiting production in 1942, long before the war was over.

I t was something as simple and basic as the placement of valves in the cylinder heads that eventually turned the tide forever in Harley-Davidson's favor and eventually led to Indian's demise.

In the pioneering days, most motorcycle engines featured their inlet valve mounted above the exhaust valve in a pocket set to the side of the cylinder. This engine layout was variously known as inlet-over-exhaust, pocket-valve, or F-head. The configuration tended to burn out exhaust valves, stranding many a rider by the side of a road to the derision of those folk who had indeed bought a horse. Still, in the first decades of American motorcycling, it was the rare engine that did not feature the F-head layout.

The next development in valve configuration arrived on the Reading-Standard motorcycle of 1906. Instead of having its valves placed above each other, the Reading-Standard mounted them side by side on the side of the cylinder, a layout known not surprisingly as a side-valve engine. In about 1910, the Thiem Manufacturing Company of St. Paul, Minnesota, followed suit, introducing a side-valve, or flathead, single. The layout offered better performance, less valve failure, and allowed the valve gear to be safely enclosed away from the dirt and grime of the road.

Side-valves were obviously a giant step into the future, but it was not until 1916 that Indian offered a side-valve engine, launching its new Powerplus lineup. It would take Harley-Davidson another decade, making the change to side-valves as late as 1929.

Lurking in the shadows was another engine design that had been experimented with in Europe on both motorcycles and automobiles: overhead-valve engines where the valves were placed above the cylinder, offering dramatically improved airflow and thus more power. But the overhead-valve engines also ran hotter and required a much more complicated valvetrain than the crude but efficient pushrod system that drove most side-valves.

Still, the writing was on the wall: Overhead valves were the route to more power. Indian experimented with a series of short-lived eight-valve overhead-valve racers in 1911. In 1916, Harley-Davidson ventured to build a series of eight-valve overhead-valve racers with the assistance of English engineer Harry Ricardo. But with years of development in their heads, the side-valve Indians still proved their worth against the OHV Harleys. After World War I, however, the tables began to turn, and the OHV engine powered Harley's Wrecking Crew to dominate all comers.

Yet neither Harley nor Indian offered an overhead-valve engine for the street. Tradition was certainly a roadblock, but the cost of developing a reliable OHV valvetrain was also a problem. So, Harley-Davidson and Indian fans remained content with their F-head and side-valve rides throughout the 1910s, 1920s, and most of the 1930s.

Some in North America saw the tide turning. Colonel Albert L. Pope offered his first V-twin in 1912 with technical innovations that were miles ahead of the Indians and Harleys of the day. The Pope Model L boasted pushrod-operated overhead valves powering its 61-cubic-inch (1,000cc) engine to 15 hp. The Pope also rode on plunger rear suspension some three decades before most other American motorcycles.

The same was not the case in Europe, however. The ferocious competition on the road and track pushed companies to work overtime in developing overhead-valve engines. By the dawn of the 1930s, most every major European motorcycle maker that had hopes of staying in business had overhead-valve models for sale.

By the mid-1930s, the American motorcycle industry was in trouble. Harley and Indian had battled with each other for decades, but now they were up against a more daunting foe in the form of the Great Depression, which was slowing motorcycle sales to a trickle. Harley's sales

alone were cut almost in half from 1929 to 1931, and cut in third again by 1933. In addition, a handful of European motorcycles were also beginning to invade the grand old makers's turf, stealing trophies from out of the hands of the faithful and winning away some buyers with their dazzling OHV machinery.

A secret weapon was needed.

In 1931, Bill Harley began developing Harley-Davidson's future in the form of a radical new engine. Built on the foundation of a new "sump oiler" bottom end, this 61-cubic-inch (1,000cc) motor would be crowned by an overhead valvetrain. Development would continue for five long years while the Motor Company endured the Depression and dealers begged for a new model.

Production of the new 61 OHV model was finally approved for 1935—and then cancelled at the last minute due to further engine problems. Even after the future was unveiled to the enraptured dealers on November 25, 1935, and "Cactus" Bill Kennedy emptied his six-shooter into a chandelier in joy, it would be several long, hard months before the first production cycles were shipped to lucky dealers. Many dealers could not even get a 61 OHV until mid-1936, and these they kept as showroom samples so they could write orders and pray for future delivery.

Indian, however, saw the future in a different light. The Wigwam stood stalwart behind its tried and true Chief, Scout, Thirty Fifty, and Four models, and made the decision not to update their flathead engines with overhead valves.

At the same time, Indian looked to the successful British vertical-twin motorcycles as inspiration. In 1945,

Indian's new owner, Ralph B. Rogers, bought the Torque Engineering Company of Plainfield, Connecticut, which had created a modular engine prototype penned by former Indian engineer G. Briggs Weaver. The modular vertical cylinder was topped by overhead valves, and Indian looked down the road to producing a single, twin, and four. The single and twin finally entered Indian's lineup alongside the venerable Chief and Scout in 1948 after several setbacks.

Indian was banking on its new vertical engine, but it was a bad bet. The new machines suffered numerous niggling large and small problems, but most importantly, the dedicated Indian faithful did not take to them. In their minds, Indians were supposed to be V-twins. It would be better to update the classic models or rekindle the grand old Four.

At almost the same time as Indian's all-American version of the British vertical twin made its debut, the true British twins invaded North America in droves. British currency had been devalued simply to increase the country's flagging exports, and Triumph, BSA, and Norton twins began to roll onto America's roads.

By the end of the 1940s, Indian was ailing. In 1950, Rogers resigned. The British invasion that began with imported motorcycles now outpaced Indian; a British marketing conglomerate headed by J. L. Brockhouse took over the reins of the proud old firm.

Indian did not succumb easily. The great Chief soldiered on with much the same specifications until 1953, by which time Harley had developed its Panhead, a further refinement from the 61 OHV Knucklehead that sparked the revolution. Indian made an attempt to resurrect it V-twin heritage by joining forces with the British Vincent concern to supply its glorious engine to be mounted in Indian chassis, but the project never came to pass. After Brockhouse's takeover, Indian put its name on the side of Royal Enfield, Horex, Norton, and Velocette gas tanks, and imported a number of two-stroke and mini-bikes, all in a last-ditch effort to stay alive. By the mid-1950s, the company was essentially gone, living on as a marketing ploy and a label to be licensed to the highest bidder.

Today, dispute over the Indian badge continues as various entrepreneurs try to revive the lineage. The name may never be allowed to rest in peace. Meanwhile, Harley-Davidson thrives on a decision made in 1931 to build an overhead-valve version of its classic V-twin.

Proud Harley-Davidson riders pose with
their mount for the family Brownie.

Harley-Davidson riders scrapbook,
circa 1920s–1950s.

Tom Swift and His Motor-Cycle

By Victor Appleton

The pioneering days of motorcycling came during an era when gee-whiz gizmos of all sorts were wowing the minds of people everywhere. Airplanes, automobiles, dirigibles, wireless radios—the list goes on and on.

Victor Appleton's series of Tom Swift novels from the 1910s played on this fascination. In each book, young Tom proved his genius with the modern world's latest mechanical marvel. And he beat out no-good crooks, down-and-dirty bad guys, and other evildoers along the way!

This excerpt from *Tom Swift and His Motor-Cycle, or Fun and Adventures on the Road* depicts how Tom won rights to his machine—and then went on to perfect its mechanicals.

When Tom reached the prostrate figure on the grass at the foot of the old oak tree, the youth bent quickly over the man. There was an ugly cut on his head, and blood was flowing from it. But Tom quickly noticed that the stranger was breathing, though not very strongly.

"Well, he's not dead just yet!" exclaimed the youth with a sigh of relief. "But I guess he's pretty badly hurt. I must get help—no, I'll take him into our house. It's not far. I'll call dad."

Leaning his wheel against the tree Tom started for his home, about three hundred feet away, and then he noticed that the stranger's motor-cycle was running at full speed on the ground.

"Guess I'd better shut off the power!" he exclaimed. "No use letting the machine be ruined." Tom had a natural love for machinery, and it hurt him almost as much to see a piece of fine apparatus abused as it did to see an animal mistreated. It was the work of a moment to shut off the gasolene and spark, and then the youth raced on toward his house.

"Where's dad?" he called to Mrs. Baggert, who was washing the dishes.

"Out in one of the shops," replied the housekeeper. "Why, Tom," she went on hurriedly as she saw how excited he was, "whatever has happened?"

"Man hurt—out in front—motor-cycle smash—I'm going to bring him in here—get some things ready—I'll find dad!"

"Bless and save us!" cried Mrs. Baggert. "Whatever are we coming to? Who's hurt? How did it happen? Is he dead?"

"Haven't time to talk now!" answered Tom, rushing from the house. "Dad and I will bring him in here."

Tom found his father in one of the three small machine shops on the grounds about the Swift home. The youth hurriedly told what had happened.

"Of course we'll bring him right in here!" assented Mr. Swift, putting aside the work upon which he was engaged. "Did you tell Mrs. Baggert?"

"Yes, and she's all excited."

"Well, she can't help it, being a woman, I suppose. But we'll manage. Do you know the man?"

"Never saw him before to-day, when he tried to run me down. Guess he doesn't know much about motor-cycles. But come on, dad. He may bleed to death."

Father and son hurried to where the stranger lay. As they bent over him he opened his eyes and asked faintly:

"Where am I ? What happened?"

"You're all right in good hands," said Mr. Swift. "Are you much hurt?"

"Not much—mostly stunned, I guess. What happened?" he repeated.

"You and your motor-cycle tried to climb a tree," remarked Tom with grim humor.

"Oh, yes, I remember now. I couldn't seem to steer out of the way. And I couldn't shut off the power in time. Is the motor-cycle much damaged?"

"The front wheel is," reported Tom, after an inspection, "and there are some other breaks, but I guess—"

"I wish it was all smashed!" exclaimed the man vigorously. "I never want to see it again!"

"Why, don't you like it?" asked Tom eagerly.

"No, and I never will," the man spoke faintly, but determinedly.

"Never mind now," interposed Mr. Swift "Don't excite yourself. My son and I will take you to our house and send for a doctor."

"I'll bring the motor-cycle, after we've carried you in," added Tom.

"Don't worry about the machine. I never want to see it again!" went on the man, rising to a sitting position. "It nearly killed me twice to-day. I'll never ride again."

"You'll feel differently after the doctor fixes you up," said Mr. Swift with a smile.

"Doctor! I don't need a doctor," cried the stranger. "I am only bruised and shaken up."

"You have a bad cut on your head," said Tom

"It isn't very deep," went on the injured man, placing his fingers on it. "Fortunately I struck the tree a glancing blow. If you will allow me to rest in your house a little while and give me some plaster for the cut I shall be all right again."

"Can you walk, or shall we carry you?" asked Tom's father.

"Oh, I can walk, if you'll support me a little." And the stranger proved that he could do thin by getting to his feet and taking a few steps. Mr. Swift and his son took hold of his arms and led him to the house. There he was placed on a lounge and given some simple restoratives by Mrs. Baggert, who, when she found the accident was not serious, recovered her composure.

"I must have been unconscious for a few minutes," went on the man.

"You were," explained Tom. "When I got up to you I thought you were dead, until I saw you breathe. Then I shut off the power of your machine and ran in for dad. I've got the motorcycle outside. You can't ride it for some time, I'm afraid, Mr. —er" and Tom stopped in some confusion, for he realized that he did not know the man's name.

"I beg your pardon for not introducing myself before," went on the stranger. "I'm Wakefield Damon, of Waterfield. But don't worry about me riding that machine again. I never shall."

"Oh, perhaps," began Mr. Swift.

"No, I never shall," went on Mr. Damon positively. "My doctor told me to get it, as he thought riding around the country would benefit my health. I shall tell him his prescription nearly killed me."

"And me too," added Tom with a laugh.

"How—why—are you the young man I nearly ran down this morning?" asked Mr. Damon, suddenly sitting up and looking at the youth.

"I am," answered our hero.

"Bless my soul! So you are!" cried Mr. Damon. "I was wondering who it could be. It's quite a coincidence. But I was in such a cloud of dust I couldn't make out who it was."

"You had your muffler open, and that made considerable dust," explained Tom.

"Was that it? Bless my existence! I thought something was wrong, but I couldn't tell what. I went over all the instructions in the book and those the agent told me, but I couldn't think of the right one. I tried all sorts of things to make less dust, but I couldn't. Then, bless my eyelashes, if the machine didn't stop just after I nearly ran into you. I tinkered over it for an hour or more before I could get it to going again. Then I ran into the tree. My doctor told me the machine would do my liver good, but, bless my happiness, I'd as soon be without a liver entirely as to do what I've done to-day. I am done with motorcycling!"

A hopeful look came over Tom's face, but he said nothing, that is, not just then. In a little while Mr. Damon felt so much better that he said he would start for home.

"I'm afraid you'll have to leave your machine here," said Tom.

"You can send for it any time you want to," added Mr. Swift.

"Bless my hatband!" exclaimed Mr. Damon, who appeared to be very fond of blessing his various organs and his articles of wearing apparel. "Bless my hatband! I never want to see it again! If you will be so kind as to keep it for me, I will send a junk man after it. I will never spend anything on having it repaired. I am done with that form of exercise—liver or no liver—doctor or no doctor."

He appeared very determined. Tom quickly made up his mind. Mr. Damon had gone to the bathroom to get rid of some of the mud on his hands and face.

"Father," said Tom earnestly, "may I buy that machine off him?"

"What? Buy a broken motor-cycle?"

"I can easily fix it. It is a fine make, and in good condition. I can repair it. I've wanted a motor-cycle for some time, and here's a chance to get a good one cheap."

"You don't need to do that," replied Mr. Swift. "You have money enough to buy a new one if you want it. I never knew you cared for them."

"I didn't, until lately. But I'd rather buy this one and fix it up than get a new one. Besides, I have an idea for a new kind of transmission, and perhaps I can work it out on this machine."

"Oh, well, if you want it for experimental purposes, I suppose it will be as good as any. Go ahead, get it if you wish, but don't give too much for it."

"I'll not. I fancy I can get it cheap."

Mr. Damon returned to the living room, where he had first been carried.

"I cannot thank you enough for what you have done for me," he said. "I might have lain there for hours. Bless my very existence! I have had a very narrow escape. Hereafter when I see anyone on a motor-cycle I shall turn my head away. The memory will be too painful," and he touched the plaster that covered a cut on his head.

"Mr. Damon," said Tom quickly, "will you sell me that motor-cycle?"

"Bless my finger rings! Sell you that mass of junk?"

"It's not all junk," went on the young inventor. "I can easily fix it; though, of course," he added prudently, "it will cost something. How much would you want for it?"

"Well," replied Mr. Damon, "I paid two hundred and fifty dollars last week. I have ridden a hundred miles on it. That is at the rate of two dollars and a half a mile—pretty expensive riding. But if you are in earnest I will let you have the machine for fifty dollars, and then I fear that I will be taking advantage of you."

"I'll give you fifty dollars," said Tom quickly, and Mr. Damon exclaimed,
"Bless my liver—that is, if I have one. Do you mean it?"

Tom nodded. "I'll fetch you the money right away," he said, starting for his room. . . .

"I have the money for the motor-cycle," and he drew out the bills. "You are sure you will not regret your bargain, Mr. Damon? The machine is new, and needs only slight repairs. Fifty dollars is—"

"Tut, tut, young man! I feel as if I was getting the best of you. Bless my handkerchief! I hope you have no bad luck with it"

"I'll try and be careful," promised Tom with a smile as he handed over the money. "I am going to gear it differently and put some improvements on it. Then I will use it instead of my bicycle."

"It would have to be very much improved be fore I trusted myself on it again," declared Mr. Damon. "Well, I appreciate what you have done for me, and if at any time I can reciprocate the favor, I will only be too glad to do so. Bless my soul, though, I hope I don't have to rescue you from trying to climb a tree," and with a laugh, which showed that he had fully recovered from his mishap, he shook hands with father and son and left.

"A very nice man, Tom," commented Mr. Swift. "Somewhat odd and out of the ordinary, but a very fine character, for all that."

"That's what I say," added the son. "Now, dad, you'll see me scooting around the country on a motor-cycle. I've always wanted one, and now I have a bargain."

"Do you think you can repair it?"

"Of course, dad. I've done more difficult things than that. I'm going to take it apart now, and see what it needs. . . ."

Tom had graduated with honors from a local academy, and when it came to a question of going further in his studies, he had elected to continue with his father for a tutor, instead of going to college. Mr. Swift was a very learned man, and this arrangement was satisfactory to him, as it allowed Tom more time at home, so he could aid his father on the inventive work and also plan things for himself. Tom showed a taste for mechanics, and his father wisely decided that such training as his son needed could be given at home to better advantage than in a school or college.

Lessons over, Tom hurried to his own particular shop, and began taking apart the damaged motor-cycle.

"First I'll straighten the handle-bars, and then I'll fix the motor and transmission," he decided. "The front wheel I can buy in town, as this one would hardly pay for repairing."

Tom was soon busy with wrenches, hammers, pliers and screw-driver. He was in his element, and was whistling over his task. The motor he found in good condition, but it was not such an easy task as he had hoped to change the transmission. He had finally to appeal to his father, in order to get the right proportion between the back and front gears, for the motor-cycle was operated by a sprocket chain, instead of a belt drive, as is the case with some.

Mr. Swift showed Tom how to figure out the number of teeth needed on each sprocket, in order to get an increase of speed, and as there was a sprocket wheel from a disused piece of machinery available, Tom took that. He soon had it in place, and then tried the motor. To his delight the number of revolutions of the rear wheel were increased about fifteen per cent

"I guess I'll make some speed," he announced to his father.

"But it will take more gasolene to run the motor; don't forget that. You know the great principle of mechanics—that you can't get out of a machine any more than you put into it, nor quite as much, as a matter of fact, for considerable is lost through friction."

"Well, then, I'll enlarge the gasolene tank," declared Tom. "I want to go fast when I'm going."

He reassembled the machine, and after several hours of work had it in shape to run, except that a front wheel was lacking.

"I think I'll go to town and get one," here. marked. "The rain isn't quite so hard now."

In spite of his father's mild objections Tom went, using his bicycle, the chain of which he had quickly repaired. He found just the front wheel needed, and that night his motor-cycle was ready to run. But it was too dark to try it then, especially as he had no good lantern, the one on the cycle having been smashed, and his own bicycle light not being powerful enough. So he had to postpone his trial trip until the next day.

He was up early the following morning, and went out for a spin before breakfast. He came back, with flushed cheeks and bright eyes, just as Mr. Swift and Mrs. Baggert were sitting down to the table.

"To Reedville and back," announced Tom proudly.

"What, a round trip of thirty miles!" exclaimed Mr. Swift

"That's what!" declared his son. "I went like a greased pig most of the way. I had to slow up going through Mansburg, but the rest of the time I let it out for all it was worth."

"You must be careful," cautioned his father. "You are not an expert yet."

"No, I realize that. Several times, when I wanted to slow up, I began to back-pedal, forgetting that I wasn't on my bicycle. Then I thought to shut off the power and put on the brake. But it's glorious fun. I'm going out again as soon as I have something to eat. That is, unless you want me to help you, dad."

"No, not this morning. Learn to ride the motor-cycle. It may come in handy."

Neither Tom nor his father realized what an important part the machine was soon to play in their lives.

Chapter 3

The Need for Speed

The sport of **racing** merits special **consideration** whether in and of itself or whether for its singular values. This sport that you cultivate requires a certain force of character, a **harmonious force** of the **whole body** whose energy manifests itself above all in the loyalty and in the disciplines of life. But more efficacious and more exalted is the reality of your symbolic race toward the glory of eternal life. Since you are loyal to the Christian life and **you want to conquer** not just a trophy that can be passed on to other hands, but a holy, **indestructible crown.**

—Pope Pius XII speaking to motorcycle racers, 1950s

How Many Lives Must Be Sacrificed to Speed?

By Arthur Davidson

Arthur Davidson needs little introduction. After all, it's his family's name that graces the gas tanks.

Arthur and his brothers Walter and William, as well as Bill Harley, had differing views on the need for speed. While Walter was racing his Harley-Davidson in different kinds of events, Arthur was railing against the dangers of motorcycle competition. In the pages of *The Harley-Davidson Dealer* magazine, Arthur condemned motordrome racing and warned dealers against supporting racers.

This 1914 article from the *Dealer* describes a horrific motordrome crash that not only killed two riders but six spectators as well and sparked national outrage. The essay sums up Arthur's views—and those of the fledgling Harley-Davidson Motor Company as well. At least in those early years.

The news that Eddie Hasha, John Albright and six spectators met death at the Vailsburg Motordrome, at Newark, N. J., on September 8th, was no doubt startling to everyone, but to none more so than the writer for the reason that a close friendship had existed, for some time, between Eddie Hasha and myself, dating back to the time at Dallas, Texas, when Hasha was starting his racing career.

At that time we had a racing machine shipped to Dallas, and Eddie Hasha was given a chance to ride against Robert Stubbs, and defeated him. From then on his entry into the racing game was fast and remarkably successful.

Not so very long ago, Mr. Hasha took up the selling of Harley-Davidson motorcycles in Dallas, but the race track fever got him again and he went back to it. And, while it was with very deep regret that I heard the story of his death, as well as that of John Albright, I was not a great deal surprised, as I had expected it to come in the course of events. But to cause the death of spectators was more than any of us had predicted.

When we read history, it tells about the Roman chariot races, in which they drove like mad, with but one thought: "To win." If a few lives were lost, what of it? The audience must be entertained. The more thrilling and death-defying, the better the show.

The Romans demanded the sacrifice of many lives in what they were pleased to call their "sports." When the gladiators entered the arena they said: "We, who are about to die, salute you." Whether a vanquished fighter should be spared or put to death was signified by the spectators. "Thumbs up" meant "let him live" and "thumbs down" meant "kill him."

We consider ourselves better civilized than the Romans. Perhaps we are a trifle less bloodthirsty. But the fact remains that there is some public demand for what are called "thrills" and that there are enough promoters and venturesome spirits to satisfy the demand. In fact, the demand is stimulated by the promoters and the performers.

Now, after the Newark accident, what is the result? Newspapers are calling the race tracks "Murderdromes" and one paper in Ohio declared motorcycles "murdercycles." Thousands of lines of the worst kind of publicity were given to this affair and it will take at least an equal number of lines of good publicity to overcome the bad, if such a thing is possible.

When parents read these awful newspaper accounts and their son has a motorcycle, it causes them worry. We know of several cases where riders have been compelled to dispose of their machines, because of the fears of the rest of the family. This refers not only to motordromes but to race tracks as well.

The Harley-Davidson Motor Company has often been asked why it did not take part in the racing game. Our answer is: "We do not believe in it." And we have reasons for that answer.

Before going into those reasons, let us make the statement that the Harley-Davidson Motor Company can build just as good and as fast racing machines as any of the companies that are building them today. This is a broad statement, but we can prove it, because we did it previous to the time we dropped racing.

We can build freak racing machines, eight valves, auxiliary forks, lightened moving parts and everything "skinned" down to racing. But of what benefit would it be to us? We don't sell these freak racers.

They would not teach us anything in the way of design, because their design is altogether different than that of a road machine. They would be of no service, except possibly

to amuse racing fans, make a little money, for the promoters, and incidentally, secure a few records, which might be of use in selling our stock machines.

Perhaps you wonder why this was written. It was for no other purpose than to place emphasis on the stand we take regarding the racing game, its benefits and injuries to the motorcycle industry. A year ago we did not believe very much in the racing game; today we believe a great deal less, and we hope to see the time that it will be abolished completely.

But, no doubt, it will take more human sacrifices before the "speed craze" dies out. We are for the safe, sane rider, who uses his machine both for business and pleasure and enjoys his motorcycle as it was designed to be used.

This talk will not give us back our friends. I feel keen, personal loss in the death of Mr. Hasha. We were very close friends and his tragic death affected me greatly. On a number of occasions Hasha and I had discussed the racing game. He looked forward to the day when he hoped to get out of the game safely.

Now Hasha has gone to his death, sacrificed on the altar of the speed mania and I, his friend, am preaching the moral. Some may think that it is in poor taste for me to use Hasha's death to point the moral, but I know how Eddie Hasha felt about the racing game, and I certainly know how I feel about it.

How many more good fellows must sacrifice their lives this way? It surely is to be hoped that the sacrifice of the eight lives at Newark has not been in vain.

Motorcycle race posters, circa 1910s–1920s.

Bert Wilson's Twin Cylinder Racer

By J. W. Duffield

Bert Wilson was a fictional boyhood hero who came alive in a book series written by J. W. Duffield in the 1910s and 1920s. Like the stars of the Horatio Alger rags-to-riches tales or the Hardy Boys mysteries, Bert overcame all adversity to win, proving the American ideal that the dreams do come true.

Duffield's hero differed from the Alger and Franklin W. Dixon books in that he wrote tales of sporting derring-do. And his tales stood out from other motorcycling books of the day—such as the Big Five Motorcycle Boys or the Motorcycle Chums—by being well written and truly exciting.

Published in 1914, *Bert Wilson's Twin Cylinder Racer* ended with a big race on one of the boardtrack motordromes that Arthur Davidson had tried to rally the fans against. Duffield's account seems true to life, and may be the sole surviving description of this most extreme of motorcycling sports.

The big motordome was gayly decorated with flags and bunting, in honor of the Fourth, and there was just enough breeze stirring to give them motion. A big military band played patriotic and popular airs, and, as the spectators filed into their seats in a never-ending procession, they felt already the first stirrings of an excitement that was to make of this a night to be remembered through out a lifetime.

An hour before the time scheduled for the race to begin every seat in grandstand and bleachers was taken, and people were fighting for a place in the grassy infield. Very soon, even that was packed with as many spectators as the managers felt could be disposed of with safety. They were kept within bounds by a stout rope fence stretched between posts. At last every available foot of space was occupied, and the gates were closed. Thousands were turned away even then, although there were over sixty thousand souls within the stadium.

The motordrome had been constructed to hold an immense crowd, but its designers had never anticipated anything like this. So great was the interest in the event, that most of those who could not gain admittance camped down near the gates to get bulletins of the progress of the race, as soon as possible.

It was an ideal night for such an event. The air was soft and charged with a thousand balmy odors. The band crashed out its stirring music, and made the blood of the most sluggish leap and glow. Suddenly the arc lights suspended at short intervals over the track blazed out, making the whole place as light as day.

Then, as every detail of the track was plainly revealed, thousands drew a deep breath and shuddered. The track was banked at an angle of approximately thirty-eight degrees, with three laps to the mile. It seemed impossible to many that anything on wheels could cling to the precipitous slope, that appeared to offer insecure footing even for a fly.

Near the bottom, a white band was painted around the entire circumference, marking the actual one-third of a mile. At the bottom of the track there was a level stretch, perhaps four feet wide, and beyond that the smooth turf, bordered at a little distance by a dense mass of spectators confined within the rope fence. Above the track tier after tier of seats arose.

Opposite the finish line, the starter's and judge's pavilion was built. Here all the riders and machines that were to take part were assembled, and it presented a scene of the utmost bustle and activity. Tom and Dick were there, anxiously waiting for Bert to emerge from his dressing room, and meanwhile inspecting every nut and bolt on the "Blue Streak." Despite the recent changes made in it, the faithful motorcycle was still the same staunch, dependable machine it had always been, but with even greater speed capabilities than it had possessed before.

Of course, there were many who claimed that Bert could never have a chance of winning without a specially built racer, and he had been urged a score of times to use such a mount. But he had refused without the slightest hesitation.

"Why," he always said, "I know what the old 'Blue Streak' will do, just as well as I know what I am capable of. I know every whim and humor of it, and just how to get the last ounce of power out of it. I've tested it a thousand times. I know it will stand up to any work I put it to, and I'd no more think of changing machines now than I would of trying a new system of training two days before I was to enter a running race. No, thanks, I guess I'll stick to the old 'Blue Streak.'"

Motorcycle race posters, circa 1910s–1930s.

Dick and Tom were still busy with oil can and wrench when Bert emerged from his dressing room. He was dressed in a blue jersey, with an American flag embroidered on breast and back. His head was encased in a thick leather helmet, and a pair of heavy-glassed goggles were pushed up on his forehead.

He strode quickly over to where his chums were working on his mount, and they shook hands heartily. "Welll" he exclaimed gaily, "how is the old 'bus' to-night? Everything O.K., I hope?"

"It sure is," replied Dick. "Tom and I have gone over every inch of it, and it seems in apple-pie order. We filled your oil tank up with oil that we tested ourselves, and we know that it's all right. We're not taking any chances."

"That's fine," exclaimed Bert, "there's nothing more important than good oil. We don't want any frozen bearings to-night, of all nights."

"Not much!" agreed Tom, "but it must be pretty nearly time for the start. It's after eight now."

Even as he spoke, a gong tapped, and a deep silence descended on the stadium. Excitement, intense and breathless, gripped every heart. A burly figure carrying a megaphone mounted a small platform erected in the center of the field, and in stentorian tones announced the conditions of the race.

Seven riders, representing America, France, England, Italy, and Belgium, were to compete for a distance of one hundred miles. The race was to begin from a flying start, which was to be announced by the report of a pistol. The time of each race was to be shown by an illuminated clock near the judge's stand.

Jay Springsteen gets lowdown and mean on his Harley-Davidson XR-750.

Harley-Davidson racers,
circa 1910s–1920s.

The man with the megaphone had hardly ceased speaking when the roar of several motorcycle exhausts broke forth from the starting platform and the band crashed into a stirring march.

Then a motorcycle appeared, towing a racer. Slowly it gathered headway, and at last the rider of the racing machine threw in the spark. The motor coughed once or twice, and then took hold. With a mighty roar his machine shot ahead, gathering speed with every revolution, and passing the towing motorcycle as though it were standing still.

In quick succession now, machine after machine appeared. It was Bert's turn to start, and, pulling his goggles down over his eyes, he leaped astride the waiting "Blue Streak."

"Go it, old man!" shouted Dick and Tom, each giving him a resounding buffet on the shoulder, "show 'em what you're made of."

"Leave it to me," yelled Bert, for already the towing motorcycle was towing him and the "Blue Streak" out onto the track. They went at a snail's pace at first, but quickly gathered momentum.

As he came into view of the gathered multitude, a shout went up that made the concrete structure tremble. This was repeated twice and then the spectators settled back, waiting for the start.

When he felt he was going fast enough, Bert, by a twist of the right grip, lowered the exhaust valves, and the next second he felt the old "Blue Streak" surge forward as though discharged from a cannon. It required a speed of fifty miles an hour even to mount the embankment, but before he had gone two hundred yards he had attained it. He turned the front wheel to the slope, and his machine mounted it like a bird.

Never had he sensed such gigantic power under him, and he felt exalted to the skies. He forgot everything in the mad delirium of speed; tremendous, maddening speed. Every time he opened the throttle a trifle more he could feel it increase. Eagerly, resistlessly, his mount tore and raged forward, whistling through the air with the speed of an arrow. In a few seconds he was abreast of the riders who had started first, and who were jockeying for a good position. There was little time for maneuvering, however, for now the riders were fairly well bunched, and the starter's pistol cracked. The race had started!

And now Bert found himself competing with the crack racers of the world. Each was mounted on the best machine the genius of his countrymen could produce, and each was grimly resolved to win. The "Blue Streak" and its rider were indeed in fast company, and were destined to be put to a test such as seldom occurs in even such strenuous racing as this.

Bert was riding high on the track at the start, and he resolved to make use of this position to gain the lead. He opened the throttle wide, and the "Blue Streak" responded nobly. So great was the force of the forward spurt that his hands were almost wrenched from the handlebars. He held on, however, and at the end of the second lap was even with the leader, a Frenchman.

Bert turned his front wheel down the slope, and swooped toward the bottom of the track with a sickening lurch. A vast sigh of horror went up from the closely packed stands. But at the last second, when within a foot of the bottom of the incline, Bert started up again, and with a speed increased by the downward rush shot up to the white band.

He hugged this closely, and reeled off mile after mile at a speed of close to a hundred miles an hour. Leaning down until his body touched the top frame bar, he coaxed ever a little more speed from the fire-spitting mechanism beneath him.

But the Frenchman hung on doggedly, not ten feet behind, and a few feet further back the English entrant tore along. In this order they passed the fifty-mile mark, and the spectators were standing now, yelling and shouting. The rest of the field had been unable to hold the terrific pace, and had dropped behind. The Belgian entrant had been forced to drop out altogether, on account of engine trouble.

The leaders swept on and gradually drew up on the three lagging riders. A quarter of a lap—half a lap—three-quarters of a lap—and amid a deafening roar of shouting from the spectators Bert swept past them. He had gained a lap on them!

The English and French entries were still close up, however, both hanging on within three yards of Bert's rear wheel. They reeled off mile after mile, hardly changing their positions by a foot. Suddenly there was a loud report that sounded even above the roar of the exhausts, and a second later Bert fell to the rear. His front tire had punctured, and it was only by the exercise of all his skill and strength that he had averted a horrible accident.

"It's all over. It's all over," groaned Tom. "He's out of the race now. He hasn't got a chance."

Dick said nothing, but his face was the color of chalk. He dashed for the supply tent, and emerged carrying a front wheel with an inflated tire already on it, just as Bert pulled up in front of them and leaped from his mount. His eyes were sunken, with dark rings under them, but his mouth was set and stern as death.

"On with it, Dick, on with it," he said, in a low, suppressed voice. "Let's have that wrench, Tom. Hold up the front fork, will you?"

He worked frantically, and in less than forty seconds had substituted the new wheel carrying the inflated tire in place of the old.

Flinging down the wrench, he sprang into the saddle, and with willing strength Dick and Tom rushed him and his machine out onto the track, pushing with all the might of their sinewy young bodies. At the first possible moment Bert shot on the power, and the engine, still hot, started instantly. In a second he was off in wild pursuit of the flying leaders.

As he mounted the track, he was seen to lean down and fumble with the air shutter on the carburetor. Apparently this had little effect, but to Bert it made all the difference in the world. The motor had had tremendous strength before, but now it seemed almost doubled. The whole machine quivered and shook under the mighty impact of the pistons, and the hum of the flywheels rose to a high whine. Violet flames shot from the exhaust in an endless stream.

The track streamed back from the whirling wheels like a rushing river. It seemed to be leaping eagerly to meet him. The lights and shadows flickered away from him, and the grotesque shadow cast by his machine weaved rapidly back and forth as he passed under the sizzling arc lights.

The spectators were a yelling mob of temporary maniacs by this time. The Frenchman and Englishman had passed the eighty-mile mark, and Bert was still a lap and a half behind. He was riding like a fiend, coaxing, nursing his machine, manipulating the controls so as to wring the last ounce of energy from the tortured mass of metal he bestrode.

Slowly, but with deadly persistence, he closed the gap between him and the leaders. Amidst a veritable pandemonium from the crazed spectators he passed them, but

Race posters, circa 1950s–1980s.

MOTORCYCLE RACES

CLASS A-

EVERY Wed. NITE

STARTING at

8.30 PM

SPEEDWAY

WINDY CITY

MOTORCYCLE CLUB

4th ANNUAL

HILL CLIMB

at the FAMOUS JANDUS HILL.

200 Ft. Hill-75 Percent Grade-at CARY, ILL.

Thrilling Amatuer and Novice Events **CHAMPION PROFESSIONALS**

MAY 25

Rain **June 8** Date

THRILLS AND SPILLS

Come and see riders like Joe Petrali, Art Erlenbough, Swede Anderson, Ed Wagner, Dynamite Smith, Squibby and many others.

ACTION GALORE

A. M. A. Sanction 1101

1:00 p. m.

...ral Standard Time

→ Take Illinois State Highway 19 or 22 to Cary. Then Follow 80-Mile Per-Gallon Arrow One Mile S-still had one lap to make up in fifteen miles. Shortly after passing them, he was close on the three remaining competitors, who were hanging on in the desperate hope of winning should some accident befall the leaders.

Suddenly, without any warning, something—nobody ever learned what—went wrong. They became a confused, tangled mass of blazing machine and crumpled humanity. Bert was not twenty feet behind them, and men turned white and sick and women fainted. It seemed inevitable that he would plow into them traveling at that terrific pace, and add one more life to the toll of the disaster.

Bert's mind acted like a flash. He was far down on the track, and could not possibly gain a position above the wreckage, and so skirt it in that way. Nor did he have time to pass beneath it, for men and machines were sliding diagonally down the steep embankment.

With a muttered prayer, he accepted the last chance fate had seen fit to leave him. He shot off the track completely, and whirled his machine onto the turf skirting it.

The grass was smooth, but, at Bert's tremendous speed, small obstacles seemed like mountains. The "Blue Streak" quivered and bounded, at times leaping clear off the ground, as it struck some uneven place. For what seemed an age, but was in reality only a few seconds, Bert kept on this, and then steered for the track again. If his machine mounted the little ridge formed by the beginning of the track proper, all might yet be well, if not—well, he refused to even think of that.

The front wheel hit the obstruction, and, a fraction of a second later, the rear wheel struck. The machine leaped clear into the air, sideways. Bert stiffened the muscles of his wrists until they were as hard as steel, to withstand the shock of landing. The handlebars were almost wrenched from his control, but not quite, and once more he was tearing around with scarcely diminished speed.

By great good fortune, the riders involved in the accident had not been hurt seriously, although their machines were total wrecks, and they hobbled painfully toward the hospital tent, assisted by spectators who had rushed to their aid.

Bert was now less than half a lap behind the flying leaders, but he had only four miles in which to make it up. At intervals now he leaned down and pumped extra oil into the engine. This added a trifle of extra power, and as he rushed madly along the "Blue Streak" lived up to its name nobly. At the beginning of the last mile he was only about three lengths behind. The vast crowd was on its feet now, shouting, yelling, tossing hats, gesticulating. They were worked up to a pitch of frenzy absolutely indescribable.

As Bert crept grimly up, nearer and nearer, the place became a veritable Bedlam. Now the racers had entered the last lap; only a third of a mile to go, and Bert was still a length behind. The exhaust of the racing motorcycles united in one hoarse, bellowing roar, that seemed to shake the very earth.

Then Bert reached down, and with the finish line but a short hundred yards ahead, opened wide the air shutter on the carburetor. His machine seemed to almost leave the track, and then, tearing forward, passed the Frenchman, who was leading. As he crossed the finish line, Bert was ahead by the length of a wheel!

The uproar that burst forth then defied all description. As Bert, after making a circuit of the track, finally brought the "Blue Streak" to a standstill, a seething mob rushed toward him, waving hats and flags, and shouting frantically and joyfully.

Never had **he sensed** such **gigantic power** under him, and **he felt exalted** to the skies. He forgot everything in the **mad delirium** of speed; tremendous, maddening speed.

—J. W. Duffield, *Bert Wilson's Twin Cylinder Racer,* 1914

MOTORCYCLE

3 ★ *RACES*

CLARK COUNTY FAIRGROUNDS
SPRINGFIELD, OHIO
SATURDAY NIGHT - 8:00 P. M.
MAY 22

9 EVENTS - TIME TRIALS 6 P.M.

Admission $1.50 tax included
Children under 12 admitted FREE
when accompanied by Parents

SPONSORED BY
Springfield Pirates Motorcycle Club

AMA Sanction No. 21104

MOTORCYCLE
RACES

every **WEDNESDAY** night

SANTA FE SPEEDWAY
9100 S. WOLF RD. 3 Mi. So. of Junction Interstates 55 & 284

Race posters, circa 1950s–1980s.

The Grandstand Complex

By Horace McCoy

Horace McCoy was one of the founders of the hard-boiled school of tough-guy writing. Along with Dashiell Hammett, Raymond Chandler, and others, McCoy started out penning his tales for the pulps—cheap men's magazines of the 1920s, 1930s, and 1940s. But along the way, he turned his penny-a-word prose into true poetry.

McCoy was also the author of 1935's *They Shoot Horses, Don't They?* His first novel, it became an American classic—a tersely written, well-crafted, and boldly bleak look at the Depression era and the effects it had on the hearts and minds of Americans.

Working for pulps such as *Detective Action Stories, Battle Aces, Western Trails*, and the famous *Black Mask*, McCoy wrote about everything from bi-plane dogfights to gumshoeing the mean streets to Indian ambushes—all without ever having experienced such exploits.

"The Grandstand Complex" followed in this vein. While McCoy probably never raced on the speedways, he sure could talk the talk.

Tony Lukatovich had finished the Florida season a few points ahead of me, but I had got them back (with plenty to spare) the first four weeks in Los Angeles. That L.A. track was made to order for me. I had so much confidence in it, and in my JAP motor, that after the first week I stopped wearing the steel cap on my left foot and the polo belt I used to protect my abdomen. This made it more dangerous for me in case of a bad spill, but it looked spectacular to the crowds. You have to be a showman to be a success in motorcycle racing. Finally, to live up to the publicity I was getting in the newspapers, and to prove that my winning of last year's national championship was no accident, I discarded my crash helmet, substituting a simple leather helmet such as aviators used to wear. Everybody said I was a damn fool for doing this. If my head ever smacked the track or the guard rail at fifty-five or sixty that leather helmet would have been absolutely no protection. My skull would have cracked like an eggshell. I knew that and so did the crowd. The majority came out just to hear somebody's skull crack (you may not think you can hear a skull crack with all those exhausts popping, but you can, you most certainly can) or to see somebody's brains spilled in the dirt, but so far the customers had been disappointed. At the end of the first four weeks I was the big favorite in L.A. I was out in front in individual points, and with the Long Beach team matches coming up, and the national awards but a month away, I looked like a cinch to repeat the championship.

Tony Lukatovich was very jealous of my popularity and you would have thought that every point I collected was a year off his life. He had been the runner-up in the national last year and he had definitely made up his mind he was not going to finish second again. I don't think he wanted the championship title as much as he did the glory that went with it. He was a grandstander, a great grandstander. He was a great rider, too, but it was the cheers of the crowd he wanted. These were meat and drink to him. Give him a crowd big enough and let them all root for him and he was the greatest motorcycle racer who ever lived. He would pull turns and slides and finishes that none of the others of us would even dare think about. In Florida when he was leading in points and was the star attraction, where the crowd was for him to a man, he was a broadsiding maniac. He was more than that; he was a genius.

But the Florida track was short, one sixth of a mile, and the L.A. track was longer, one fifth of a mile. Those seventy-two yards made a difference. On the longer track Tony's judgment, his intuition, was a fraction bad. His timing slipped just enough to keep him from winning consistently.

"It's only your imagination," I told him one day, lying, trying to cheer him up.

"I haven't got any imagination. You're the guy who's got all the imagination. You go to hell," he said.

"All right, if that's the way you feel about it," I said. "I was only trying to help you out."

"I don't need any help from you," he said. "You go to hell."

After that he got nastier and nastier and finally I stopped speaking to him at all. Then he began taking all sorts of reckless chances on the turns and doing trick riding in the homestretch, trying to show up the rest of us. But instead of impressing the crowds with his ability

103

he only gave them the idea that he was a wild man out there trying to kill some of the other riders.

I never did get really sore at him because I knew what was the matter. He simply wanted to become a favorite with the customers and get them pulling for him. He was starving for lack of glory. But the harder he tried the worse he looked. In every race I was knocking his ears down. I was concentrating on piling up all the points I possibly could so that if I had a spill that put me in the hospital I would have enough points to coast to the championship. I didn't expect to go to the hospital; I mean I wasn't looking forward to it, but in motorcycle racing you never can tell, especially when you have a wild man who hates your guts riding behind you.

Tony was trying so desperately to win, was looking so bad, the committee notified him that unless he got back some of his old-time form they would have to give him a handicap. This was like telling Joe Louis that unless he improved they were going to match him with Barney Ross. Tony raved and yelled and screamed and put on an act in front of the stands, challenging the committee to a fight, individually or collectively, kicking up the dirt and throwing his equipment all over the infield. He rushed over to the loudspeaker microphone and was trying to make a speech to the crowd when Jack Gurling, the promoter, collared him and threatened him with a suspension. That cooled Mr. Lukatovich, but I knew from the look of his face that there was blood on the moon.

That night after the races he came over to my room. I invited him in, thinking he probably wanted to talk things over.

"The team races with Long Beach are next week," he said.

"That's right," I said.

"And you and I race again as the number-one team?"

"I suppose we do," I said.

"And if we win this time we get permanent possession of the cups?"

"That's right. We've got two legs on 'em now and if we win this time we get permanent possession. Did you get back your cup from your mother?"

Tony always sent all the trophies and cups he won back home to his mother in Ohio, so she could show the neighbors how well he was going.

"No, I didn't," he replied.

"You didn't? Don't you think you ought to get it?"

"I can't," he said. "It would break her heart. She thinks it's mine already."

"It probably will be," I said, "but if we should happen to lose it might be embarrassing for you not to have the cup."

"We won't lose," he said. "But I didn't come over here to talk about that. I want to talk about us—you and me."

"Go ahead," I told him.

"Do you think you're a better rider than I am?" he asked.

"How do you think I won the championship last year—with cigarette coupons?"

"You think you are then?"

"I don't think anything about it. I know damn well I am."

"Do you think you've got as much nerve as I have?"

"I wouldn't know much about that. But I've got more skill, which is a damn sight more important."

"All you've got is a swelled head," he said. "Why have you got it in for me?"

"You must be daffy," I said. "I haven't got it in for you. The only trouble with you is you're jealous. As long as you're the fair-haired boy with the fans and get all the newspaper publicity, everything is roses. The moment somebody else does, you curl up. You can't take it, Tony."

"Is that so?" he said, jumping up, grabbing me by the coat lapel.

"Sit down," I said. He had that blood-on-the-moon look on his face again. "I don't know what's eating you," I said, "but whatever it is, I don't want any part of it. Suppose you beat it."

He said nothing, standing there and looking at me with his eyes glittering.

"Go on, beat it," I said. "Whatever grudges we've got we'll settle out there on the track."

"That's exactly what I want to do," he said. "That's exactly why I came here. I'm going to make you a proposition. I'll see how much nerve you've got."

I knew this was going to be something that was very screwy.

"There's no doubt," he said, "that we're the two best motorcycle racers in the world."

"That's right. I'm the best and you're the second best," I said.

"Okay. We'll make a bet on it."

"You know I don't bet," I said.

"Not money," he said smiling, shaking his head. "Not money. You. Bet yourself."

"I don't get you," I said.

"Your life. You," he said. "You and I race together in the team matches. If you win I'll kill myself. If I win you kill yourself. That'll leave the winner the biggest star in the game."

"Nothing doing," I said.

"Why not? There's nothing new about duels—they've been fighting them for hundreds of years. The other day I read in the paper about a couple of miners in Europe fighting a duel with sledgehammers. That's all this is—a duel. With motorcycles."

"This is the goofiest thing I ever listened to," I said. "Nothing doing."

"I told you I had more nerve than you did," he said.

"It's not a question of nerve—"

"Oh, yes, it is."

"Oh, no, it's not. It's that grandstand complex of yours. You'd rather be dead than to be second best."

"I'm slowly dying anyway," he said.

"You go right ahead and die," I told him. "Me, I'm having a fine time living."

"Well, then, it's all settled," he said, turning to go.

"Let's shake hands on it," he said, sticking out his hand.

"Why should I shake hands with you?" I asked. "You hate my guts."

"Sure, I do, sure, I do," he said, smiling. "But that's got nothing to do with it. Gentlemen always shake hands when they make a bet."

"I haven't made any bet," I said, getting sore.

"Oh, yes, you have. The team race Friday night—the race for life. Whoever loses kills himself."

He stood there smiling, his hand stuck out, waiting for my shake.

"Beat it the hell out of here," I said.

"Is it yes or no?" he asked, not moving.

"Beat it——" I said.

"All right, I'll beat it. But this is going to ruin you. I'm going to spread the word around to everybody, the newspaper reporters and everybody, that you're yellow. I'm going to tell them about the proposition to fight a duel with motorcycles and how you were too yellow to take me up on it because you thought you might lose and have to kill yourself. This'll ruin you."

Suddenly it dawned on me that he was right. This would ruin me. People wouldn't stop to figure it was a screwy proposition, they'd really think I was yellow. Soon they'd have me believing it myself.

"You polack — — — — — — — — — — —," I said, stepping over, hitting him in the face. He grabbed me, trying to hold on, but I shook him loose and began punching him in the head with my fists. He grabbed me again and we fell over a chair, breaking it, wrestling on the floor. I finally climbed to my feet, dragging him with me, and started punching him in the face some more. Then he grabbed me again, trying to hold on. I got loose and hit him back of the ear and he fell to the floor unconscious, his arms doubled under his stomach.

"Well," my mind said, "you've knocked him out and where did it get you? He's still got that axe over you. The only way to stop whatever is going to happen from actually happening is to cut the guy's tongue out. The minute he starts talking everybody will think you are yellow and they'll all go over to his side. . . . It looks like you'll have to accept the challenge."

"I suppose so," I replied to myself.

"The thing to do," my mind said, "is to win."

"I'll win, all right," I said. "I certainly don't want to have to commit suicide."

I got a wet towel out of the bathroom and rolled Tony over and began rubbing his face and wrists and pretty soon he came to.

"I'm okay," he said, sitting up.

"There's just one thing," I said. "If I do win this race how do I know you won't welsh?"

"Don't worry," he said, pushing himself up off the floor. "I won't welsh and neither will you. We'll shake hands like gentlemen do."

He stuck out his hand. I took it.

"All right, you polack — — — — — — — — — —," I said. "Now beat it."

There was a big crowd out for the team races, many of them coming from Long Beach to back their own riders. There was a lot of money bet on the races this year by the Long Beach fans because our second, third and fourth teams were weaker than usual. The men who had been our number-two team last year, and who had won easily, both had been killed on the Florida track. Tony and I looked like cinches to beat our men, but we weren't so sure about the other teams.

About 7:30 that night Tony came in the shed where I was tightening up my chain.

"How do you feel?" he asked. It was the first time he had spoken to me since the fight.

"Swell," I said, "just perfectly—damn swell. How do you feel?"

"I feel fine," he said.

"You won't feel so fine when Gurling finds you," I said. "He's been asking me questions about your cup."

"Look," he said, "everything will be all right if we win. One of us has got to win. I told Gurling my mother had mailed the cup but that it just hadn't got here yet."

"Suppose we lose?" I asked.

"We can't lose," he said. "One of us has got to win. Not only for the cup, but for another reason, too. Did you keep your dinner down tonight?" he asked, leaning over.

"What was that?" I asked suddenly, turning around, pretending I had heard something. "That was a peculiar noise. Is anybody rattling dice in here? Oh, excuse me," I said, looking at Tony. "It's you."

"Me?" he said, surprised.

"It's your teeth I hear," I said.

"You go to hell," he said, crossing to where his mechanics were checking his motor. . . .

The first event on the program was a handicap race for Class B riders, boys who had ridden only a few events. The next event was a four-lap heat, the first three to transfer to Event 7, the handicap semifinals. I won this race in 1:05:10, pretty good time. The third event was an exhibition by some local trick-riding jockies. Tony was in Event 4, the first three in this also to transfer to Event 7. He won the heat in 1:06 flat. Events 5 and 6 were for novice riders.

Tony and I were the only ones to start from scratch in Event 7, one of the two feature races of the night. This event was run in two heats, the first three in each heat to transfer to the final event, four laps, the points to count toward the national championship.

Tony and I sat in our saddles on the scratch line, saying nothing, six feet apart, while the announcer introduced us. I got the most applause. I looked at Tony, winking.

"It won't be long now," he said, winking back.

"Don't let him get your goat," my mind told me.

"Fat chance," I replied.

The starter's gun popped and my two mechanics shoved. My motor caught on the first shove.

"Good old JAP," I said to myself, giving her the gun.

There were two men in front of me. They were both handicap men. One had started from thirty yards ahead of the scratch line and the other from twenty-five. I wasn't much worried about them; they were kids on the way up, and I knew I could outgut them in a pinch. But I went right after them anyway, not taking any chances. I trailed them a full lap before I could cut down the handicap and on the backstretch I hung on their tails waiting for a hole at the turn. One of them skidded a little and I shot through. I trailed the leader down the stretch, but I took him on the front turn and went ahead. In a moment I got a flash out of the corner of my eye and I knew it was Tony making his bid. I hugged the inside railing, hoping he didn't lose his head and crash me. Tony was a maniac when he was desperate. With some riders you can make a close race out of it and give the fans a good finish and a run for their money, but not with Tony. Stay just as far in front of him as you possibly could, was my motto.

I beat him into the finish by a length. I went on around the track and went through the gate into the pits.

There was one other event before the team race—the race that meant the finish for either me or Tony. I had six or seven minutes before we were to go out, so I walked

FIFTH STRAIGHT YEAR

HARLEY-D

WINS SPRING
NATIONAL CHAM

Mike Long

Mike Long Wins 5-STAR
CLASS "A" SHORT TRACK RACE
on HARLEY-DAVIDSON *Sprint*

AVIDSON
ELD 50-MILE
IONSHIP

Carroll Resweber

SPRINGFIELD, ILL. • AUGUST 20, 1961

rroll Resweber **FIRST in 33 minutes and 54.41 sec.**

rt Markel .... **TIES FOR SECOND SPOT**

e Leonard .... **FOURTH PLACE**

L ABOVE RIDING HARLEY-DAVIDSONS

SILK SCREEN PRINTED IN U.S.A.

Dealer poster boasting of Harley-Davidson victory, 1961.

around, trying to tell myself there was nothing to get nervous about. I got a hot dog and a bottle of pop, trying to put my mind on the movies or women or something, anything except what depended on the outcome of the duel. The taste of mustard in the hot dog nauseated me and for a minute I thought I would have to check my dinner. I gagged on the pop, finally throwing it away, too.

"What the hell is this?" I asked myself. "Why am I so nervous? I've never been nervous before. I can beat that guy any day in the week."

"Let's go," said one of my mechanics.

"It's not time yet," I said.

"Sure, it is," he said. "The other race is finished. Come on—"

There was more applause when I came out onto the track. Tony and the Long Beach riders were already there, Red Dooley and Paul Jarvis, two top-notchers, not champions yet, but a couple of boys who were getting better every hour. I gave my motor to my mechanics, moving up to the starting line where they were waiting to toss for positions. Tony and I both lost and had to take the second and fourth positions. The Long Beach crowd whooped it up at this.

"Toss for us," Tony said to the starter. "You call it," he said to me.

"Never mind," I said. "You can have two."

"Okay," he said, not even thanking me.

"That was a silly thing to do," my mind said a moment after I had uttered the words. "Why didn't you toss with him? Number four is on the outside, the worst position on the track. You've deliberately put yourself in a hole in the most important race you ever rode in your life."

There was a lot of yelling . . . and then we were off. The others got away first. My motor didn't fire at once.

"Good God!" I thought.

My mechanics shoved again, harder, and this time the motor caught. The others were going into the turn, twenty yards ahead. This was a terrific handicap to give good riders and I knew I was up against it.

I settled down to business, telling myself not to get panicky, and eased into the first turn. But on the backstretch I opened up, swinging high on the outside to keep my goggles from fouling from the dirt the front riders were kicking up. At the turn I dropped down into the slot, figuring Paul Jarvis, just in front of me, would be a little too anxious and would go in a little too fast to hold his line and would therefore slide a little. He did. He left two feet between him and the inside railing and I went through without shutting off. But the impetus carried me to the outside again and I had to shut off and skid to keep from hitting the wall. I laid my left toe on the ground, pulling my motor over at an angle of about thirty degrees. I heard a gasp go up from the stands. I eased my handlebars over, opening up in the homestretch.

Tony was in second place, a full length behind Dooley. I was still twenty yards back of Tony. I was in a rotten spot. We had three laps left, just three, and I knew I was going to need everything I had to win this race. My motor was all right now that she was rolling—it was the best racing JAP in the world. This time it was up to me.

I took the front turn wide open, laying my motor over my left knee, listening for that first faint whirr that tells you the traction is slipping. When you hear that you want to get it up in a hurry, else you will have the whole thing suddenly in your lap.

. . . I fought and fought, took chances I had never taken before, used all my skill, all my anticipation, but I was getting nowhere. I had managed to cut off a few yards, but I was not close enough to make my bid. I felt satisfied this was the greatest race I had ever ridden. I would have been in front by the same distance I was now behind if I hadn't lost that one or two seconds getting started.

On the third lap Tony took the back turn wide open, a stupid thing to do, and lost a couple of yards in a slide. I picked up this much on him, going down the stretch so close that my front wheel almost touched his rear wheel. On the front turn of the last lap Dooley made his first mistake—he hit a patch of soft dirt that he should have spotted before now, and slid across it. It was a very short slide, but for an instant his back wheel spun and in that instant Tony and I had pulled up on him. It happened in the tick of a clock.

We went into the backstretch at top speed. Tony knew I was behind him and tried to shake me off, but I held on, hoping he would slide in the turn so I could take him. This was my final chance to win; if it didn't happen I was a gone gosling.

I eased over to the right a trifle to get set for the jump. Dooley was swinging wide now, trying to play safe, and I saw Tony follow him over.

"He's crazy to take a chance like that," I thought.

Just then Tony's front wheel hit Dooley's rear wheel and both motors went over, riders and all. One of the wheels struck the concrete guard rail, leaving a shower of sparks. Suddenly, the sky filled with flame. It was right in front of me.

"Good God, I'm going to pile up!" I thought, twisting my handlebars over, turning my head so the crash wouldn't put out my eyes. . . . My motor twisted and kicked and I had that awful cold feeling in the bowels that a man gets when he realizes the thing he is riding is suddenly out of control. . . . Then my wheels gripped and I righted myself and saw the starter in front of me waving the checkered flag, the winner's flag, giving the signal to me.

"Can I drop you some place?" a reporter asked, coming out of the morgue with me.

"No, thanks," I said.

"Too bad about Tony," he said. "Jesus, there wasn't much left of his face, was there? Those spokes are as bad as a meat grinder."

I looked at him steadily, trying to focus my eyes on him, but not being able to.

"Tony called me up just this afternoon," he said. "It's a funny thing, but he had a hunch something like this was going to happen."

"He did?" I said.

"Yes," the reporter said. "It was a good story. I used it as a feature in the *Bulldog*. It's out now. Read it. As a matter of fact, it was written especially for you."

"I'll get it," I said.

"Well . . . you sure I can't drop you some place?"

"I think I'll walk around a little," I said.

At the corner I was stopped by the traffic light. There was a stack of morning papers piled up by the lamp post. "Two Die In Motorcycle Race," the headline said. "Tony Lukatovich and Red Dooley killed in Long Beach—L.A. team match. . . ." I stopped, looking down at the paper. "Motorcycle Champion Resigns Career After Fatal Smash; Vows He Will Never Race Again," said a heading.

"I didn't say that," I said to myself, trying to figure the whole thing out. The next moment I knew what the reporter meant. "My God!" I said to myself, turning the corner, walking down the street very fast. . . .

Harley-Davidson racers, circa 1910s–1920s.

Chapter 4

The Birth of Bad

On the Fourth of July weekend, 4,000 members of a motorcycle club roared into Hollister, California, for a three-day convention. **They quickly tired of ordinary motorcycle thrills and turned to more exciting stunts.** Racing their vehicles down the main streets and through traffic lights, they rammed into restaurants and bars, breaking furniture and mirrors . . . **police arrested many . . . but could not restore order.**

—*Life* magazine, 1947

The consummate Harley-Davidson rebels, circa 1950s.

"A Shocking Story": The Wild One and the Ones that Weren't So Wild

By Michael Dregni

The Wild One was loosely based on events the purportedly took place during a Fourth of July celebration by motorcyclists in the sleepy little town of Hollister, California, in 1947. But the truth behind the tales has long been debated. Photographs were fixed; news reports bloated; events distorted.

In this essay, Michael Dregni looks at the various versions of one of the formative events in creating motorcycling's outlaw mystique.

I t was a movie with a reputation, as folk used to say in the old days about a "fallen" woman or a teenage juvenile delinquent.

I remember the first time I saw it, almost four decades after it was first released. It was showing at a revival theater that screened an oddball assortment of classics and forgotten movies from days past. The theater was as old as many of the movies themselves and indeed had shown some of them when they first opened. The red velvet that covered the chairs was threadbare, the seats squeaked when you sat down, and the air had the smell of popcorn from decades ago. Then, the lights dimmed and the surroundings were forgotten. Onto the screen in glorious black and white burst the opening images of a country road and the sound of motorcycles in the distance. In a flash, the title rolled across the screen: *The Wild One*.

Although decades had passed since its debut, there was still an aura to this famous—or more likely, infamous—film. It was dangerous, subversive. It even began with a warning that echoed the first lines of Dante's guided tour of Hell: "This is a shocking story. It could never take place in most American towns—but it did in this one. It is a public challenge not to let it happen again."

I t was a day that would live in infamy. Pearl Harbor was history and World War II was finally finished, but in the days after the war, some young men returning from battle had a craving for something different from the ordered life and the American dream that they had fought for. Kickstarting a motorcycle into life and riding off to find the horizon filled the bill. It was just such a ride that brought a group of motorcyclists searching for fun to the sleepy little town of Hollister, California, on the Fourth of July in 1947.

What really happened at Hollister is impossible to tell from today's vantage. There are many versions of the story of the day that changed motorcycling forever, and none of them are consistent with each other. There's one thing they all agree on, however: The story as presented in *Life* magazine and Marlon Brando's movie, *The Wild One*, was a hoax.

It all began with a photograph. Late editions of the San Francisco Chronicle on July 5, 1947, carried the first version of the story: A gang of drunken motorcyclists called the Boozefighters had invaded the town of Hollister on America's most sacrosanct day, July 4. They had raced through the streets on their motorized steeds, terrifying good people. They drank beer and brawled and distressed young damsels. Life in Hollister would never be the same.

A single photograph was sent out over the wires to news media around the country. In the photograph taken by Barney Petersen, a fat slob of a motorcyclist sat astride his Harley, surrounded by a sea of empty bottles. He clutched a couple beers in his evil claws and leered at the camera. In his eyes was a cold message: "Bar your doors and lock away your daughters because I'm coming to get you."

A photo editor at *Life* saw the photograph and marked it for use. At the time, Life held the respect of Americans like no magazine before or since. Life had told the awful story of World War II in words and photographs like Grandpa sitting down to spin a yarn in front of the fireplace after a turkey dinner with all the dressings. It was not until Walter Cronkite arrived in American living rooms every evening on the television that the news media had a more powerful single voice.

Life reported: "On the Fourth of July weekend, 4,000 members of a motorcycle club roared into Hollister, California, for a three-day convention. They quickly tired of ordinary motorcycle thrills and turned to more exciting stunts. Racing their vehicles down the main streets and through traffic lights, they rammed into restaurants and bars, breaking furniture and mirrors . . . police arrested many . . . but could not restore order."

When *Life* ran the photo with the story of the Hollister brouhaha, the awful event was catapulted into the hearts and minds of Americans everywhere. The story of Hollister had all the makings of myth. It was the modern western, with the lawless men in black riding into town to confront the good citizenry, only to be banished by a duel with the fearless lawman. It was like a glorified war movie, a blitzkrieg by minions of the evil empire upon the peace-loving townspeople. Almost overnight, a new menace was at hand, and every motorcyclist was suddenly seen as one of the dreaded Boozefighters.

Then came the movie. In 1953, *The Wild One* starring Marlon Brando opened at a theater near you. Producer Stanley Kramer and director Laslo Benedek knew a good story when they saw one. They jumped on the Hollister incident, read the news accounts, shook their heads once more at the photograph, and fashioned a fictionalized account of the event.

In the film, Marlon Brando played the leader of the Black Rebels Motorcycle Club, a cool cat named Johnny Strabler who wore a black leather jacket like a suit of armor against the world. Atop his Triumph Thunderbird, he led his gang on a Fourth of July ride up the California coast, stopping to wreak havoc at a motorcycle race before moving on to terrorize an innocent small town based on Hollister.

An early scene provided a quick Hollywood-style sociological analysis of the roots of postwar disaffection that gave birth to motorcycle gangs. A highway patrolman who had just chased away Brando's gang warns another officer.

"Where'd that bunch come from?" an officer asks, playing the devil's advocate for a theater full of moviegoers asking themselves the same question.

"I don't know," responds the other patrolman, the voice of all-knowing wisdom. "Everywhere. I don't even think they know where they're going. Nutty. Ten guys like that gives people the idea everybody that drives a motorcycle is crazy. What are they trying to prove?"

"Beats me," answers the first officer, the voice of the common people. "Looking for somebody to push them around so they can get sore and show how tough they are."

When the gang arrives in town, it makes a beeline for Bleeker's Cafe and Bar. Members drop their change into the jukebox and order up rounds of beer. One townsgirl, taken by the excitement that follows the gang, says, "Black Rebels Motorcycle Club, that's cute! Hey Johnny, what are you rebelling against?"

With studied nonchalance, Johnny answered, "Whaddya got?"

He further explained his philosophy of life to the waitress named Cathy, played by Mary Murphy. She is curious about Johnny and his gang, and queries him: "Where are you going when you leave here? Don't you know?"

Johnny: "We're just gonna go."

Cathy: "Just trying to make conversation; it means nothing to me."

Johnny: "Look, on weekends, we go out and have a ball."

Cathy: "What do you do? I mean, do you just ride around, or do you go on some sort of picnic or something?"

Johnny: "A picnic? Man, you are too square! I have to straighten you out. Now listen, you don't go any one special place, that's cornball style. You just go!" he says to a snap of his fingers. "A bunch gets together after a week. It builds up. The idea is to have a ball. Now, if you gonna stay cool you gotta wail. You gotta put something down. You gotta make some jive, don't you know what I'm talking about?"

Obviously, she doesn't have a clue.

Soon, Johnny will take Cathy for a ride on his Triumph, giving society a taste of freedom on two wheels. "I've never ridden on a motorcycle before," Cathy exclaims with delight. "It's fast. It scared me. But I forgot everything. It felt good."

Then, the true bad guy shows his face. Lee Marvin and his gang of bad bad guys ride into town. As Cathy walks home from work, Marvin on his Harley-Davidson leads his gang to encircle the woman, spinning around in a kaleidoscope of revving bikes moving in for the kill —just like the Indians circling the wagon train in a Wild West shoot-'em-up. Only Johnny can save her, whisking her away on his Triumph like a knight in shining armor.

Brando's character was confusing to 1950s audiences. He was the bad guy and the good guy at the same time. This didn't make sense: Everyone knew full well that the bad guys wore black hats and the good guys wore white. It was repeated every Saturday matinee in the horse opera at the local theater.

Now, suddenly, here was Johnny wearing a black leather jacket and a black cap, terrorizing a town with his good-for-nothing bikers—and then midway through the movie another side of his character gradually comes to light. Johnny ain't all bad. Just confused. Under the mask of that emotionless face and the armor of his jacket, he's introspective, questioning, maybe as confused about his direction in life as the audience is confused about his character. Johnny was the first anti-hero role in Hollywood.

Marlon Brando had the look down pat. "The part was actor-proof," he wrote forty years later in his autobiography, *Songs My Mother Taught Me*. That may have been a self-deprecating brag, or perhaps Brando didn't realize that in many ways he was Johnny.

Brando provided his own psychoanalysis of Johnny: "More than most parts I've played in the movies or onstage, I related to Johnny, and because of this, I believe I played him as more sensitive and sympathetic than the script envisioned. There's a line in the picture where he snarls, 'Nobody tells me what to do.' That's exactly how I've felt all my life. Like Johnny, I have always resented authority. I have been constantly discomfited by people telling me what to do, and have always thought that Johnny took refuge in his lifestyle because he was wounded—that he'd had little love as a kid and was trying to survive the emotional insecurity that his childhood had forced him to carry into adulthood. Because of the emotional pain of feeling like a nobody, he became arrogant and adopted a pose of indifference to criticism. He did everything to appear strong when inside he was soft and vulnerable and fought hard to conceal it. He had lost faith in the fabric of society and had made his own world. He was a rebel, but a strong part of him was sensitive and tender. At the time I told a reporter that 'I wanted to show that gentleness and tolerance is the only way to dissipate the forces of social destruction' because I view Johnny as a man torn by an inner struggle beyond his capacity to express it. He had been so disappointed in life that it was difficult for him to express love, but beneath his hostility lay a desperate yearning and desire to feel love because he'd had so little of it. I could have just as easily been describing myself. It seemed perfectly natural for me to play this role."

The movie was not a hit when it made its debut. Many theater-owners refused to screen such trash; others who dared to were read the riot act by do-gooders. "The public's reaction to *The Wild One* was, I believe, a product of its time and circumstances," Brando wrote. "It was only seventy-nine minutes long, short by modern standards, and it looks dated and corny now; I don't think it has aged well. But it became a kind of cult film."

The film struck a chord with a certain disaffected crowd that were tantalized by the rebellion—and by Brando's character. He was a romanticized Robin Hood on a cycle, offering would-be rebels an image to live by. Sales of black leather jackets soared, Brando related in his autobiography, and suddenly became a symbol, although what the symbol stood for was not truly understood. It was the dawn of the juvenile delinquent craze, a horror mirrored in numerous paperback potboiler novels and Hollywood films. A new star was born riding on the wave of this craze, a young actor named James Dean, who in his film A Rebel Without a Cause came to stand against everything society stood for.

Brando writes that he never expected *The Wild One* to have such an impact: "I was as surprised as anyone when T-shirts, jeans and leather jackets suddenly became symbols of rebellion. In the film there was a scene in which some-body asked my character, Johnny, what I was rebelling against, and I answered, "Whaddya got?" But none of us involved in the picture ever imagined it would instigate or encourage youthful rebellion. . . .

"After The Wild One was finished, I couldn't look at it for weeks; when I did, I didn't like it because I thought it was too violent."

Reading between the lines of Brando's autobiography, it seems obvious that The Wild One also played an important role in changing Brando's life, whether he realized it or not.

"I never knew that there were sleeping desires and feelings in our society whose buttons would be hit so uncannily in that film. In hindsight, I think people responded to the movie because of the budding social and cultural currents that a few years later exploded volcanically on college campuses and the streets of America. Right or wrong, we were at the beginning of a new era after several years of transition following World War II; young people were beginning to doubt and question their elders and to challenge their values, morals and the established institutions of authority. There was a wisp of steam just beneath the surface when we made that picture. Young people looking for a reason—any reason—to rebel. I simply happened to be at the right place at the right time in the right part—and I also had the appropriate state of mind for the role."

John Cameron was there at Hollister on the Fourth of July, 1947. He was a founding member of the Booze-fighters, a ringleader on two wheels. He remembers the events that created the myth and calls it all a hoax.

Cameron spent the best years of his life aboard a motorcycle. In a 1995 videotaped interview with motorcycle historian Paul Johnson, he read his résumé: "I been riding motorcycles since 1928. I've had pretty near Harleys all my life—except one Crocker, which is the only bike I bought new, and I still have it."

The Boozefighters were not exactly a knitting circle, but on the other hand they weren't overgrown Boy Scouts that had turned world-class delinquents either. In Cameron's mind, they were a bunch of good old boys who liked beer and bikes, just like members of the other motorcycle clubs starting up around that same time in California—the 13 Rebels, Yellow Jackets, Galloping Gooses, Hell's Angels. Most of them were former servicemen who were drawing $20 a week for the first year out of the service—the so-called 52/20 benefit—and they were eager to taste some of the freedom they had been fighting for. But as another Boozefighter said, "We never tried to hurt anybody, because we'd all been hurt in the war. Believe me, baby, all of us had suffered in that war."

Cameron related the origin of the Boozefighters: "You've heard of 'Wino Willie'?" he starts in his best grandma-telling-a-fairy-tale-to-grandchildren voice. "He was a good friend of mine." One day, just after World War II had ended, Wino Willie Forkner, Cameron, and some other buddies were spectating at a Class C race at El Cajon, California. "We were out in the parking lot, and that crazy Willie said, 'Let's put on a show!'

"Willie went riding right through the crash wall during intermission. The flag man tried to wave him off, but Willie ran right by him," Cameron related, a happy, misty-eyed look coming into his eyes at the memory. Astride his Indian Chief, Willie roared off down the straightaway at full throttle in full view of the abhorring crowd. "I thought he wasn't going to make that turn because I knew he was drunk," Cameron said. Lo and behold, Willie made the turn and blasted around the track for another lap—until he augured in while careening through a different turn.

Cathy: "I've never ridden on a motorcycle before. It's **fast.** It **scared** me. But I **forgot** everything. **It felt good."**

—*The Wild One,* 1953

"He tried to get back up again, but I ran out and pulled the two spark plug wires off his bike.

"Then here comes the law, and Willie went to jail," Cameron continued.

Willie was let loose again in ninety days, and that's when the Boozefighters got kickstarted.

"Willie belonged to a club called the 13 Rebels," said Cameron. "He went to a club meeting [after he got out of jail], and they jumped all over him about what he done. So he ripped his sweater off and quit."

Cameron and his bunch were having a beer at their chosen corner of heaven, the All American Bar in South Los Angeles, when the rebellious Willie walked in, stripped of his 13 Rebels colors. "We were sitting there drinking a little," remembered Cameron, "and Willie said we should start our own club." Someone retorted, "Yeah, but what'll we call it?" Another, well-oiled motorcyclist named Walt Porter drawled out, "Call it the Booozefighters: That's what they're mad about, your boozing and fighting."

It had a certain ring to it. Boozefighters it was.

On the other hand, the name was not exactly custom-made for public relations value, as Cameron remembered: "When that name came out, boy, we was nothing. Other clubs really looked down upon us."

Alongside Wino Willie, Cameron, and the veteran drinker, the Boozefighters were primarily made up of racers. Among the racers were two brothers, Ernie and John Roccio, who would become champion Class A speedway riders in Europe. In the 1950s, the Boozefighters collaborated to build "The Brute," a tuned Harley that peaked at 227 mph on the Bonneville Salt Flats, ridden at different times by Bobby Kelton and Jim Hunter. Mean-while, Cameron's brother, Jim, won the grueling Big Bear Run desert race. Cameron himself ran TTs, scrambles, and anything else where he was allowed to twist his throttle wide open. Their uniform was a white sweater with green sleeves, a far cry from Brando's black leather jacket.

On the 1947 Fourth of July weekend in question, the Boozefighters made up their minds to hit the road. With visions dancing in their heads of motorcycle races followed by a cold beer, they rode north out of San Diego, bedrolls strapped to the back of their bikes. Hollister appeared before them like an oasis on the never-ending road, so they turned into town and made a beeline for the local watering hole.

"All that mess never happened," Cameron said, shaking his head at memories of the *Life* photograph and *The Wild One*. On the other hand, just as Marlon Brando would say in the movie, it wasn't exactly a picnic outing, either. "Nothing happened that didn't happen at other meets," Cameron continued. "We drank a lot, maybe someone rode their motorcycle into a bar, stuff like that."

Reports differ dramatically about the number of bikers that descended on Hollister and the subsequent goings on. Some say there were upwards of 4,000 motorcyclists swarming through town, racing in the Independence Day hillclimb and scrambles, drag racing down main street, and doing everything from pioneering the art of riding motorcycles through crowded bars to razzing the vestal virgin baton-twirlers in the Independence Day parade.

News of the escapades spread, and somehow a photo was snapped that made the Boozefighters—and all cyclists everywhere—infamous.

"The war was over and *Life* magazine didn't have anything exciting," Cameron recounts, "and so they imported those people [to set up that photograph]. It was an actor. He looked like a Boozefighter named 'Fat Boy' Nelson, but it wasn't him because Fat Boy was riding a Crocker at that time [and the guy in the photo was on a Harley]."

Still, that pictured Harley had the words "Boozefighters MC" painted across its tank.

"No one was going to sit on their bike on the sidewalk and drink that many beers; the cops would run you off," Cameron shook his head and said with the voice of experience. "You could do a one-time thing like ride into a bar and then ride out again."

Whatever the truth was, the photo spoke louder than the words of a handful of Boozefighters. Cameron acknowledged the effect it had with a sorrowful shake of his head:

"That photograph changed the image of motorcycling forever. It was one of the most important things that happened to motorcycling in all eternity. That brought on the Hell's Angels and everything else. They said, 'We'll cash in on this. We'll be the bad guys.' And that started them, and it's a doggone shame."

Watching *The Wild One* these days is like climbing aboard a 1912 Harley-Davidson Silent Gray Fellow and riding off down modern-day streets—you wonder what all the fuss was about. Was this the infernal speed machine that put the fear of God into folk and inspired them to holler "Get a horse"? Movies such as *The Wild Angels*, *The Leather Boys*, *Easy Rider*, and many other biker "classics" today have a period charm. They're timepieces, practically Victorian drawing-room dramas. Hell, they're almost cute.

That's missing the point, however. Watching *The Wild One* in a revival theater from today's vantage point, it's impossible to see the movie and its message from the point of view of the audiences of 1953. Yet the images of fear and loathing that *The Wild One* once inspired toward motorcyclists and their innocent machines were real. After the film opened, you had to be a brave soul to wear a black leather jacket into your local small-town café. Many folk believed that a switchblade was the chief tool you needed to ride a cycle. And it wasn't for naught that when Honda motorcycles were launched in the United States in the early 1960s, the importer spent big bucks on its ad campaign "You Meet the Nicest People on a Honda"; the motorcycle's image needed a haircut, shave, and a new set of respectable clothes.

Today, the town of Hollister holds an annual Independence Day motorcycle race and rally that trades on the commercial value of the 1947 fracas that was once seen as threatening the end of the free world as we know it. Black leather motorcycle jackets are as common as boxer shorts, and if you're a stockbroker or dentist that doesn't own a Harley, you stand out from the crowd. *The Wild One*, once the scourge of movie theaters, is a popular video rental. The Hell's Angels even have their own Internet website.

The motorcycle has come full circle in acceptance. The outlaw biker mystique that once shocked and terrified the masses has been subjugated into the mainstream, eaten up by society, and spit out as everyday fashion.

Hollister, Roswell, and a Brave New Bro's World—1947

By Paul Garson

Paul Garson practices what he preaches. He has logged thousands of miles on bikes and has written thousands of articles on motorcycling. A long-time contributor to *Easyriders*, he was also the first editor of *Hot Bike* and former editor-in-chief of *VQ*. The culmination of his riding and researching appeared in his book *Born to Be Wild: A History of the American Biker and Bikes 1947–2002*.

In this essay, Paul examines the changing motorcycling scene following World War II—and the indelible influence it would have on everyone and anyone who threw their leg over a motorcycle in the years that followed.

Let's say you're a World War II veteran and put your back pay money in the bank, and now with a couple years' interest, you're ready to go shopping at your local Harley-Davidson dealer. What brand spanking shiny new models would you get to ogle on the showroom floor of 1947?

The range of V-twin powered models included bikes powered by the 45-cubic-inch (750cc) flathead, the 61-cubic-inch (1,000cc) OHV, and the 74-cubic-inch (1,200cc) in both flathead and OHV designs. The newly introduced 61 OHV ran $605. Milwaukee built 4,117 of the high-compression 61-inch bikes, and 6,893 of the 74-inch hi-comp FLs. What's a nice '47 Panhead going for now . . . twenty, thirty times the original MSRP?

We all like to know our roots. The genealogy of the "bad biker" starts loosely after World War II when U.S. servicemen returned home after taking part in a world conflagration that saw more than 50 million people slaughtered. It was a good war, very black and white, and they were all considered heroes, and phrases like Post Traumatic Stress Disorder did not exist. Yet, the guys, after leaving their Thompson submachine guns and Mustang P-51 fighters behind and donning their civvies, were not the same guys that left home to see war up close and personal in the European and Pacific theatres.

Upon returning home, they found it wasn't the same. Some of them climbed on motorcycles and wandered the byways and highways of America looking for answers to unanswerable questions or teamed up with their war buddies because either they felt safer in the company of their brothers under arms or they didn't quite fit back into the relatively low ebb of civilian life. Motorcycles maybe gave them back the edge they needed, the adrenaline rush they had experienced so often in combat.

In any case they were not riding into towns and burning them to the ground. That would come later. At least according to the media. And the media does like a story and often doesn't let the truth get in the way. They went looking for trouble and found it.

Lots of people were looking for trouble in the summer of 1947, but they didn't include pilot Kenneth Arnold or the Boozefighters MC. But they both started revolutions.

In the case of Mr. Arnold, he was a traveling salesman that liked to pilot his own Cessna to work. When another aircraft disappeared, he volunteered to look for it around the rugged Cascade Mountains near Seattle. He didn't find the lost plane, but he did witness nine objects flying in a V-formation against the backdrop of Mt. Baker. He estimated the boomerang-shaped vehicles were clocking 1,700 miles per hour, a tad faster than current military-issue aircraft. He told the media that they looked liked saucers skipping across water, hence the term "flying saucers" coined by some reporter. The government experts dismissed them as a flock of birds, but not so the imagination of the world.

A couple weeks later, around July 4, at a place near Roswell, New Mexico, something crashed on Mack Brazel's cattle ranch. The local military authorities announced they had found pieces of a flying disk—yep, a spaceship—and it hit the front pages. A day later, the official story changed to something more mundane: a weather balloon had crashed during the thunderstorm. And so began a controversy raging now more for than fifty years.

Meanwhile, not too far away, and on exactly the same day, in Hollister, California, a different kind of controversy was being conceived or perceived, depending how you looked at it. For some it would be the seminal event heralding the "biker culture." Culture didn't quite fit the image reported, or perpetrated, by the press.

So what happened that infamous day in Hollister? What were the facts that lead up to the fiction? Or was it fiction?

It started with the AMA deciding to bring back its popular series of races called the Gypsy Tours. As the name implies, a lot of "enthusiasts" would putt around the country enjoying the various flat-track and hill-climb venues. In those goldy oldie days of cheap gas and post-war rootlessness, it was as good a reason as any to hit the road, camping out wherever nightfall found you and your Bros, your family of motorized gypsies. Sometimes, these little hamlets were swamped by riders, their infrastructure (to use a modern buzzword) unable, or unwilling, to deal with the motley crew of what they considered "outlaws and outsiders," which was pretty much what the rough riders of the day liked to think of themselves as well. Hollister, part of the Gypsy Tour, was scheduled for a hill climb. Harley top rider Joe Leonard would be competing. People started rolling in on a Friday night.

Back then, in 1947, Hollister was called a "village." And they referred to "biker gangs" as "clubmen," i.e., motorcyclists who formed or joined clubs of like-minded enthusiasts. Into the apparently pleasant environment of clubmen came the so-called "outlaw" element. For three days, these "outlaws" terrorized the town, a scene of unruliness that ultimately required the calling up of 500 California Highway Patrol, California State Police, and local law officers to route the lawbreakers from town. The press listed the offending clubs: the Boozefighters, Galloping Gooses, Satan's Sinners, Satan's Daughters, and the Winoes. (Yes, there was a spelling problem, but apparently women were given equal opportunity to raise hell.)

It seems some of the visitors weren't interested in the official races and were staging their own burn-outs down San Benito Street, the location of Hollister's restaurants and bars. About fifty people got busted for things like public drunkenness, indecent exposure, resisting arrest. Not exactly the sacking of a city and the murder of its inhabitants, but it was too much for little Hollister.

What the press said happened during the July Fourth city celebrations came out like a riot, rampage, near-rape, and semi-pillaging of a small town by motorcycle hooligans, thugs on wheels, drunken, beer-bottle-tossing Wild Ones, all in black leather jackets and engineer boots and riding motorcycles. Somehow, all the bikes became Harley-Davidsons in the mindset (which they weren't), and the equation was born. Hollister = biker gangs running amuck = Harley-Davidson as the incendiary fuel.

It would have been great stuff for CNN, except CNN would have been there to show the real facts, not some highly massaged non-fiction fiction set piece manufactured to sell papers and magazines. That's what Bro historians will tell you now.

The Hollister hysteria is captured by the infamous black-and-white photograph taken in front of Johnnie's Bar that appeared first in the San Francisco *Chronicle*, then on the cover of the July 21st *Life* magazine showing an obviously seriously toasted guy on a Harley with a small mountain of beer bottles piled around the bike. Letters to the editor poured into the mag deploring the exploitation of the event, including one from actor/motorcyclist Keenan Wynn, pointing out that out of the 4,000 bike fans attending the Hollister celebration, only 500 contributed to the trouble, the majority of the AMA members behaving with all decorum. The indelible images in such a respected publication had their effects. The public had a

Cashing in on the infamy:
Biker movie press booklets, circa
1960s–1980s.

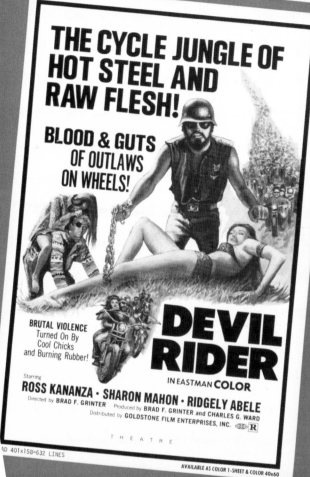

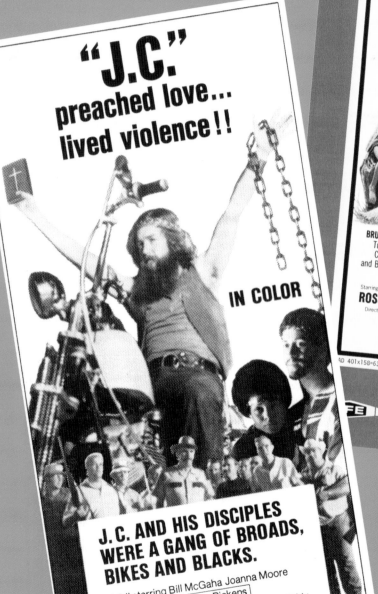

new boogey man, i.e., the bad biker. Hollister started the ball rolling, and can be credited for spawning the torrent of lurid "bad biker" melodrama that would appear in so many Hollywood films and later television. And thus the stigma was born, a bad rep bikers have been trying to overcome for half a century.

The "negative image" was re-enforced when *Life*, as part of its 25th anniversary, chose to republish the same image in July 1972 just in case the public might have forgotten what a drunken biker hooligan looked like. And of course, that image reminded everyone that bad bikers preferred Harleys, thus branding the bike guilty by association. Did it hurt Harley sales? Doubtful.

Cultural impact was listed somewhere near the effect of the Yucatan meteor on dinosaurs. As Harry V. Sucher, the official historian of the Harley-Davidson's Owners Association, stated in his 1981 book *Harley-Davidson: The Milwaukee Marvel*, when writing of the Hollister watershed event, "Others claimed that certain antisocial individuals had chosen the iconoclastic entity of the motorcycle to express their general emotions of revolt against the formal social structuring of contemporary American life." He also added that the choice of these "elements" was a stripped-down form of the Big Twin "dresser"—bikes that carried a full complement of windshields, bags, and safety equipment—and indicated a further revolt against the more conservative "class" of motorcyclists and the "wimps" who rode non-American middleweight Brit imports. He also cites a significant collateral effect, one that would in itself create its own sub-culture: the proliferation of so-called unfranchised specialty bike shops, aka chopper shops. Seems the regular dealers didn't want to be associated with the saddle tramps/ unwashed bikers element, so the so-called outlaws began opening their own shops and supporting them.

So what did happen in that sleepy California town, located inland and west about halfway between Monterey and Santa Cruz (about thirty miles south of San Jose), when some guys on motorcycles came to celebrate America's Independence Day? Years later, a letter penned by an eyewitness and sent to the editors of *Easyriders* magazine reportedly told it how it really was.

A Goose Talks About Hollister

Hey, I want to set the record straight about the Hollister hassle. I was one of the Galloping Gooses there, and I'm writing to tell you that *Life*'s version of what happened was bullshit.

That photo of the two dudes was staged by a *Life* photographer. (I have it on good authority that the two dudes that posed for the photo were paid a visit and shown the errors of their ways.)

The bash started with the AMA (American Motorcycle Association) officials refusing to let the Gooses participate in the event unless they removed the Gooses patch from their backs. The symbol was a large fist giving the finger. AMA's demand went over the Gooses like a fart in church, and as a result the Gooses were "outlawed" from the event. This was probably the origin of the term *outlaw*, although the AMA had no doubt outlawed other bikers and clubs from participating in other events prior to this time; however, this hassle received the most notoriety.

We had about twelve to fifteen members at that time. When we were outlawed we headed for town along with another club that was there too—the Booze Fighters [*sic*]. At that time I think they had about 25 members. It's been so long, I don't remember the other clubs that were there, although I think you were wrong about the 13 Rebels—I think they turned AMA prior to Hollister.

Here's a photo of me and my bike at that time. It's a 1936 VLH Harley. The engine was built up to a healthy 90.98 cubic inches. It went like hell—between the time it blew up on me.

Old Goose
Los Angeles, CA

Maybe you've seen the patch on a vest or jeans jacket: "1%." Call it a badge of honor or a refutation of the status quo, it refers to the image of the outlaw biker as being both a unique rarity and someone happily occupying the margin of society. The phrase was penned, not deliberately, by Lin Kuchler, then secretary of the AMA, when describing the Hollister incident: "The disreputable cyclists were possibly one percent of the total number of motorcyclists, only one percent are hoodlums and troublemakers." This sounded kind of cool to a bunch of the hardcore Bros, and they responded by accepting rather than refuting the onerous term, taking it as their own.

Years later in Japan, the builders of Honda motorcycles would belatedly capitalize on this onerous distinction when they came out with the phrase, "You meet the nicest people on a Honda." In Hollister, and in similar rowdy incidents occurring in its wake, you wouldn't find the nicest people, as least by society's definition back in the late 1940s. Meanwhile, a large majority of police motor officers across the country were mounted on basically stock Harley-Davidsons which both served to solidify the image of Harley in a positive light, but also polarized the "outlaw element" on their custom bobbed-fendered hot rod bikes into the other camp.

Townsgirl: "Black Rebels Motorcycle Club, that's cute! Hey Johnny, what are you rebelling against?"

Johnny: "Whaddya got?"

—The Wild One, 1953

The Tale of Grandpa and the Bottle of, uh, Milk . . .

By Bill Hayes

Bill Hayes writes passionately about the things he loves and knows best—from motorcycles to the blues to martial arts. It's little surprise that his essays, columns, and fiction have appeared in a wide range of magazines, including *Easyriders*, *Thunder Press*, *Biker*, *Real Blues*, and *Black Belt*.

Bill's book *The Original Wild Ones: Tales of the Boozefighters Motorcycle Club*, published by Motorbooks International, may be his masterpiece—at least for now. Hooking up with members of the venerable club, he recounts their tales in a grand verbal history of the glory days.

This excerpt looks at the founding of the Boozefighters and the fracas at Hollister that would make them more infamous in their time than even the Hell's Angels.

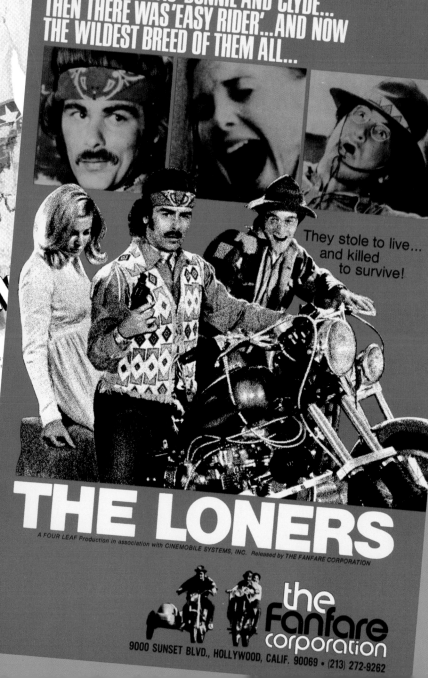

Biker movie press booklets,
circa 1960s–1980s.

Long before a spate of chopper-building programs flooded cable television, before one-percenter motorcycle clubs blurred the distinction between fame and infamy, and even before those outlaw clubs became targets for federal undercover agents in search of contraband and lucrative book deals, the Boozefighters Motorcycle Club—the original wild ones—backfired onto the American motorcycle scene like a fat-jetted Harley V-twin engine. These young men, restless World War II veterans eager to exercise the freedom they had risked their lives to preserve, fueled by hooch and pretty girls, unconsciously established the archetype of "biker."

One summer weekend in 1947, the BFMC gunned the stroked engines of their hopped-up Indians and Harleys and set out in search of a little fun. Instead they made history. A sensation-seeking press exaggerated their boisterous antics at the Fourth of July celebration in the sleepy little town of Hollister, California, and in the process created the biker lifestyle.

A few grizzled old bikers who participated in this seminal event are still alive today. A few of them even continue to ride motorcycles and wear the fabled patch of the Boozefighters MC: the three-starred bottle.

Sometimes they have a little explaining to do. A grizzled old biker usually observes the world in a slightly different light than a five-year-old girl.

Usually.

"Grandpa, why do you have that bottle of milk on the back of your vest?"

Old 'n' grizzled wasn't about to begin a long, morally tinged ramble about the difference between milk and moonshine, which one's good for you, which one's not, and why. Instead he answered with a smile and a kid-like shrug that simply said, "Just because." And to a little girl that was OK, that was reason enough. Her grandpa is a member of the original wild ones: The Boozefighters Motorcycle Club. The "bottle" is the centerpiece of the patch, a sacred green icon that symbolizes a brotherhood and a heritage that few are ever fortunate enough to experience. Is it actually supposed to be a bottle of milk? Probably not. But that really is left up to the imagination. The Peter Pan eye-of-the-beholder that is the fanciful essence of an innocent five-year-old is, in many ways, what also fuels the Boozefighters.

The truth is that the founding fathers of the original wild ones were really just big kids themselves, simply trying to recapture some of the youthful fun they lost out on due to the innocence-destroying interruption of a very adult evil known as World War II.

There were no excuses, no laments, no protests. The country needed young soldiers. They went. War changes everyone. And everything. When young vets like Willie Forkner, Robert Burns, and George Manker returned home, it was difficult to forget the horrors of what they had seen. It was hard to shake off the ingrained military regimentation. It was impossible to shed some of the cold-sweat guilt that comes with surviving while so many others did not. And there was an unnerving restlessness in trying to adapt to the calmness and serenity of "normal" living after drowning in chaos. It was easy, however, to adopt an "I don't fit in" kind of attitude. It was easy for returning vets to feel more comfortable with one another than with those from "the outside."

The recipe had been written. The mix was almost complete. All that was needed was the addition of a potent ingredient to spice up the social soup. Something like, say, racing fast motorcycles. The races and rally organized by the American Motorcyclist Association Gypsy Tour in 1947 boiled the soup into a fiery jalapeno-laced stew.

The green stitched bottle that the five-year-old asked her old gramps about was very different from the real bottles that were gathered from the streets of Hollister by an energized photojournalist during that infamous weekend. The image on that patch is very different from the horde of broken and empty bottles that were carefully arranged around the seemingly drunk and woozy non-Boozefighter (identified as Eddie Davenport or Don Middleton, depending on the source) by San Francisco *Chronicle* photographer Barney Peterson.

The resulting picture was not exactly a work of art that might have emerged from the all-American portfolios of Ansel Adams, Norman Rockwell, or Grant Wood. No. Instead, we were treated to an urban-ugly portrait of the tipsy "model," astride a "nasty, fire-breathing, Milwaukee-steel dragon," viciously framed by those stale-smelling empties and jagged glass shards.

When that twisted version of American Gothic leaped out at the sophisticated readers of *Life* magazine's July 21, 1947, issue, a frightening chill blew through the calm kingdom air. Some of the common village folk wanted to head for the hills, and some wanted to take up pitchforks, sickles, and torches against the strange new beast.

Some wanted to tell the whole story. Sort of. Filmmaker Stanley Kramer produced *The Wild One* six years later, and the snarling cat was out of the bag. The question is, of course, just how sharp were that cat's claws really?

But more than a half-century has already passed, and the legend has grown. The embroidered green bottles went on in 1946, Hollister swept up all that busted brown glass in 1947, *The Wild One* rolled out on black-and-white celluloid at the end of 1953, and the always colorful stories, tales, and traditions have never stopped.

Today, as in 1946, surviving BFMC members are more concerned with carrying on the most important Boozefighter tradition of all: Having fun. One of the early members, Jack Lilly, has a credo that is woven into the very fabric of that holy green patch when it comes to having a good time: "Do it now!" They did. And they still do.

When that cat flew out of the bag, the popularized fear was that he was bent on shredding and hunting prey. In reality that fast, sleek animal was just living up to his reputation for curiosity and playful prowling. For wanting to sniff out every aspect of life. Eat, drink, fool around, chase an occasional mouse, cough up a hairball or two after a tad too much consumption, and, in general, just enjoy the heck out of living.

"Every original Boozefighter I've met," club historian Jim "JQ" Quattlebaum says, "—Wino, J. D. and Jim Cameron, Red Dog, Jim Hunter, Roccio, Les, Gil, Lilly, and Vern Autrey—all exhibit signs that they are made of common threads: Spirited and daring character, challenging competitiveness, strong bonding friendship, a caring and giving nature, the love of motorcycling, and brotherhood with bikers. They're honest and law-abiding citizens, but not beyond the embellishment of a good story." Even in their old age they've stayed active. No rocking chairs for them! Still riding motorcycles as long as their health and bodies would allow.

"Yeah, they let off a lot of steam, partied hearty, got jailed for getting drunk, got a lot of speeding tickets, and occasionally duked it out with redneck bar patrons that hassled them . . . and sometimes they fought with each other. Then they'd sit down together and laugh about it over a beer.

"But no original ever got put in jail for a serious crime like murder or drugs. They got along with all other MC clubs, sponsored races, baseball games, and different events with other clubs. They never considered themselves outlaws the way that term is used today. This was a term that the AMA applied to riders and clubs who didn't follow the structured AMA racing rules back in the 1940s.

"And the originals didn't discriminate toward any ethnic, religious, or political group. Wino said, 'We fought side by side for all Americans to have freedom of choice.'

"That freedom also extended to the members' choice of bikes to ride, as long as they could keep up! Indians and Harleys were the most available, so they were the most used. However, many old BFers started acquiring the Triumph because of its improved racing speed. Hendersons and other pre–World War II bikes were used, too. When the BSA was introduced in the 1950s, it became the bike of choice for the still-racing BFers, like Jim Hunter, Jim Cameron, Ernie and Johnny Roccio.

"Present day BFMC requires members to ride an American or World War II–allied brand of bike. But some exceptions are made in some chapters for special consideration. 'Brooklyn' is allowed to ride a touring Moto Guzzi in honor of his grandfather, who fought with the Italian underground resistance against the Germans.

"The present-day Boozefighters revere our originals and the club's founders for their intent, purpose, and priorities: Family, job, and club brotherhood. We're family men, engaged in legitimate businesses and careers, enjoying getting together as a social group for parties, rides, and special events. We're into this thing strictly for having harmless, good clean fun. We couldn't care less about 'territory' and things like that.

"We don't push religion on anyone but we do have a national chaplain, 'Irish Ed' Mahan, who, in a nondenominational way, conducts Bible study class every Tuesday night, performs legal marriages and funerals, and visits members that request special counseling or have illness issues. He also conducts Easter sunrise services at our clubhouse every year. It's attended by a lot of friendly clubs.

"And we're involved in giving back to society through fund-raising, toy runs, March-of-Dimes, Wish With Wings and such. We have a blood bank for members. We're active in motorcycle rights organizations, and many of us are state delegates to our respective political parties.

"We believe in peaceful coexistence with all clubs, but we don't wear support patches for any other organization. And we don't believe in displaying any antisociety or anti-American items."

Apparently some of the original members' priorities and the club's eventual evolution based on those principles were neglected just a bit in *The Wild One*. But, with another shrug of the shoulders, that, too, is OK. The Boozefighters are comfortable with who they are. And who they were. They're very proud of their founders. And they're happy with the continuance of the all-important "fun" tradition.

They're content with their personalities being somewhere in between Brando's "Johnny," Marvin's "Chino," and the brilliant 1940s/1950s abandon of, oh maybe, a Red Skelton or a Jackie Gleason.

In a letter dated September 18, 1946, the San Francisco Boozefighter prez, Benny "Kokomo" McKell, wrote to the L.A. chapter to order four club sweaters for his newest members. They had just passed the rigorous series of seven tests required of a "prospect":

1. Get drunk at a race meet or cycle dance.

2. Throw lemon pie in each other's faces.

3. Bring out a douche bag where it would embarrass all the women (then drink wine from it, etc.).

4. Get down and lay on the dance floor.

5. Wash your socks in a coffee urn.

6. Eat live goldfish.

7. Then, when blind drunk, trust me ("Kokomo") to shoot beer bottles off of your heads with my .22.

Would Johnny or Chino do all that?

No.

Would Skelton or Gleason?

Probably.

Would the Boozefighters?

Just ask 'em.

So, are all of the tales and legends surrounding the Boozefighters sworn gospel? JQ answers that (more or less) in an interesting discussion about memory and motorcycle lore:

"If you ask me today what I did last night, I'd be hard pressed to remember all the details precisely right. I know I started off with 65 or 70 dollars in my pocket and got home with about 7. For the life of me I can't remember what I spent the money on. But to get the story more accurate, that doesn't count that $100 bill I had stashed away for an emergency. Man, I hope I didn't blow that, too. . . .

"Ask the original wild ones what happened fifty years ago and they, too, are hard pressed to remember the precise facts. Once, sitting with three such old-timers, I witnessed a heated—but friendly—debate about what club one of them raced for during the Hollister melee. They finally all agreed on one thing: Whether it was the 13 Rebs, Yellow Jackets, or Boozefighters, they all had one heck of a good time, excluding the jail time for rowdiness, of course.

"I had a good time last night, too. (That is, unless I can't find my $100 bill.)

"But anyway, if Patrick Henry had said, 'If I don't get my rear end outta here, I'm gonna get it shot off,' and some historical writer quoted him as actually saying, 'Give me liberty or give me death,' then what kind of respect would you have for that writer? As historian, I've had to dig deep into the facts about the Boozefighters, and there are times I wished I hadn't found out that some stories just weren't so. But then again, the more I dug, the more I found out that there are great stories that were never told.

"They need to be told, so we'll tell them. Some are fantastic, but I'll let the listener or reader sort out what they want to believe. Most importantly, though, the telling of these stories will be geared to the essence of truth as the old-timers wanted to remember it."

And the heart of that truth—those stories—beats with the same wide-eyed wonder that drives the fertile imagination of that inquisitive five-year-old.

Is there milk in that bottle, some 90-proof hooch, or a genie that will pop out and take us directly into a unique and exotic land, a growling jungle that members of the button-down, mainstream, overly protected, boy-in-the-bubble society fear, envy, and would give their eye teeth to journey into?

Maybe it's all three.

Chapter 5

Born to Be Wild

The concept of the
'motorcycle outlaw'
was as uniquely American as jazz.
Nothing like them
ever existed.
In some ways, they appeared to be a kind of
half-breed anachronism,
a human hangover
from the era of the Wild West.

—Hunter S. Thompson, *Hell's Angels: A Strange and Terrible Saga*, 1967

The Motorcycle Gangs: Losers and Outsiders

By Hunter S. Thompson

Hunter S. Thompson was a relatively unknown and struggling journalist in the early 1960s when he stumbled on the story that would make his name. A native of Louisville, Kentucky, he began writing as a sports columnist in Florida before turning freelance.

Then he met the Hell's Angels.

He first wrote about the Angels in the May 17, 1965 issue of *The Nation* in a well-crafted, tightly penned article that was an odd blend of apologia and celebration. Obviously, Hunter felt a kinship.

Inspired, he went undercover with the Angels and produced the book that may be his masterpiece, 1967's *Hell's Angels: A Strange and Terrible Saga*. As the book's biographical note states, Hunter's "research . . . involved more than a year of close association with the outlaws—riding, loafing, plotting, and eventually being stomped." His writing is passionate; the prose is up close and personal, uninhibited and offensive, fueled by whiskey and exhaust fumes. *Hell's Angels* marks the dawn of a new style of over-the-top participatory writing that became known as gonzo journalism.

Here is the original piece from *The Nation*, an article that launched two legends—the Hell's Angels and Hunter S. Thompson.

Last Labor Day weekend newspapers all over California gave front-page reports of a heinous gang rape in the moonlit sand dunes near the town of Seaside on the Monterey Peninsula. Two girls, aged 14 and 15, were allegedly taken from their dates by a gang of filthy, frenzied, boozed-up motorcycle hoodlums called "Hell's Angels," and dragged off to be "repeatedly assaulted."

A deputy sheriff, summoned by one of the erstwhile dates, said he "arrived at the beach and saw a huge bonfire surrounded by cyclists of both sexes. Then the two sobbing, near-hysterical girls staggered out of the darkness, begging for help. One was completely nude and the other had on only a torn sweater."

Some 300 Hell's Angels were gathered in the Seaside–Monterey area at the time, having convened, they said, for the purpose of raising funds among themselves to send the body of a former member, killed in an accident, back to his mother in North Carolina. One of the Angels, hip enough to falsely identify himself as "Frenchy of San Bernardino," told a reporter who came out to meet the cyclists: "We chose Monterey because we get treated good here; most other places we get thrown out of town."

But Frenchy spoke too soon. The Angels weren't on the peninsula twenty-four hours before four of them were in jail for rape, and the rest of the troop was being escorted to the county line by a large police contingent. Several were quoted, somewhat derisively, as saying: "That rape charge against our guys is phony and it won't stick."

It turned out to be true, but that was another story and certainly no headliner. The difference between the Hell's Angels in the paper and the Hell's Angels for real is enough to make a man wonder what newsprint is for. It also raises a question as to who are the real hell's angels.

Ever since World War II, California has been strangely plagued by wild men on motorcycles. They usually travel in groups of ten to thirty, booming along the highways and stopping here and there to get drunk and raise hell. In 1947, hundreds of them ran amok in the town of Hollister, an hour's fast drive south of San Francisco, and got enough press to inspire a film called *The Wild One*, starring Marlon Brando. The film had a massive effect on thousands of young California motorcycle buffs; in many ways, it was their version of *The Sun Also Rises*.

The California climate is perfect for motorcycles, as well as surfboards, swimming pools and convertibles. Most of the cyclists are harmless weekend types, members of the American Motorcycle Association, and no more dangerous than skiers or skin divers. But a few belong to what the others call "outlaw clubs," and these are the ones who—specially on weekends and holidays—are likely to turn up almost anywhere in the state, looking for action. Despite everything the psychiatrists and Freudian casuists have to say about them, they are tough, mean and potentially as dangerous as a pack of wild boar. When push comes to shove, any leather fetishes or inadequacy feelings that may be involved are entirely beside the point, as anyone who has ever tangled with these boys will sadly testify. When you get in an argument with a group of outlaw motorcyclists, you can generally count your chances of emerging unmaimed by the number of heavy-handed allies you can muster in the time it takes to smash a beer bottle. In this league, sportsmanship is for old liberals and young fools. "I smashed his face," one of them said to me of a man he'd never seen until the swinging started. "He got wise. He called me a punk. He must have been stupid."

The most notorious of these outlaw groups is the Hell's Angels, supposedly headquartered in San Bernardino, just east of Los Angeles, and with branches all over the state. As a result of the infamous "Labor Day gang rape," the Attorney General of California has recently issued an official report on the Hell's Angels. According to the report, they are easily identified:

The emblem of the Hell's Angels, termed "colors," consists of an embroidered patch of a winged skull wearing a motorcycle helmet. Just below the wing of the emblem are the letters "MC." Over this is a band bearing the words "Hell's Angels." Below the emblem is another patch bearing the local chapter name, which is usually an abbreviation for the city or locality. These patches are sewn on the back of a usually sleeveless denim jacket. In addition, members have been observed wearing various types of Luftwaffe insignia and reproductions of German iron crosses. [Purely for decorative and shock effect. The Hell's Angels are apolitical and no more racist than other ignorant young thugs.] Many affect beards and their hair is usually long and unkempt. Some wear a single earring in a pierced ear lobe. Frequently they have been observed to wear metal belts made of a length of polished motorcycle drive chain which can be unhooked and used as a flexible bludgeon ... Probably the most universal common denominator in identification of Hell's Angels is generally their filthy condition. Investigating officers consistently report these people, both club members and their female associates, seem badly in need of a bath. Fingerprints are a

Biker meet in the good old days before all the craziness struck, circa 1950s. *Library of Congress*

very effective means of identification because a high percentage of Hell's Angels have criminal records. In addition to the patches on the back of Hell's Angels' jackets, the "One Percenters" wear a patch reading "1%-er." Another badge worn by some members bears the number "13." It is reported to represent the 13th letter of the alphabet, "M," which in turn stands for marijuana and indicates the wearer thereof is a user of the drug.

The Attorney General's report was colorful, interesting, heavily biased and consistently alarming—just the sort of thing, in fact, to make a clanging good article for a national news magazine. Which it did; in both barrels. *Newsweek* led with a left hook titled "The Wild Ones," *Time* crossed right, inevitably titled "The Wilder Ones." The Hell's Angels, cursing the implications of this new attack, retreated to the bar of the DePau Hotel near the San Francisco waterfront and planned a weekend beach party. I showed them the articles. Hell's Angels do not normally read the news magazines. "I'd go nuts if I read that stuff all the time," said one. "It's all bullshit."

Newsweek was relatively circumspect. It offered local color, flashy quotes and "evidence" carefully attributed to the official report but unaccountably said the report accused the Hell's Angels of homosexuality, whereas the report said just the opposite. *Time* leaped into the fray with a flurry of blood, booze and semen-flecked wordage that amounted, in the end, to a classic of supercharged hokum: "Drug-induced stupors . . . no act is too degrading . . . swap girls, drugs and motorcycles with equal abandon . . . stealing forays . . . then ride off again to seek some new nadir in sordid behavior . . ."

Where does all this leave the Hell's Angels and the thousands of shuddering Californians (according to *Time*) who are worried sick about them? Are these outlaws really going to be busted, routed and cooled, as the news magazines implied? Are California highways any safer as a result of this published uproar? Can honest merchants once again walk the streets in peace? The answer is that nothing has changed except that a few people calling themselves the Hell's Angels have a new sense of identity and importance.

After two weeks of intensive dealings with the Hell's Angels phenomenon, both in print and in person, I'm convinced the net result of the general howl and publicity has been to obscure and avoid the real issues by invoking a savage conspiracy of bogeymen and conning the public into thinking all will be "business as usual" once this fearsome snake is scotched, as it surely will be by hard and ready minions of the Establishment.

Meanwhile, according to Attorney General Thomas C. Lynch's own figures, California's true crime picture makes the Hell's Angels look like a gang of petty jack rollers. The police count 463 Hell's Angels: 205 around L.A. and 233 in the San Francisco–Oakland area. I don't know about L.A. but the real figures for the Bay Area are thirty or so in Oakland and exactly eleven—with one facing expulsion—in San Francisco. This disparity makes it hard to accept other police statistics. The dubious package also shows convictions on 1,023 misdemeanor counts and 151 felonies—primarily vehicle theft, burglary and assault. This is for all years and all alleged members.

California's overall figures for 1963 list 1,116 homicides, 12,448 aggravated assaults, 6,257 sex offenses, and 24,532 burglaries. In 1962, the state listed 4,121 traffic deaths, up from 3,839 in 1961. Drug arrest figures for 1964 showed a 101 percent increase in juvenile marijuana arrests over 1963, and a recent back-page story in the *San Francisco Examiner* said, "The venereal disease rate among [the city's] teen-agers from 15–19 has more than doubled in the past four years." Even allowing for the annual population jump, juvenile arrests in all categories are rising by 10 per cent or more each year.

Against this background, would it make any difference to the safety and peace of mind of the average Californian if every motorcycle outlaw in the state (all 901, according to the state) were garroted within twenty-four hours? This is not to say that a group like the Hell's Angels has no meaning. The generally bizarre flavor of their offenses and their insistence on identifying themselves make good copy, but usually overwhelm—in print, at least—the unnerving truth that they represent, in colorful microcosm, what is quietly and anonymously growing all around us every day of the week.

"We're bastards to the world and they're bastards to us," one of the Oakland Angels told a *Newsweek* reporter. "When you walk into a place where people can see you, you want to look as repulsive and repugnant as possible. We are complete social outcasts—outsiders against society."

A lot of this is a pose, but anyone who believes that's all it is has been on thin ice since the death of Jay Gatsby. The vast majority of motorcycle outlaws are uneducated, unskilled men between 20 and 30, and most have no credentials except a police record. So at the root of their sad stance is a lot more than a wistful yearning for acceptance in a world they never made; their real motivation is an instinctive certainty as to what the score really is. They are out of the ball game and they know it—and that is their meaning; for unlike most losers in today's society, the Hell's Angels not only know but spitefully proclaim

exactly where they stand.

I went to one of their meetings recently, and halfway through the night I thought of Joe Hill on his way to face a Utah firing squad and saying his final words: "Don't mourn, organize." It is safe to say that no Hell's Angel has ever heard of Joe Hill or would know a Wobbly from a Bushmaster, but nevertheless they are somehow related. The I.W.W. had serious plans for running the world, while the Hell's Angels mean only to defy the world's machinery. But instead of losing quietly, one by one, they have banded together with a mindless kind of loyalty and moved outside the framework, for good or ill. There is nothing particularly romantic or admirable about it; that's just the way it is, strength in unity. They don't mind telling you that running fast and loud on their customized Harley 74s gives them a power and a purpose that nothing else seems to offer.

Beyond that, their position as self-proclaimed outlaws elicits a certain popular appeal, however reluctant. That is especially true in the West and even in California where the outlaw tradition is still honored. The unarticulated link between the Hell's Angels and the millions of losers and outsiders who don't wear any colors is the key to their notoriety and the ambivalent reactions they inspire. There are several other keys, having to do with politicians, policemen and journalists, but for this we have to go back to Monterey and the Labor Day "gang rape."

Politicians, like editors and cops, are very keen on outrage stories, and state Senator Fred S. Farr of Monterey County is no exception. He is a leading light of the Carmel–Pebble Beach set and no friend to hoodlums anywhere, especially gang rapists who invade his constituency. Senator Farr demanded an immediate investigation of the Hell's Angels and others of their ilk—Commancheros, Stray Satans, Iron Horsemen, Rattlers (a Negro club), and Booze Fighters—whose lack of status caused them all to be lumped together as "other disreputables." In the cut-off world of big bikes, long runs and classy rumbles, this new, state-sanctioned stratification made the Hell's Angels very big. They were, after all, Number One. Like John Dillinger.

Attorney General Lynch, then new in his job, moved quickly to mount an investigation of sorts. He sent questionnaires to more than 100 sheriffs, district attorneys and police chiefs, asking for more information on the Hell's Angels and those "other disreputables." He also asked for suggestions as to how the law might deal with them.

Six months went by before all the replies where condensed into the fifteen-page report that made new outrage headlines when it was released to the press. (The Hell's Angels also got a copy; one of them stole mine.) As a historical document, it read like a plot synopsis of Mickey Spillane's worst dreams. But in the matter of solutions it was vague, reminiscent in some ways of Madame Nhu's proposals for dealing with the Vietcong. The state was going to centralize information on these thugs, urge more vigorous prosecution, put them all under surveillance whenever possible, etc.

A careful reader got the impression that even if the Hell's Angels had acted out this script—eighteen crimes were specified and dozens of others implied—very little would or could be done about it, and that indeed Mr. Lynch was well aware he'd been put, for political reasons, on a pretty weak scent. There was plenty of mad action, senseless destruction, orgies, brawls, perversions and a strange parade of "innocent victims" that, even on paper

and in careful police language, was enough to tax the credulity of the dullest police reporter. Any bundle of information off police blotters is bound to reflect a special viewpoint, and parts of the Attorney General's report are actually humorous, if only for the language. Here is an excerpt:

On November 4, 1961, a San Francisco resident driving through Rodeo, possibly under the influence of alcohol, struck a motorcycle belonging to a Hell's Angel parked outside a bar. A group of Angels pursued the vehicle, pulled the driver from the car and attempted to demolish the rather expensive vehicle. The bartender claimed he had seen nothing, but a cocktail waitress in the bar furnished identification to the officers concerning some of those responsible for the assault. The next day it was reported to officers that a member of the Hell's Angels gang had threatened the life of this waitress as well as another woman waitress. A male witness who definitely identified five participants in the assault including the president of Vallejo Hell's Angels and the Vallejo "Road Rats" advised officers that because of his fear of retaliation by club members he would refuse to testify to the facts he had previously furnished.

That is a representative item in the section of the report titled "Hoodlum Activities." First, it occurred in a small town—Rodeo is on San Pablo Bay just north of Oakland—where the Angels had stopped at a bar without causing any trouble until some offense was committed against them. In this case, a driver whom even the police admit was "possibly" drunk hit one of their motorcycles. The same kind of accident happens every day all over the nation, but when it involves outlaw motorcyclists it is something else again. Instead of settling the thing with an exchange of insurance information or, at the very worst, an argument with a few blows, the Hell's Angels beat the driver and "attempted to demolish the vehicle." I asked one of them if the police exaggerated this aspect, and he said no, they had done the natural thing: smashed headlights, kicked in doors, broken windows and torn various components off the engine.

Of all their habits and predilections that society finds alarming, this departure from the time-honored concept of "an eye for an eye" is the one that most frightens people. The Hell's Angels try not to do anything halfway, and anyone who deals in extremes is bound to cause trouble, whether he means to or not. This, along with a belief in total retaliation for any offense or insult, is what makes the Hell's Angels unmanageable for the police and morbidly fascinating to the general public. Their claim that they "don't start trouble" is probably true more often than not, but their idea of "provocation" is dangerously broad, and their biggest problem is that nobody else seems to understand it. Even dealing with them personally, on the friendliest terms, you can sense their hair-trigger readiness to retaliate.

This is a public thing, and not at all true among themselves. In a meeting, their conversation is totally frank and open. They speak to and about one another with an honesty that more civilized people couldn't bear. At the meeting I attended (and before they realized I was a journalist) one Angel was being publicly evaluated; some members wanted him out of the club and others wanted to keep him in. It sounded like a group-therapy clinic

in progress—not exactly what I expected to find when just before midnight I walked into the bar of the De Pau in one of the bleakest neighborhoods in San Francisco, near Hunters Point. By the time I parted company with them—at 6:30 the next morning after an all-night drinking bout in my apartment—I had been impressed by a lot of things, but no one thing about them was as consistently obvious as their group loyalty. This is an admirable quality, but it is also one of the things that gets them in trouble: a fellow Angel is *always right* when dealing with outsiders. And this sort of reasoning makes a group of "offended" Hell's Angels nearly impossible to deal with. Here is another incident from the Attorney General's report:

> On September 19, 1964, a large group of Hell's Angels and "Satan's Slaves" converged on a bar in the South Gate (Los Angeles County), parking their motorcycles and cars in the street in such a fashion as to block one-half of the roadway. They told officers that three members of the club had been recently asked to stay out of the bar and that they had come to tear it down. Upon their approach the bar owner locked the doors and turned off the lights and no entrance was made, but the group did demolish a cement block fence. On arrival of the police, members of the club were lying on the sidewalk and in the street. They were asked to leave the city, which they did reluctantly. As they left, several were heard to say that they would be back and tear down the bar.

Here again is the ethic of total retaliation. If you're "asked to stay out" of a bar, you don't just punch the owner—you come back with your army and destroy the whole edifice. Similar incidents— along with a number of vague rape complaints—make up the bulk of the report. Eighteen incidents in four years, and none except the rape charges are more serious than cases of assaults on citizens who, for their own reasons, had become involved with the Hell's Angels prior to the violence. I could find no cases of unwarranted attacks on wholly innocent victims. There are a few borderline cases, wherein victims of physical attacks seemed innocent, according to police and press reports, but later refused to testify for fear of "retaliation." The report asserts very strongly that Hell's Angels are difficult to prosecute and convict because they make a habit of threatening and intimidating witnesses. That is probably true to a certain extent, but in many cases victims have refused to testify because they were engaged in some legally dubious activity at the time of the attack.

In two of the most widely publicized incidents the prosecution would have fared better if their witnesses and victims *had* been intimidated into silence. One of these was the Monterey "gang rape," and the other a "rape" in Clovis, near Fresno in the Central Valley. In the latter, a 36-year-old widow and mother of five children claimed she'd been yanked out of a bar where she was having a quiet beer with another woman, then carried to an abandoned shack behind the bar and raped repeatedly for two and a half hours by fifteen or twenty Hell's Angels and finally robbed of $150. That's how the story appeared in the San Francisco newspapers the next day, and it was kept alive for a few more days by the woman's claims that she was getting phone calls threatening her life if she testified against her assailants.

Then, four days after the crime, the victim was arrested on charges of "sexual perversion." The true story emerged, said the Clovis chief of police, when the woman was "confronted by witnesses. Our investigation shows she was not raped," said the chief. "She participated in lewd acts in the tavern with at least three other Hell's Angels before the owners ordered them out. She encouraged their advances in the tavern, then led them to an abandoned house in the rear . . . She was not robbed but, according to a woman who accompanied her, had left her house early in the evening with $5 to go bar-hopping." That incident did not appear in the Attorney General's report.

But it was impossible not to mention the Monterey "gang rape," because it was the reason for the whole subject to become official. Page one of the report—which *Time's* editors apparently skipped—says that the Monterey case was dropped because ". . . further investigation raised questions as to whether forcible rape had been committed or if the identifications made by victims were valid." Charges were dismissed on September 25, with the concurrence of a grand jury. The deputy District Attorney said "a doctor examined the girls and found no evidence" to support the charges. "Besides that, one girl refused to testify," he explained, "and the other was given a lie-detector test and found to be wholly unreliable."

This, in effect, was what the Hell's Angels had been saying all along. Here is their version of what happened, as told by several who were there:

One girl was white and pregnant, the other was colored, and they were with five colored studs. They hung around our bar—Nick's Place on Del Monte Avenue—for about three hours Saturday night, drinking and talking with our

Riding with class, circa 1930s–1940s.

riders, then they came out to the beach with us—them and their five boyfriends. Everybody was standing around the fire, drinking wine, and some of the guys were talking to them—hustling 'em, naturally—and soon somebody asked the two chicks if they wanted to be turned on—you know, did they want to smoke some pot? They said yeah, and then they walked off with some of the guys to the dunes. The spade went with a few guys and then she wanted to quit, but the pregnant one was really hot to trot; the first four or five guys she was really dragging into her arms, but after that she cooled off, too. By this time, though, one of their boy friends had got scared and gone for the cops—and that's all it was.

But not quite all. After that there were Senator Farr and Tom Lynch and a hundred cops and dozens of newspaper stories and articles in the national news magazine—and even this article, which is a direct result of the Monterey "gang rape."

When the much-quoted report was released, the local press—primarily the *San Francisco Chronicle*, which had earlier done a long and fairly objective series on the Hell's Angels—made a point of saying that the Monterey charges against the Hell's Angels had been dropped for lack of evidence. *Newsweek* was careful not to mention Monterey at all, but the *New York Times* referred to it as "the alleged gang rape" which, however, left no doubt in a reader's mind that something savage had occurred. It remained for *Time*, though, to flatly ignore the fact that the Monterey rape charges had been dismissed. Its article leaned heavily on the hairiest and least factual sections of the report, and ignored the rest. It said, for instance, that the Hell's Angels initiation rite "demands that any new member bring a woman or girl [called a 'sheep'] who is willing to submit to sexual intercourse with each member of the club." That is untrue, although, as one Angel explained, "Now and then you get a woman who likes to cover the crowd, and hell, I'm no prude. People don't like to think women go for that stuff, but a lot of them do."

We were talking across a pool table about the rash of publicity and how it had affected the Angels' activities. I was trying to explain to him that the bulk of the press in this country has such a vested interest in the *status quo* that it can't afford to do much honest probing at the roots, for fear of what they might find.

"Oh, I don't know," he said. "Of course I don't like to read all this bullshit because it brings the heat down on us, but since we got famous we've had more rich fags and sex-hungry women come looking for us that we ever had before. Hell, these days we have more action than we can handle."

California, Labor Day weekend . . . early, with
ocean fog still in the streets,
outlaw motorcyclists
wearing chains, shades and greasy Levis roll out
from damp garages, all-night diners and cast-off
one-night pads in Frisco, Hollywood, Berdoo and
East Oakland, heading for the Monterey peninsula,
north of Big Sur. . . .
The Menace is
loose again....

—Hunter S. Thompson, *Hell's Angels: A Strange and Terrible Saga,* 1967

Harleys, Choppers, Full Dressers, and Stolen Wheels

By Sonny Barger

Ralph "Sonny" Barger is a proud one-percenter. As president of the Oakland chapter of the Hell's Angels Motorcycle Club in its glory days, he was one of the figureheads that stamped and stomped the indelible image of the outlaw biker into the world's consciousness.

Sonny tells his tale in the 2000 autobiography *Hell's Angel: The Life and Times of Sonny Barger and the Hell's Angels Motorcycle Club.* The book never pulls any punches nor comes close to an apology—it even includes a summary of his rap sheet as an appendix. Obviously, the Hell's Angels—now incorporated—are more chic than ever.

Sonny followed with 2002's *Ridin' High, Livin' Free: Hell-Raising Motorcycle Stories* and a novel in 2003, *Dead in 5 Heartbeats.* Today, his Web site offers a full array of Sonny-branded products, from T-shirts to his own beer.

This excerpt from *Hell's Angel* is focused on motorcycles—a hymn to Harley-Davidsons done the Hell's Angels way.

If anybody deserves anything in this whole bike-riding world, it's Sonny.

He led the way.

You see people wearing their fucking patches, "Ride to live, Live to ride." Yeah, right. As soon as the shit comes down, their bike is the first thing they sell.

Sonny is the one who pushed the bike-riding lifestyle.

There wasn't an outlaw type of lifestyle as there is today until

he created it.

—Oakland Hell's Angels president Cisco Valderrama

I've always been crazy about motorcycles. When I was a kid, the Oakland motorcycle cops used to park in front of my house, waiting to catch drivers rolling the stop sign on the corner. Oakland Police Department cops rode Harleys and Indians, the latter a V-twin flathead. Man, I was in awe of their bikes. Even though I really didn't like cops, I'd walk up and talk with them just as an excuse to look at their bikes. Once, one of the motorcycle cops was kick-starting his bike and my dog King freaked out and bit him. Figuring they would throw King in the pet slammer, I grabbed him and ran off. Later that night the police knocked on our door. Luckily my father smoothed things out, and they allowed us to keep King if we promised not to let him leave the house until his rabies quarantine expired.

Motorcycles became the thing to ride in California after World War II. A lot of the GIs coming home from the Pacific who didn't want to return to some boring life in Indiana or Kentucky chose to stick around California. A motorcycle was a cheap mode of transportation, kind of dangerous and perfect for racing and hanging out. Plus they could ride together, just like they were back in the service again. California and its sunshine became the center of motorcycle culture, and for years there were more motorcycles registered in the state of California than in all the other states combined.

I bought my first motor scooter, a Cushman, when I was thirteen. Cushmans had small wheels and the motor mounted on a tin scooter-type frame. An oval box on top of the frame served as the seat. After you kick-started them, little gearshifts and a two-speed shifter made them go. We could throttle those suckers up to forty miles per hour. Mustangs looked like miniature motorcycles with a Briggs & Stratton motor and a fairly small gas tank. During the early fifties when Cushmans and Mustangs were really popular, a brand-new Mustang cost a few hundred bucks, but a used Cushman went for around twenty dollars. So we rode Cushmans.

I was bored stiff with school. I wanted to ride. A guy named Joe Maceo drove demolition derby hardtops for a Signal gas station around the corner from where I lived. Joe was twenty-one (old and wise to a fourteen-year-old like me). They called the cars hardtops. They were those neat little '32 Fords. We'd weld a roll bar over the top of these Fords and nobody cared if they got wrecked or not. Joe and his buddy Marty let me paint the numbers on the hardtops, and on Saturday nights we'd all go down to the races at the Cow Palace in San Francisco and watch Joe smash up those wrecks.

My brother-in-law Bud (sister Shirley's husband) bought used cars and fixed them up for extra cash. Bud and Shirley had a big backyard filled with old heaps that he would buy on the cheap and we'd both work on. I liked working on cars, but I really dug motorcycles. Compared to a car, a bike is a much more personal thing. You can pull the motor off, spread it all out on your workbench, and not have your head stuck down in the hood of some big hunk of steel.

A trailer rental shop opened up next door to my house, and the guy who ran the yard owned a bike too. He let me work for him, and he would take me out for rides on his Norton motorcycle. Riding the Norton, I realized how much more powerful they were than Cushmans or Mustangs.

I saved my dough and bought my first real motorcycle when I was eighteen after being discharged from the Army. The average motorcycle rider was still a little older than I was. I was always the younger guy riding out in front with my friends, most of whom were in their middle twenties. The big bike companies in those days were BSA, Triumph, Norton, Harley-Davidson, and Indian. I went for the Harley and got myself a used 1936 model that, counting tax and license, set me back $125. Gasoline was nineteen cents per gallon, so now I had a cheap way to cruise the streets of Oakland. I was finally on the loose.

Motorcycles were built on rigid frames then, which meant they would vibrate when you rode them. When you hit bumps or a pothole there wasn't a lot of flex on the frame. The constant vibration caused a lot of parts and pieces to come loose and fall off, sometimes when you were riding. You had to constantly wrench up your bike just to keep it shipshape.

Messing around with motorcycles is something I do best. It seems I've been working on motorcycles all my life, modifying them, chopping them, customizing them to my own taste, then changing my mind, breaking them down, and starting over again.

The original Harleys were flatheads. A flathead literally means the head of the engine is flat and it has valves on the side like a flathead Ford engine. My 1936 Harley had overhead valves, instead of valves on the side going up and down. These were called knuckleheads, because they had a big aluminum block on the side where the pushrods went, looking like a knuckle. In 1948, Harley changed over to a tin cover called a panhead, which evolved in 1966 to an aluminum cover called a shovelhead. Different engine heads never overlapped on Harleys; when they changed, they changed across the board. In 1984, Harley converted to a different-looking engine they call an Evolution head.

Harley has enjoyed a huge share of the large-bike market for decades. They control about fifty percent of cruiser sales, with Japanese bikes making up the other half. As a result, they often act a little high and mighty toward their customers.

An official at Harley-Davidson was once quoted as saying, "Enough bikes is too many, and if we make enough, we lose mystique." While they keep saying they're building more and more each year, up until a couple of years ago I believe Harley-Davidson intentionally held back production to stir up demand. Now there are companies like Titan, American Eagle, and American Illusion imitating Harley's Softail model. That's the fifties-styled bike all these new riders want. Softail-type bikes look like rigid-frames but really aren't, and they don't necessarily ride "soft" either. Although they're equipped with shock absorbers, if you ride them over fifty-five miles per hour on the open road you're not going to experience a smooth ride. The motor is not rubber-mounted; it's not much different from a 1936 Harley in the ride. They still tend to break and vibrate if you ride them too fast. For riders who just want to ride down to the bar every Saturday night, the Softail is Harley's bestselling bike for modern times, and the design incorporated the cool look of the chopper. In 2000, Harley came out with an 88B motor that is counterbalanced and does not vibrate.

Titan, American Eagle, and American Illusion make what they call "clone bikes," and although some of these models are manufactured in America, they often don't make their own engines and are just copies of Harleys.

Their credo is violence....Their God is hate and they call themselves 'THE WILD ANGELS'

AMERICAN INTERNATIONAL presents
PETER FONDA · NANCY SINATRA
THE WILD ANGELS
PANAVISION & PATHECOLOR
Co-starring BRUCE DERN and DIANE LADD
PRODUCED AND DIRECTED BY ROGER CORMAN
WRITTEN BY CHARLES GRIFFITH
MEMBERS OF HELL'S ANGELS OF VENICE, CALIFORNIA

WILD AND WICKED

...living with no tomorrow!

MOTORCYCLE GANG

starring ANNE NEYLAND · STEVE TERRELL · JOHN ASHLEY · CARL SWITZER
with RAYMOND HATTON · RUSS BENDER · JEAN MOORHEAD · SCOTT PETERS
ALEX GORDON · Executive Producer SAMUEL Z. ARKOFF · Directed by EDWARD L. CAHN

WILD AND WICKED

...living with no omorrow!

MOTORCYCLE GANG

starring ANNE NEYLAND · STEVE TERRELL · JOHN ASHLEY · CARL SWITZER
with RAYMOND HATTON · RUSS BENDER · JEAN MOORHEAD · SCOTT PETERS
Screenplay by LOU RUSOFF · Produced by ALEX GORDON · Executive Producer SAMUEL Z. ARKOFF · Directed by EDWARD L. CAHN
AN AMERICAN-INTERNATIONAL PICTURE

"Wild and Wicked": Biker movie advertising lobby
cards, circa 1950s–1980s.

But Hell's Angels started riding Harley-Davidsons mostly because, unlike today, they didn't have much choice. In 1957, it was either ride a Harley or settle for a Triumph or BSA. They'd already stopped building Indians. It's always been important for Hell's Angels to ride American-made machines. In terms of pure workmanship, personally I don't like Harleys. I ride them because I'm in the club, and that's the image, but if I could I would seriously consider riding a Honda ST 1100 or a BMW. We really missed the boat not switching over to the Japanese models when they began building bigger bikes. I'll usually say, "Fuck Harley-Davidson. You can buy an ST1100 and the motherfucker will do 110 miles per hour right from the factory all day long." The newest "rice rockets" can carry 140 horsepower to the rear wheel, and can easily do 180 miles per hour right out of the box. While it's probably too late to switch over now, it would have been a nice move, because Japanese bikes today are so much cheaper and better built. However, Japanese motorcycles don't have as much personality.

I ride a Harley FXRT because it's their best model for people who put on a lot of miles. Harley doesn't make them anymore, but they're the best of both worlds—it's a good bike for long distances and also handles and corners well on the short runs. It's not as heavy as their other dresser models, but they ride a little faster, and they still come with saddlebags for traveling. But my FXRT is lucky if it does ninety, that is, until I work on it. After you work on it, you make it unreliable. I always say, the faster a Harley, the less reliable. New Triumphs can do a quarter mile in ten seconds. If you get a Harley street bike to run a quarter mile like that, it's a bomb. The worst thing about it is that once you get a Harley going that fast, you can't

stop it. Right now, Hell's Angels are stuck with Harleys, or maybe we're stuck with each other. Someday we'll be smart enough to walk away.

A Harley FXR is the bike of choice for most Hell's Angels today. FXRs have a rubber-mounted motor on a swing-arm frame. A swing arm means the frame houses left and right shock absorbers in the back section for better road flex. Harley developed the FXR as a reaction to bike riders like the Hell's Angels who preferred more stripped-down bikes. The FXR and the FXRT are basically the same bike. The FXR is more stripped-down, while the FXRT was designed as a touring bike with saddlebags and a fairing, which is the plastic piece that holds the windshield and reduces the wind on the rider.

The FXR is an efficient bike for speed and distance. For years most Hell's Angels usually rode rigid-frame bikes. Nowadays they're switching over to FXRs because they're riding out of state more, going longer distances, and riding faster.

As far as what Harley manufactures, the FXR handled and rode the best, so everybody bought them. After 1993, Harley-Davidson stopped making the FXR. When the 1999 limited series came out, they were list-priced at $17,000. Because of demand, the shops sold them for as much as $25,000. The Dyna Glide has since replaced the FXR. In my opinion it's not as good a bike because it doesn't handle as well as an FXR.

What it's really all about with a Harley-Davidson is the sound . . . everybody loves that fucking rumble. Another thing Harley owners really crave about their bikes is the low-end torque, the raw power coming out of the gate. It runs out pretty quick once you get up past ninety miles an hour. Most Harley riders don't care about high speed, they'd rather have that low-end torque, the one that gurgles down in your groin and gives you the feeling of power. The Japanese bikes, while they *have* the power, they don't quite have the *feeling* of power. You can hook a rope up to a Harley and pull a Mack truck. You can't do that with a Japanese bike. Even though the power is there, you'd tear the clutch right out.

In the early sixties, Honda had an ad, "You meet the nicest people on a Honda." That really turned the Hell's Angels off and knocked Harley for a loop with the average consumer. Honda had such tiny bikes, 50cc and 100cc bikes, the biggest one being a 450cc. Later, when they started coming out with 900, 1100, and 1200 and even those big 1500cc bikes, man, that's some machinery Harley can't touch. Kawasaki and some of the Japanese sport bikes have better brakes and more horsepower and handle easier.

What Harley has is brute horsepower. A brand-new Harley comes with about forty-nine to fifty-two horsepower to the rear wheel. After I've done a little work on mine, I'll get eighty-one horses to the rear wheel.

Up until 1984, Harley-Davidsons were famous for leaking oil. Even when they were brand-new, they leaked, and dealers had to put pieces of cardboard under them in the showroom. Early Harleys came with oil leaks because the tin primary cases had ineffective cork gaskets around them. Sometimes the motors weren't machined properly. If you didn't start your bike for a week, the oil accumulated through the oil pump and into the crankcase. Once you started it, it spit oil all over the ground. After stricter quality control and extra research and development at the factory, they eventually took care of the problem with the new Evolution motor.

If you fix an older Harley right, they won't leak. You'll *never* find a drop of oil under my bike because I refuse to believe motorcycles have to leak. What I do is make sure all the seals are quality, that everything is sealed up right. If I see oil seeping, I wash the parts and replace the gaskets. I guess I'm a bit of a fanatic. The only time you'll see a drop of oil under my motorcycle is after I've run it hard at high speeds. One drop comes out of the breather tube as a result of condensation a while after stopping. I probably could solve that by installing a one-way PCV valve that only lets the engine breathe in, keeping the oil from leaking out. But I'd rather let that single drop continue to leak, because I still want my engine to breathe out.

With speed limits being raised across the United States, I recently installed a RevTech six-speed transmission by Custom Chrome, Inc., in my bike. Having a sixth gear instead of a normal five-speed is like an overdrive and it's really nice. You can hit ninety-five miles per hour and not have your engine rev up. It relieves stress on the motor. If you're doing ninety-five on the highway and turning 5,000 revolutions per minute, you can now do the same speed and only be turning 3,500 rpm. I'm also awaiting my eighty-eight-cubic-inch CCI RevTech motor to go along with the six-speed transmission.

Harley-Davidson has yet to convert to six speeds, while some Jap bikes are already going up to seven speeds. I believe most Harley riders will want to convert to six speeds. When we had three speeds, riders wanted four. When Harley went to four speeds, people dreamed about five-speed motorcycles. Harley six-speed bikes are only a matter of time.

Even though average Harley enthusiasts like the Softail and drive short distances, they'll instinctively want what the Hell's Angels want—faster horses and more efficient overdrive. Motorcycles went to bigger motors (from eighty inches to eighty-eight to ninety-five) because riders like the Hell's Angels kept pushing for more. When the rubber meets the road, the yuppies and the RUBbers (rich urban bikers) will want what we want.

Hell's Angel "choppers" were born when we started taking the front fenders off our bikes, cutting off the back fender, and changing the handlebars. When you watch *The Wild One*, check out the bikes. Lee Marvin and his crew were riding Harleys and Indians with cut front fenders. They hadn't gone to smaller tanks or different wheels. When the Hell's Angels came along, we started taking our bikes apart, improving them and fucking with Harley's formula designs.

When you'd buy a new motorcycle it came equipped with standard features. First we would take the windshields off, then throw out the saddlebags and switch the big old ugly seat (with springs) with a smaller, skinny seat. We didn't need all of those lights either. We converted the oversized headlight to a smaller beam, replaced the straight handlebars with a set of high bars, and replaced the bigger gas tanks with small teardrop-shaped tanks. We used old Mustang motorcycle gas tanks until the mid-fifties, when we started using narrow Sportster gas tanks. The tanks were changed for looks, because the wide and thick stock tanks on a Harley covered up the top of the motor. The design of the bike became radically streamlined, the curvature of the body narrow and sleek. It looked cooler if the front end was longer with a skinny front wheel. Plus you could see the whole motor, a real extra for a street machine.

Next we'd toss the front fender, then cut the back one or make an even thinner fender from the tire cover mount of a 1936 Ford. That made a beautiful back fender for a Harley with a sixteen-inch tire, and it was practical too.

The standard color on Harley frames used to always be black. The gas tank and fenders would be another color. When we built our own bikes we made the frames the same color as the gas tanks and molded it so you didn't see any welding marks. We'd chrome every part we could and install dual carburetors. The results of all the customizing we did were a lot of trophies at the competitions.

I painted myself like a pumpkin to match the new orange of my motorcycle on Halloween night at the Fillmore, 1968. Someone who worked at the Bay Bridge brought me some orange spray cans, so I painted my bike with what soon became "Oakland Orange." It was kinda a bright racing orange. During the Oakland Hell's Angels' 1960s days, orange became a very popular color, and a lot of Oakland members painted their bikes that color. Forget the symbolism, it was free paint.

We painted our death heads and designs on the gas tanks. Tommy the Greek, an old car painter in Oakland, was our man. You immediately recognized Tommy the Greek's designs because he had a *very* distinctive flame design. Big Daddy Roth picked up on Tommy's style too. Von Dutch was another artist whose customized paintwork was admired, especially in SoCal. There were other artists like Len Barton in the Bay Area, Gil Avery in Fresno, Art Hemsel, and Red Lee who were well known for painting cool designs on gas tanks. Arlen Ness, who is one of the leading sellers of bike parts today, got his start as a bike painter. When the Harleys came fresh from the factory, guys like Arlen would take them apart and paint everything one color to match, using fancy shades like candy-apple red.

As opposed to choppers, "full dressers" are motorcycles that keep all of the original manufacturer's pieces on, plus they add accessories like fancy Plexiglas windshields, mud flaps, leather saddlebags, aerials for their radios with raccoon tails on them, extended fenders with a lot of chrome, and *lots* of lights. Too much useless gear, man. The street term for full dressers is "garbage wagons," and in the old days you'd never catch a Hell's Angel on one of them. The casual weekender who was going down to visit his mother-in-law usually rode a full dresser. Or maybe off-duty cops.

These days if I was just a long-distance rider, I'd go for the Harley-Davidson Road King. The Road King is better than Harley's Dyna Glide for long distances. The Road King is a rubber-mounted, stripped-down version of the full dresser. It still has saddlebags and the fairing, but doesn't have stuff like a radio and the big passenger seat.

The Hell's Angels crafted a whole different type of motorcycle. Just like Corvette and Thunderbird helped create the sports-car look for Ford and Chevy, we created the chopper look from Harley-Davidsons. Hell's Angels didn't buy a lot of parts. We made them. I made the first set of high bars that I ever had from the chairs of those old chrome tables in the fifties with Formica tops. You'd get a set of those chairs and they were one inch thick and already bent. You cut off the two ends of the chair, and bang, you had a set of high bars.

Some of the other ways we'd modify our bikes were when we took the rigid front end of one bike, cut it off,

took another rigid, cut *it* off, and welded them together to make the front end six inches longer. By extending the front end of the bike out, the frame dropped lower. Then we'd install the narrow fenders, grab rails, and sissy bars. We made our own sissy bars and foot pegs, molding them out of metal, bending and welding them to our own specifications. By the late 1960s and early 1970s, we might chop a bike to make it sit lower, but we didn't usually cut the frame. It only seemed that way since our seats sat way back, right up on the rear fender.

The only parts we had to buy were for the internal engine and transmission parts. I've probably spent half of my life in a garage so I always have a garage full of spare parts. We'd cut down the flywheels on the left side to make them lighter so the bike would take off quicker. For top-end performance for the long hauls, a heavier flywheel was better, but it was important to us to take off quick.

It was a macho thing to have what we called suicide clutches and jockey shifts, where you would shift gears with your left hand and operate a clutch system with your left foot. Before bikes had electronic ignitions, we would install magnetos to eliminate the need for batteries and coils. A magneto generates electricity for the spark plugs when you kick-start the bike. It was just another way to slim down our choppers.

For the quick takeoff as well, we put in new cams and solid push rods, installed bigger valves and new pistons, punched out the carburetor, and put closer-ratio gears inside the transmission with bigger sprockets to make our motorcycles accelerate faster. Everything had to do with takeoff.

It was like a locomotive about ten miles away. It was the Hell's Angels in "running formation" coming over the mountain on Harley-Davidson 74s. The Angels were up there somewhere weaving down the curves on Route 84, gearing down

thragggggggh

—and winding up, and the locomotive sound got louder and louder until you couldn't hear yourself talk any more . . .

thragggggggh

—here they came around the last curve, the Hell's Angels, with the bikes, the beards, the long hair, the sleeveless denim jackets with the death's head insignia and all the rest, looking their most royal rotten. . . .

—Tom Wolfe, *The Electric Kool-Aid Acid Test,* 1968

The back wheels were changed to an eighteen-inch wheel, and a twenty-one-inch was used for the front. From the axle down, an eighteen-inch rim with a 450x18 tire leaves four and a half inches of tire from the rim to the ground. A twenty-one-inch wheel leaves you only about two and a half inches of tire, so while it really doesn't raise or lower the bike that much, it makes it significantly narrower and faster because of less tire on the ground.

The best deals for bikes were used Harley-Davidsons that the police departments sold. By the way, they still auction them today. Two hundred bucks in the sixties would buy about six or seven thousand dollars in bikes and parts today. The highway patrol—in the days of shovelhead engines—would put twenty thousand miles on bikes before rebuilding them. After forty thousand miles, they'd send them to their academies. Their reasoning was they thought the bikes suffered too much metal fatigue. When the academy was through with them, they'd auction them off, which is when we would buy them. One of the reasons Hell's Angels have stayed loyal to Harley-Davidsons is that a Harley can always be rebuilt, no matter what happens to it unless it catches on fire and burns. That's why you can still see 1936 Harleys on the road today. They are indestructible if you maintain them.

In the early sixties, the serial number on a motorcycle didn't really matter. They were on the left side of the engine case, and if the number matched your pink slip, you were okay, whether it was a factory number or inscribed with a punch. The cops then didn't give a shit if you had lights or license plates. Once bikes started getting stolen, the law got more particular. The vehicle registration laws tightened up and there started being a few more rules. Now even frames have ID numbers.

A lot of the guys in the club would experiment with different things. We'd move our brake to the middle of the bike, replacing the old one with a hydraulic model. Harley-Davidson picked up on that modification and put it on all of their stock bikes. We also changed the kickstands by taking them off the front of the bike and moving them to the middle. Then Harley started doing that on their Sportsters and later on the Big Twins. For kick-start mechanisms, one of the things I always did was cut the kick-start pedal in half and add an inch and a half so you could start a lot easier. To make a motorcycle start, you have to spin the motor enough, and the faster you spin the motor, the easier it starts. If, like me, you weighed 150 pounds and you leaned into the pedal, that extra inch and a half would increase the kick. If you weighed over 250 pounds like Junkie George or Big Al, starting a bike was a snap.

We designed and built a bike that ran damn smooth, using the least amount of parts and accessories. Choppers were stripped down for speed, looks, and ultimate discomfort. After we got *through* with them, they weren't the easiest bikes to ride, but what the hell, at least we looked cool. It became a style and look: a bitch bar (sissy bar) so your chick could lay back. When we'd ride down the street, people would check us out and that was what it was all about.

The government started getting nervous about motorcycle clubs chopping up their bikes. Laws were passed, and as club members started raking bikes and putting on long front ends, the highway patrol helped pass laws regulating handlebar height. For a while, we ran with no front brakes. We didn't need them. A small spool wheel with nice long spokes and no front brakes looked real nice.

THIS GANG
THOUGHT
IT WAS
TOUGH...

'til it found
a new type
of hell...
THE BRIDE
OF SATAN!

WEREWOLVES ON WHEELS

STARRING STEPHEN OLIVER · SEVERN DARDEN

Produced by PAUL LEWIS Associate Producer STUART FLEMING Music by DON GERE Written by DAVID M. KAUFMAN & MICHEL LEVESQUE Directed by MICHEL LEVESQUE

A SOUTH STREET PRODUCTION, INC. Released by THE FANFARE CORPORATION LITHO IN U.S.A. 4

71/259

He Squealed
On His Gang...And
The Word Was Out...
WASTE HIM !

JOE SOLOMON presents

RUN, ANGEL, RUN!

Hear Tammy Wynette Sing "Run, Angel, Run!"

COLOR

STARRING WILLIAM SMITH VALERIE STARRETT

RESTRICTED - Persons under 18 not admitted unless accompanied by parent or adult guardian.

with LEE de BROUX · GENE SHANE · EUGENE CORNELIUS
PAUL HARPER · DAN KEMP

PRODUCED BY JOE SOLOMON ASSOCIATE PRODUCER PAUL RAPP DIRECTED BY JACK STARRETT
STORY BY RICHARD COMPTON SCREENPLAY BY JEROME WISH AND V.A. FURLONG

A FANFARE FILM PRODUCTIONS RELEASE

Biker movie advertising lobby cards,
circa 1950s–1980s.

Then a law was passed requiring front brakes. Some of our handlebars were well over shoulder height. The law was uptight and arbitrary that handlebars should be at shoulder level and no higher. They claimed you couldn't control the bike if your handlebars were too high, which is nuts. We tried to explain to lawmakers that above-shoulder-level handlebars were more comfortable on long rides. The dumb-fuck politicians didn't even consider that's how the everyday person controls their car. Look at people as they drive their cars and notice how they place their hands: On top of the steering wheel—well above shoulder level. It's natural. But I guess since we the Hell's Angels did it, they had to get us for something.

In the early days of motorcycling, nobody even thought about wearing a helmet. Now, of course, there are laws in many states. While I was in jail in 1991, California finally passed its helmet law. In the sixties, I was instrumental in keeping the helmet law off the books. There was a San Francisco assemblyman named John Foran who crusaded relentlessly to pass the first helmet law. I was always in his face, fighting him, and for three or four years, I beat him every time. The final time we clashed, he came up to me and said, "You know, Sonny, next year I'm presenting a bill in front of the assembly that says only *you* have to wear a helmet."

As a club it became our personal mission, so we rode to Sacramento to fight their laws on the steps of the capitol building. It always brought out the news cameras when the Hell's Angels helped lead the battle against helmet laws, because the motorcycle industry was too chickenshit to wage a visible fight against the California assembly. The motorcycle industry was caught in a huge public relations dilemma. They didn't want to see the law passed either, but they were afraid of looking like they weren't safety-conscious. Motorcycle manufacturers never wanted the law passed, because wearing a helmet implied that a motorcycle wasn't safe. The Hell's Angels didn't mind being labeled the bad guys should the law pass. We were used to it.

It's funny when you think about it now, but in order to look cool and have our own look, we cannibalized Harleys to the point where Harley dealers didn't even want us near their shops. We'd destroyed the original Harley design and image by taking stuff off "their" bikes and replacing them with our very own parts. Some Harley-Davidson shops refused to sell us anything. Members used to have to send in their old ladies to pick up parts.

To Harley-Davidson, we made motorcycle riding look bad. Even if we did, we also made them tons of dough for the notoriety of us riding Harley-Davidsons. In the 1950s, people were so intimidated by Harleys that if you rode one sometimes you wouldn't get waited on in restaurants or they wouldn't give you a room at a motel.

I think the Hell's Angels are responsible for a lot of the current designs and workmanship on modern motorcycles. When you look at current custom Softail motorcycles (not the full dressers) you see a lot of our design innovations. Our chopper motorcycles inspired even kids' bicycles, like the Schwinn Sting Ray with its banana seat and gooseneck handlebars. It was only a matter of time before everybody on top would cash in on selling custom motorcycle parts. Custom motorcycles and bike-riding gear has become a bigger business than ever. Thank the Hell's Angels for that.

Stolen bikes have always been a major, let's say, preoccupation with clubs like ours. The Hell's Angels have a rule that with any bike riders who come over and party with us, you cannot steal their motorcycle if it's parked in front of the clubhouse or in front of a member's house. Now that's fair, isn't it? In 1967, three Angels, Big Al Perryman, Fu Griffin, and Cisco Valderrama, stole twenty-seven motorcycles in one day. It's gotta be some kind of world record. The story goes that there were twenty-seven bikers from this nameless club from California that came down to party with the Richmond Hell's Angels one weekend. The clubhouse got raided and everybody went to jail. Cisco needed a twenty-one-inch skinny front wheel, but he knew we had this rule not to steal any bike stuff parked in front of the clubhouse. Cisco knew about the party and all the jailing that went on, so hey, who was gonna miss a front wheel? But a rule is a rule. That's when Big Al and Cisco came up with the scheme of stealing all the bikes. Fuck the front wheel, they wanted the whole enchilada. They rolled all the bikes down the block and parked them there overnight. The next day they figured they were fair game—they weren't in front of an Angels clubhouse anymore and nobody else had stolen them. Fu drove them down in Cisco's '65 Impala convertible and they started bringing them back two by two to Oakland and stashing them at Fu's house. When they were through they had a bike shop, twenty-seven to be exact, all for one lousy front wheel. They stripped them all down and now they had a big—a really big—parts shop.

Then I found out about it.

Cisco and Big Al were in trouble again. They'd fucked up. I told them they'd crossed a thin line between right and wrong, so I made them return every bike. Actually, since they had already been stripped down, we had to have each guy come over to Fu's house and pick up his stolen motorcycle in a box.

But what goes around comes around, because one year later, in 1968, my bike, my honey, my pride, my joy, got ripped off, and boy was I pissed.

Sweet Cocaine. I couldn't believe anybody would steal my beautiful hand-built bike. *Sweet Cocaine* was featured on the album cover of the *Hell's Angels '69* soundtrack. I built it from the ground up, and never a wrench was turned on that bike without the sweet sniff of cocaine. When I finished that bike, I built a miniature Sportster version of the same model for my girlfriend Sharon, calling hers *Little Cocaine.*

I was in Hayward at a jewelry store buying my sister a ring when I heard two ladies who were working in the store talking.

"He must be in his car, because I don't see his motorcycle."

"Are you referring to me?" I asked them. "My bike's right outside."

I walked outside, and sure enough *Sweet Cocaine* was gone. The two ladies had called the cops, but when the police showed up, I told them I had walked to the store. There must have been some mistake. Inside, my guts were on fire, but on the outside I didn't want any cops involved in the search. I remained calm. I got on the phone and called for an emergency meeting with the club.

Biker movie advertising lobby cards,
circa 1950s–1980s.

"Everybody looks for my bike," I told everyone in a rage. "Nobody, and I mean nobody, rides a motorcycle in this town until I get *Sweet Cocaine* back."

Sharon manned the phones at home while everybody else scoured the area. The first calls came in and someone reported seeing a pink Cadillac near the jewelry store. I went from bar to bar, grilling people, asking about the bike, the Cadillac, anything. I wanted the fucking thing back *now*. Meanwhile, every known bike thief was calling. Rick Motley, one of the better-known bike thieves—now dead—called the house and told Sharon he would rather have the Army, the Navy, the Marines, and the Green Berets after him than Sonny Barger and the Hell's Angels looking for *Sweet Cocaine*.

Then we got a vital lead. The Cadillac proved to be a dead end. Some delivery guy outside the jewelry store had seen a guy riding away on a bike, wearing a vest with only a bottom rocker. With a rough description of the guy and the color of his patch, we narrowed it down real quick to a club called the Unknowns. We knew which bar they hung out in, so we raced over there and grabbed up a couple of them fast and asked them what their prospects were up to. Prospects are prospective members who'll do anything, anytime, to anyone just to get into a club. I asked about their prospects because they were crazy motherfuckers with no brains, no history, and usually no future. According to one of the members, yeah, a couple of prospects were tearing down a bike they had just stolen. I told them, "That bike is mine, motherfucker, and you're going to help me get it back."

The prospects who stole the bike didn't know whom it belonged to. The guys who *told* them to steal it probably knew it was mine. I had the registration by the back license plate in a clear round glass tube. The guys tearing it down for parts that night had everything unbolted, but when they got to the registration holder, they knew they were in deep, deep shit. Rather than return *Sweet Cocaine*, they dumped it into the Oakland Estuary.

We rounded up everybody who was responsible, tied them up, and took them over to my house on Golf Links Road. Sharon was supposed to keep an eye on them, but it was a good thing we tied them up because it was so late at night Sharon kept falling asleep clutching her gun. Every half hour or so, the front door would open and another accomplice was tossed into the living room. When we found the last guy the punishment began. One at a time we bullwhipped them and beat them with spiked dog collars, broke their fingers with ball peen hammers. One of them screamed at us, "Why don't you just kill us and get it over with?"

Then we took their motorcycles, sold them, and disbanded their club.

Moral of the story—don't get caught stealing a Hell's Angels' bike, especially if it's the president's.

Butthole Shifters and Suicide Clutches

By Tobie Gene Levingston

Before Rosa Parks took her historic bus ride, before Martin Luther King Jr., Malcolm X, and Huey Newton and the Black Panthers spoke out for equal rights, the East Bay Dragons Motorcycle Club was already making a revolutionary statement. They were a group of African-American men who had joined together to stand up for themselves, bravely risking life and limb in battling the white status quo. And they rode Harley-Davidsons.

When Sonny Barger formed the Oakland Hell's Angels in 1957, a few miles up East 14th Street in East Oakland, a young African-American transplant from Louisiana named Tobie Gene Levingston was inspired. In 1959, he organized the Dragons, a loosely knit, all-black men's club, one of the first of its kind. Soon, they became the East Bay Dragons MC, and Tobie Gene was the club's first and only president, still reigning and riding after forty-plus years.

Tobie Gene tells his story in *Soul on Bikes: The East Bay Dragons MC and the Black Biker Set*, published by Motorbooks International. It's a slice of underground American culture you're unlikely to read in any history book.

This excerpt from *Soul on Bikes* details the club's inspirations, founding, and glory days.

Nineteen fifty-nine. In the eyes of the City of Oakland and the O.P.D., the East Bay Dragons Car Club's goose was cooked. After Joe's automotive assault on the Snow Building, our name was virtually mud with the city. We were, in essence, banned from being issued any permits for our events or having access to renting any of the available halls for our dances. Without dances, the party was truly over. No parties meant no ticket sales, which meant no fundraising, no Tobie money. The end of the club seemed near. The East Bay Dragons were destined to wither and die.

Once again, I looked to Wilton for an answer. Big Wilton was a trendsetter with my crowd. If he said, "Shut up," we'd shut up. If he pointed at someone and said, "Get him," everybody would get him. As the oldest (and the smartest) Levingston, he stayed one step ahead of his brothers by developing an interest in motorcycles. Not just any motorcycle: a black Harley-Davidson full dresser. Back in the day, there weren't a lot of black men riding Harleys in and around the Oakland streets. But they could be had. Motorcycles of all makes were stashed in garages and underneath porches. Black GIs used them as cheap transportation after they were discharged from the military or relocated to Oakland and Richmond from the South. As many of them became God-fearing family men, their motorcycles gave way to the traditional family car and were shoved into the back of the garage or downstairs in the basement.

At the same time, our car club members waged a different battle on the domestic home front. Not a lot of families during the late 1950s had two or three cars parked in the driveway like they do now. Families needed that one car in the garage to run errands to keep the household going, especially on weekends. It was harder and harder for our members to tie up the car during weeknights, weekends, or the wee hours to hang out with their brothers. Since many of us were now married men, we still needed some kind of alternative vehicle to buy us freedom and time away from the crib.

Harleys weren't exactly a dime a dozen in East and West Oakland. They were hard to come by. There were two Harley dealerships in Oakland, but damned if most black men had an extra $600 or $700 to sink into a brand new motorcycle. It wasn't unusual to pick up a raggedy Harley for 40 or 50 bucks and fix it up yourself. Most important, in the late 1950s and early 1960s, the kind of Harley-Davidsons we pictured in our minds weren't the kind that sat on the showroom floors.

But none of us knew how to ride much less fix up the darned things. Maybe Wilton had the answer. He had joined an all-black motorcycle club called the Star Riders. The Star Riders had been around as a riding club for a long time. They had chapters in Los Angeles and Oakland and were made up mostly of older black guys, plus a few women riders. As a carry-over from their military days, the Star Riders' members wore spiffy matching uniforms. They donned black shirts, white neckties, black pants, white-and-black helmets, and shiny black leather patrolman's boots. They primarily, if not exclusively, rode fully loaded Harley-Davidsons, American-made bikes. A full dresser was the polite term for them. We called them "garbage wagons." They were equipped with everything that came with a Harley plus more. Saddle bags. Fenders. Safety mirrors. Low handlebars. High seats. Whitewall tires. Windshields. Lights all up and down the bike. Bullhorns. Front brakes intact. A raccoon tail flapping in the wind. Wilton's Harley had lots of chrome, which influenced us a lot. The best way to avoid riding a boring black bike was to chrome the daylights out of it. But all in all, full dressers were motorcycles that the Dragons wouldn't be caught dead riding. More on all that later.

The Star Riders frequently held dances, but they were much more formal than our car club bashes. Members would arrive decked out in suits and tuxedos, escorted by their wives, who wore mink stoles and evening dresses. Their dances were very straight-laced, uptown affairs. Wilton fit right in. But only in my mother's dreams would Joe Louis and I be wearing a tuxedo to a dance. The Star Riders could party for days. Of course, my crew was much younger, friskier, and more raggedy. The remnants of the East Bay Dragons Car Club were anything but Star Rider material.

The Star Riders weren't by any means the first all-black motorcycle club on the set. A lot of early black MCs were drill team riders. One of the premier pioneer motorcyclists on the West Coast is a friend of mine named Don Myers, aka Snake. In 1953, Don, a black man, was a member of the Berkeley Tigers. That club predated the Star Riders and was originally a drill team. They wore colors on their backs and slick matching green and yellow sweaters with their names embroidered on the front. Their membership spanned nearby northern California cities like Vallejo, San Rafael, and San Francisco. By 1955, a portion of their membership staged a rebellion and sneaked off together to have their bikes painted black. Snake hated the idea of matching black bikes, so the next club meeting was a volatile showdown between the black bikes and Don's pals who wanted to maintain a sense of individuality when it came to the color and designs of their motorcycles.

"We're all gonna paint our bikes black, and next we're going to wear black and white uniforms just like the Star Riders," the Berkeley Tigers leader pronounced.

"Not on my watch," sneered Snake. Don demanded a vote and quickly went down in flames. So Snake walked away with a band of dissenters like George, Fat Daddy, Capers, Chief, and a few others. He formed the California Blazers. That same year in Hollister, Snake came in second with the prettiest bike in California. He rode into the judge's circle on his '49 Harley FL clad in dirty Levi's, popping wheelies and cutting donuts. To this day, Snake still wears his California Blazers patch while members of the next two generations of his family, son Pac Man and nephew Lil Al, have become East Bay Dragons.

Besides the Tigers and the Blazers, there were other black or mixed clubs cutting donuts on Bay Area back roads. Drill team trick riders performed on Bay Area streets in tight formation, turning figure eights, standing upright on moving bikes, being featured in parades and competitions, sometimes in front of California governors. One of the earliest black clubs in northern California was the Bay View Rockets, which started up in 1951. There were also the Buffalo Riders, the Space Riders, the Jolly Riders, the Peacemakers, and the Safari Riders.

There were also the Roadrunners out of Richmond. Richmond was a rough-and-tumble city for bike riders to

Wild and wicked... living with no tomorrow!

—Ad slogan for the movie *Motorcycle Gang*, 1957

congregate. You could ride to a nightspot like the Savoy Club and not make it out with your bike, or even alive for that matter, if you didn't know somebody local. It was a dangerous town to ride through. The Hell's Angels started an early chapter there.

Then, of course, there were the Rattlers in San Francisco. The Rattlers were a mixed club, though mostly black, who had chapters up and running in Frisco and Los Angeles. By mixed, I mean they had a couple of white boys as members. They rode Harley choppers and full dressers. James "Heavy" Evans, the motorcycle-racing king of California, joined the Rattlers as a founding member on Christmas Eve 1955. Other early members included president Ellis White, Jake Stewart, Lonnie Lee, Porky Pete, Big Foot Charles, and Big Spoon, brother of the famous blues singer, Jimmy Witherspoon. In San Francisco, the three clubs that mixed it up were the Hell's Angels, the Gypsy Jokers, and the Rattlers. The Rattlers' turf was the Fillmore district. Like Oakland's Seventh and Market, the Fillmore at night in San Francisco was brimming with pimps, whores, card sharks, thieves, and murderers. The Rattlers kept a hole-in-the-wall clubhouse right on the corner of Ellis and Fillmore Streets. If you could handle yourself on the streets of the Fillmore, you were tough enough. The Rattlers held their dances at the downstairs Fillmore Theater and the auditorium around the corner. The Star Riders turned up at their dances.

As for the fate of our car club, I talked to my friend Sonny Barger, president of the Oakland Hell's Angels. I went to Sonny and said, "Sonny, how do you guys get your permits?"

"Hell," Sonny said, "we don't have no hard time getting party permits. We just go down to the police station and get us one. Ain't no problem."

But we were having a problem. I said fuck it. Everybody get us some motorcycles.

Sonny and I knew each other pretty well from the streets. He grew up across town on the west side, but our paths crossed regularly. By 1959, his Oakland chapter of the Hell's Angels was up and running, going strong. They were—how would you say it?—visible and organized. They rode chops—stripped-down motorcycles known as choppers.

These white guys were scary and tough and rode whenever and wherever they felt like it and did what they pleased. As motorcycle riders, they were second to none. As a brotherhood they were so tight, whenever they met, they'd lock lips and kiss.

The Angels owned the streets of Oakland and virtually ruled the town. Hollywood, TV, and the newspapers were in awe of them. They were something to aspire to. I remember the Hell's Angels way back when they rode in a great big wedge. It wasn't a long two-bike pack like today. The Angels took up both sides of the street, and if they were coming your way, look out!

The members of our car club respected them and looked up to them, particularly Angels like Sonny, Zorro, Tiny, and Terry the Tramp. But Sonny was the cool head in a storm, a natural-born leader of men, a good listener, an arbiter, and a tough customer when it came to fronting his mob and keeping order within the ranks.

If we were going to become a foremost motorcycle club, an MC, the Angels were an ideal model. But first we had to learn how to ride motorcycles. We needed a teacher, bikes, and a safe place to learn to ride. Enter Wilton, his Harley, a rabbit field, and Bigge Road.

Wilton taught me how to ride his Harley. There was a large dusty field down the road from Brookfield Village filled with rabbits. Wilton and I hunted rabbits with our rifles; that's how rural it was at the time. I learned not only how to ride a Harley there, but also how to lay it down. Learning to ride meant learning to fall. As soon as I got the feel of riding and shifting, my brothers and Hooker learned next. Damn near all of our early motorcycle comrades learned to ride on that rabbit field, mainly on Wilton's bike.

Hooker was hooked; he immediately went out and bought a '49 Harley EL with droopy saddlebags. It had a kickstand that would pull the entire bike up, the back wheel jacked up off the ground. It was a bitch to start with its funky distributor. Hooker cranked that thing forever and got bruises up and down his leg. Then Hooker taught Benny Whitfield how to ride. Benny picked up an old Knucklehead and taught the next guy what he learned, and so on and so on—just like the way my family raised its ten kids in Louisiana.

Soon four or five of us were up and riding with confidence on 105th Avenue. Some of us rode Harley 74 FLs. Hooker scored a little 61 EL, but he found the bike slow, too hard to keep up with the rest of us. So he took it to the Harley shop and had them punch up the motor, polish the head, bore it out, polish the barrels inside, and put a cam in it. Soon Hooker's front wheel could barely stay on the ground. He created a monster on the drag strips with that bike.

Incidentally, that rabbit field was the same land on which the Oakland Coliseum arena was built, where the Raiders, Warriors, and Athletics now play. We moved our training grounds to a deserted street called Bigge Road, right off Ninety Eighth Avenue. The Bigge Crane Company stood at the end of the long stretch. Many a Dragon learned how to ride, shift, and fall off their bikes on Bigge Road.

Once we were up and riding, Hooker and I joined an MC called the Peacemakers. Don Myers rode with the Peacemakers for a quick minute. They were a club that accommodated both male and female members. Compared to the Hell's Angels, the Peacemakers were a G-rated, family-oriented outfit. They hosted Sunday picnics and after-church get-togethers. Riding with the Peacemakers taught Hooker and I what we didn't want in a club. When it came to staging dances, the Peacemakers were careless and sloppy. The club didn't make that much money.

During one meeting, the president and his wife started going at it. Arguments between men and women in the Peacemakers became commonplace. The Peacemakers who had their wives with them in the club bickered continuously. It got to the point that if a guy in the club supported another woman's idea, it created suspicion in the ranks. "You must be going with that bitch. That's why you're on her side."

It was bad enough when a woman would sweet talk two different half-drunk club members at a dance, and they'd end up fist fighting over a pretty woman they never even knew.

Hooker and I looked at each other and shook our heads. It was worse than when Buzzy joined the car club.

"Enough of this nagging and arguing. If we get our own MC up and going, we're not going to allow women to join."

Hair in the wind, Billy Lane rides full bore into Savannah.
Photograph © Russ Bryant

Hooker's wife, my cousin, floated the suggestion about women members, Dragonettes if you will. We put a stop to that right away. Hooker agreed. The constant bickering was exactly what members of a motorcycle club wanted to get away from. I'm not saying that women don't have good ideas when it comes to groups and organizations. I'm just saying that women, particularly strong black women, have a tendency to push their way into things.

Personally, I dig women riders. The Rattlers had ladies in their club, and that was cool. I'm just saying that for us, the idea of a more laid-back, funky, Harley-only motorcycle club exclusive to East Bay black men seemed like an idea whose time had come. Like the car club, we wanted an MC that would be a brotherhood and also a getaway from the everyday grind of work and family pressures.

After I started riding, I rode over to a Rattlers' dance with my brother Wilton and another Star Rider named Johnny L. The Rattlers were a badass group. They had all kinds of raggedy motorcycles parked out front of their tiny clubhouse in the Fillmore. I rode a little chop with a 19-inch wheel on the front, a 16 on the rear, and a shift on the side. I'd heard the skinny on the street.

"Man, when you ride your bike over to the Rattlers, you better be careful or they'll steal it."

I stood outside the clubhouse all night and watched my bike. Nobody was going to heist my precious wheels. Inside the clubhouse, two big Rattlers, Big Brown and Mule, sat face to face at a table, their steely eyes locked in mortal combat. Their arms were as big as tree trunks. The Rattlers had arm wrestling contests on most Friday and Saturday nights. Everybody threw down their money and placed bets on who would be the winner. I stood there amazed as these two went at it all night long.

In the early days, a few women wore Rattler colors on their backs, and some of the women were as tough as the guys. One member, honest to God, would talk shit and cuss you out. She'd whoop your ass in a minute. Years later, there she was, sitting at our clubhouse bar wearing a dress with a friend from Los Angeles. I laughed out loud. All these years I didn't know she was a woman. That's how tough she was. I gave her the respect she was due.

By 1959, just as the country was about to enter a new decade, the East Bay Dragons Car Club began its gradual transition from a car club to a motorcycle club. The East Bay Dragons MC was born. In making the switch, we decided to hold onto our name and patches and sew them on black Levi jackets with the sleeves cut off. In switching from cars to bikes, we found that some of the members we had lost while we were a car club had returned with vigor and enthusiasm as motorcycle-riding Dragons. While most of the black and mixed clubs rode full dressers, we modeled ourselves after the Hell's Angels. We rode our own chopped Harley-Davidsons.

From the start, the East Bay Dragons MC membership was exclusively black and Harley-only. Full dressers and Japanese bikes were strictly forbidden, except for Albert Guyton, who stubbornly demanded he ride a full dresser. We took his matter to a vote at one of our meetings. We compromised and let Albert slide by, assigning him as the rider who carried the tools (or "the garbage") on all of our runs. Other than Albert, everybody else rode chops. The earliest members included most of the original car club guys—Hooker, Joe Louis, Jonas, Van Surrell, Sonny Wash, Popsy, Johnny Mendez, Benny Whitfield, MacArthur, and me. We'd meet anywhere we could, in Hooker's garage, at Sonny Wash's duplex. We set up stakes at Miss Helen's Barbeque on Eighty Fifth Avenue. Miss Helen encouraged us early, set aside a portion of her restaurant for us to meet after closing, and kept a steady stream of chicken and ribs on the table. Helen became the patron saint of the East Bay Dragons MC. We loved her.

When it came to putting our bikes together, we set up what I called "the assembly line" in my garage. Just like when we worked on our cars, quite a few members became instantly mechanically inclined with motorcycles. When most of us first started riding, members showed up at my garage with nothing but a pink slip and the bike in a box. From the rainy months of November to early March when the sun would start shining, you would find us busy in my garage getting ready for the start of the traditional bike-riding season. As we all worked on our bikes, we'd talk, laugh, and drink a few beers. We'd gamble too; play cards, dice, and dominos. November became the time to figure out how to make your bike run faster and slicker and look prettier.

We found motorcycles much easier to work on—or tear down—than cars. Also, since we were tearing down our bikes, practically reinventing them, it made no sense to buy a brand new Harley, unless it was a new Sportster, which everybody saw and wanted after Zorro from the Hell's Angels got one. Not that we could afford them, anyway.

Working on a half dozen cars would practically take up most of the street or a yard. But half a dozen motorcycles could be worked on in my garage, rain or shine. Plus, different members developed different skills. Popgun, aka Popsy, was always in hurry and the first to get his bike up and rolling. After he'd true his own wheels, he'd help out wiring the remaining bikes. The electrical stuff, headlights and taillights, was the tricky part. Guys would be proficient at different aspects of repair and customization, and we could pool our newfound talents to put together a fleet of motorcycles that would be distinctively "East Bay Dragons"—chopped, colorful, and roaring out the door sideways.

Hooker and I chopped the first bike. We threw away the saddlebags. We removed the front fender. We cut off half the back fender. There was a Harley shop on Eighty Fourth Avenue, right next to the fish shop in case we got in trouble, needed a part, or had a question. We enlarged the stroke and bore of the engine so that the bike would be faster, capable of much higher speeds than any Harley off the showroom floor.

Whatever we could possibly chrome, we'd take over to the chrome shop down on Forty Seventh Avenue. What we couldn't afford to chrome, we added what we called "Mexican chrome." We took off the front wheel and sprayed the spokes with silver spray paint. We moved the license plate to the side. We built our own sissy bars and brake mechanisms. We took the springs out of the seat and laid it down on the rigid frame. We switched gas tanks to the smaller Sportster "peanut" tanks. We shot the pegs up or put tachometers on the gas tanks. We installed extended front ends. A few of us even went to Alameda College and took up shop. We made up extensions, risers for the handlebars, and screws for the front wheels.

Movie press booklets, circa 1960s–1980s.

THEY LIVE HARD...THEY LOVE HARD...
"ANGELS DIE HARD!"

CHOPPER OUTLAWS!..
riding their hot
throbbing machines
to a brutal climax
of violence!

IN COLOR

THEIR BATTLE CRY-
"KILL THE PIGS!"

ORIGINAL
SOUNDTRACK
ALBUM
NOW ON
UNI RECORDS!

STARRING
TOM BAKER · WILLIAM SMITH

SPECIAL GUEST STAR
R.G. ARMSTRONG · WITH ALAN DeWITT · GARY LITTLEJOHN · RITA MURRAY · CARL S...

EXECUTIVE PRODUCERS JANE SCHAFFER AND JAMES TANENBAUM · PRODUCED BY CHARLES BEACH DICKERSON · WRITTEN AND DIRECTED BY F...

A New World Pictur...

They ride to love...
They ride to kill!

THE PEACE KILLERS

A Damocles Production "THE PEACE KILLERS" starring Clint Ritchie, Jess Walton, Paul Prokop and Lavelle Roby as Black Widow.
Produced by Joel B. Michaels. Directed and Edited by Douglas Schwartz. Screenplay by Michael Berk.
Based on an original story by Diana Maddox and Joel B. Michaels. From TRANSVUE PICTURES CORP. • Color by Deluxe.

R

ONE SHEET

We rode with suicide clutches, which you engaged with your foot instead of your left hand. Others had tank shifts as opposed to foot shifts. We called that a butthole shift. We put a rod with a knob on the side of our transmissions with the suicide clutch. Shifting uphill was impossible. We replaced the mufflers with straight pipes. Eighteen-inch tires went on the front wheel, 16-inchers on the back. We constantly got tickets for our high bars and ape hangers.

Soon our bikes developed a unique style. Metalflake paint jobs. We became the original "rainbow coalition." Everybody rode a bike of a different color.

"What color you gonna paint your bike?" Sonny Wash might ask MacArthur. Whatever Mac said, Sonny chose a different shade of the spectrum. Everybody picked a color different from their other riding brothers. Whatever you chose, I did something different.

We also got pretty competitive when it came to our bikes, whether we were building them or racing them. Colors varied between turquoise blue, yellows (Benny Whitfield's specialty), loud metalflake orange, deep purples, even pink with black trim. We kept our enameled bikes shining with glass wax and our chrome glistening.

Our main painter was Harry Brown. Joe Louis found him at his shop in Hayward. A youngster named Arlen Ness painted Harley frames and was an early supporter of the East Bay Dragons and many black riders. Another painter in Berkeley named Sal painted matching flames on our helmets. Sal, an old Italian guy, was a leftover from the shoot 'em up gangster days of West Oakland.

We used a lot of guys for chrome and paint, but none matched Tommy the Greek. He did all of our striping from his studio workshop in Berkeley. The Greek was known all over the Bay Area (and beyond) for his striping technique. We loved Tommy. He was crazy. The Greek was a steady-handed artist. He did all of his painting freehand, no taping. We'd show up at his shop on Foothill Boulevard on Saturday. He had a little bitty motorcycle that he kept in a closet. He would come roaring out of the closet and chase you around the shop on his miniature motorcycle. Sometimes when he sprayed a bike with a clear coating, he'd take his teeth out and spray the stuff into his mouth and get high on his own paint supply. Whenever we'd pull up, we'd yell into the Greek's domain, "Hey Tommy! You through with our bikes?"

"Shit no! Ain't even started yet!"

Tommy was the master striper. Nothing crazy, just real clean, cool, and neat. He was great with flames and teardrops. That was his signature. Cadillac cars would drive down the street bearing his stripes and teardrops. Dudes in the know would see them and holler out from the street corner, "Greek!"

We also went down to San Pablo Avenue and visited old Walt at his Harley shop. He had a line on the old highway patrol and city PD motorcycles put up for auction. Walt was over 70, but he wasn't too old to drag race old Knuckleheads, Panheads, and Sportsters out at Fremont Drag Strip.

We would soon stage our very first bike inspection on Washington's Birthday weekend. Members wheeled their bikes over to my place for the final once over. We decided that to be a Dragon and remain in good standing, your bike not only had to be in top running order, but it also had to sparkle and shine up to extreme standards. March bike inspections are still an annual tradition to this day.

Movie press booklet, circa 1960s–1980s.

The East Bay Dragons MC started out as a melting pot of different bike-riding cultures. We liked how the Hell's Angels dressed, fought, and carried themselves. They rode Harley choppers exclusively. They sewed their scary patches onto cut-off denim or leather jackets and vests. They wore their jeans greasy. No corny uniforms or gaudy full dressers.

But we also liked how the Star Riders were organized. They could put on dances, picnics, and staged major events in the black community. We admired the Rattlers for their ability to hang tough and stand up to their white, two-wheeler counterparts.

Some black clubs required their members have jobs. We liked that. My rule was that you had to adhere to what I called "the legal hustle." When you're making a living for your family, you're hustling some kind of way. The illegal hustles were the kinds of scams that the police could pick you up on, which would then draw heat on the club. We wanted to avoid that bullshit. We elected officers, including a president, vice president, road captain, and business manager. We also learned from Buzzy, the white dude during our car club days. To be in the East Bay Dragons MC, members would have to be exclusively black, ride Harleys, and be gainfully employed.

We would keep the police off guard with our wits. We didn't take any crap, nor, as a rule, did we start any.

We might be peaceful one minute, ass kickers the next. We worked well within the black community, but we maintained our own independence. A pack of black riders would freak the living daylights out of the neighboring towns, communities, and police departments. That was okay. From the very start, we intentionally made it difficult for law enforcement to simply pigeonhole the East Bay Dragons as outlaws. Like the Angels, we wanted to be colorful and visible when it came to our public profile. We wanted to add spectacle to the streets wherever the pack rode. But the Oakland black community would be our domain.

More importantly, we wouldn't fall into the territorial trap. We refused to even claim our own neighborhood streets. We wanted to avoid that gangster, Al Capone stuff. Instead, we'd ride from one community to another with pride and confidence. I liked it that when someone on the streets, black and white, male and female, cops and bike riders, whoever, saw us, they didn't quite know what to make of us. We were unusual and special. An East Bay Dragons MC member didn't neatly fit into any biker box or easy category.

Were we nice guys or outlaws? We were no saints. Would a member help you fix your car or kick your ass? Try your luck and find out. Sometimes a little fear and uncertainty was a good thing.

Hard riders!

Mounted on burning steel! . . .
with only their leathers between
them and Hell!

Ad slogan for the movie *The Sidehackers*, 1969

Chapter 6

The Good, the Bad, and the Legendary

I don't want a
pickle,
I just want to ride on my
motor-sickle.

—Arlo Guthrie, "The Motorcycle Song"

Harley-Davidsons Fit for the King

By Evan Williams

Evan Williams has never truly recovered from the influence of his two early heroes, Evel Knievel and Elvis Presley. Their legend and style kickstarted Evan's life.

Evan covers the AMA Superbike series for Superbikeplanet.com. His work has also appeared in *Roadracer X*, *Roadracing World*, and various regional motorcycle magazines. He also writes an online column for the AMA's website at AMASuperbike.com.

This article looks back at Evan's inspiration, Elvis, and the King's own love of motorcycling.

Sometimes it's not easy to be a motorcyclist. Avoiding random lane-changers, road-rage psychotics, and just run-of-the-mill geranium brains in two-ton steel cages all help make motorcycling a pastime for the alert and skilled cyclist. All bike enthusiasts know the feeling—it's a jungle out there.

But for the moment, let's pretend differently. Let's crank up the time machine, and set the controls for August 14, 1977 and the location for Memphis, Tennessee. You are the King of Rock 'n' Roll and a lifelong bike enthusiast; you are Elvis Aaron Presley, AMA member number 94587.

Speaking of jungles, let's say you're lounging in the Jungle Room at Graceland, and decide it's time to go for a ride. You give a call out to your girlfriend, Ginger Alden, and ask her not to fetch you another peanut-butter-and-banana sandwich, but your leather jacket, because you two are going for a ride. And when the King decided to go for a ride, nothing could deter him.

"Don't forget where he came from," Elvis's guitarist Scotty Moore told the Memphis *Commercial Appeal*. "Elvis was still a kid when he died. He never grew up. It was usually things he hadn't had a chance to do when he was growing up."

If you were Presley, you'd stroll over to the garage, and decide which toy you would fire up for a ride into Southhaven. It could be a vintage chopper, or a Honda Dream, or perhaps a trike. But most likely it would be a Harley Dresser that Elvis preferred. "Most of the bikes he had that I saw him ride—the FLH, the Dressers, police-type bikes—were bigger and close to the ground,"

says Ron Elliott, the proprietor of Supercycle, a Memphis bike shop were the King took care of his (motorcycle) business. "They were more predictable and handled better (than some of his other machines)."

But first, we'd look for a member or two of our entourage, the Memphis Mafia, to ride along with us. "Elvis was real big on getting a lot of his friends to ride with him. . . . I guess it was hard for him to go anywhere by himself. The fans just swamped him everywhere he went, even down here (in Memphis)."

You've had health problems over the past few years, and you're not getting any younger, but it all fades away on your bike. The promise of the open air hits you as you roll down the hill and out the Graceland gate, maybe head towards the Circle G ranch you own right across the Mississippi state line. You are reminded of the early days, when you first bought that little Harley stroker when the money started rolling in. Of the wild California times, when you and the guys (and girls) rode up and down the coast. About getting one day away from touring in the early 1970s and coming back to ride downtown in Memphis.

You are wearing an open-face helmet, but onlookers invariably know it's you. They all double take, wave, or look for their cameras, and more than a few have trouble keeping in their lanes. If anything, the frenzy fans show at concerts is increased when they see Elvis on the streets. To circumvent the hoopla, most of your rides are at night, like this one.

Looking around at the neighborhood, you'd remember that this place was a quiet little neighborhood when you

Would-be automotive mogul Preston Tucker aboard his Knucklehead, circa 1930s.

bought Graceland in the 1950s, but twenty years have brought plenty of commercialization to the area. The smells of magnolias have been replaced with urban exhausts, but the ride still replenishes energy to your psyche.

As the ride ends, you realize it's never quite long enough. You roll through the gate and feel a twinge of sorrow. Perhaps now is the time in your life to cut back on the constant touring and relax a bit. Enjoy life, ride your bike more. You've told others that you want to make this tour your "best one ever," but part of you wonders why you can't give it a break. Perhaps delve into some serious film roles, and spend more time with your daughter, Lisa Marie.

But it wasn't meant to be. Two days later, Elvis would be dead and his fans would be in a mourning period that to this day really hasn't ended.

He may have been a superstar, but Elvis was just like us. He was a bike nut and enjoyed nothing more than getting out on the open road to clear his mind. Elvis could often be seen motoring around the streets of Memphis, or Los Angeles during his movie days. "He rode a lot; cold weather, warm weather, whenever he was in town," says Elliott.

Elvis's love affair with bikes wasn't a short-lived whim. He bought a Harley Hummer when he first received some of his Sun Records money in the mid-1950s. His last ride was two nights before his death on August 16, 1977. In between, he owned and rode Harleys, Hondas, and Triumphs, as well as trikes, snowmobiles, shifter carts, and almost every other motorized toy you could imagine. Not only did the King play a motorcyclist on the big screen, he lived the part.

Elvis's first Harley Hummer was a 125cc utilitarian machine that was designed to be an entry-level bike rather than an enthusiast's ride. According to Elliott, the King quickly grew tired of the little two-stroker and decided to step up to a bigger bike. Of course, it would be a Harley.

"It was a 1956 Model K," says Marty Rosenblum, Harley-Davidson's archivist. An 883cc machine that was to evolve into the Sportster model, Elvis's red machine came at a perfect time to help cement his image as a 1950s icon. There were a series of photos taken of Presley in black leather gear on the K Model. Some say these are the definitive Elvis photos from the 1950s.

"He appeared on the cover of our May 1956 *Enthusiast* magazine with the bike." says Rosenblum. The article was also one of the first public announcements Elvis had switched to the RCA label from Sun, after Sam Phillips sold Elvis's contract.

According to Rosenblum, Elvis ended up giving the bike to a friend to store when he joined the U.S. Army after being drafted in 1958.

Elvis's Harley has been the subject of a widely propagated urban legend with the birth of the Internet. In the tale, an enthusiast buys a basket-case H-D out of a barn, begins restoring it, and has trouble acquiring parts. He calls a dealer and gives them the VIN of the bike. Depending on the version of the story you are hearing, either Harley CEO Jeff Blustein or *Tonight Show* host Jay Leno calls the new owner and offers millions for the bike. The caller tells the enthusiast to check under the seat, which is engraved with, "To Elvis, from James Dean."

Riding through the desert from Vegas to Palm Springs on America's Main Street. *Photograph © Russ Bryant*

Sorry, but it appears scouring America's barns for the King's missing Harley will be a futile effort.

Harley has owned Elvis's bike since the early 1990s, when the Motor Company acquired it from one of Elvis's pals. It is (and always has been) in excellent condition. Harley has traced the numbers back, and has confirmed its bike is the original model Elvis bought and rode.

And the truth is, James Dean never bought Elvis a Harley.

Rebel with a cause: Clark Gable and his Big Twin, circa 1930s.

After Elvis returned from his stint in the Army, he moved to Los Angeles and resumed his career by starring in Hollywood movies. Motorcycles played a major part in his life during this period; they weren't just used for recreation, but as a preferred means of transportation.

People living in early 1960s Los Angeles have plenty of tales of Elvis and his bikes: Presley running out of gas with a starlet pillion and without any cash to fill the tank. Elvis rescuing a starving dog while on a bike ride up the coast. Presley's entourage having a dozen crated Triumphs delivered, then spending all night assembling them. Elvis's neighbors complaining about the noise. Presley buying a truckload of Honda Dreams when they first reached the

United States. Elvis and a beautiful costar sneaking away from the set for a bike ride.

Just how much is fact and how much is legend is now uncertain.

The thirty-two movies he made helped the world associate Elvis with motorcycles. Presley rode a Honda Dream in 1964's *Roustabout*, a Triumph in 1968's *Stay Away, Joe*, and a Harley Big Twin in 1967's *Clambake*. He took his love of motorcycles seriously.

At some point in the late 1960s, Elvis had a custom Harley chopper built to keep up with the trends of the day. Red and black, it had a high-rising sissy bar and plenty of chrome. Elvis kept the bike at Graceland and was seen riding it around Memphis.

"The chopper had an extended front end," said Elliott. "It wasn't a radical chopper at all. The forks were probably no more than extended six inches, maybe even four inches. But whenever you do anything like that to one, it does adversely effect the front. I don't think he liked all the adventure."

Elvis's chopper, like a child's toy, disappeared eventually and was replaced by other motorcycles. It was re-discovered after his death.

"No one even knew he rode the doggone thing," says Elliott. "(After his death) we went out to pick up some vehicle for an 'Elvis on Tour' show. We went down and picked up one of the three wheelers, a snowmobile, the pink Jeep, and his Uncle Vester said, 'Why don't you pick up the chopper?'" Elvis's cousin Billy Smith and everyone there had a blank look on their faces, because no one knew he still had it.

"In the garage was the chopper, with thirty bicycles piled up on top of it. Remarkably, it hadn't hurt the paint very much. We brought it down here and restored it, rebuilt the engine. The thing didn't have 500 miles on it. It was in like-new condition, but they wanted everything to run perfectly."

Elvis caught the trike bug in the mid 1970s. Presley's health was not at the best during this time period, reportedly due to glaucoma, an enlarged colon, and prescription drug dependence. "He had gotten, I guess, more comfortable with three wheels," says Elliott.

Elvis bought several three-wheelers, although he continued to acquire and ride Harleys. The first trike was a Rupp Centaur, which utilized a 340cc Kohler two-stroke snowmobile engine. It was German-built and a racy red, with a centrifugal clutch mated to its transmission. But the Rupp gave him reliability problems, and he soon purchased another trike from Elliott.

The new trike had a 1600cc VW engine in it and the flashy styling of the period with a custom paint job guaranteed to turn heads. It had a chrome front end with a skinny front tire in the front, but massive rear tires and lots of bodywork covering the VW mill. Custom built in Memphis by SuperCycle, one word that would aptly describe the machine is "disco."

Okay, I know what you're thinking. Most self-respecting motorcycle enthusiasts look at trikes with utter disdain. But Elvis didn't. Shortly afterward, Presley came back and bought another one.

"He liked what he liked," Joe Esposito, part of the Memphis Mafia, once told a journalist. "It didn't matter if it cost a million dollars and another cost a dime. If he liked it, he would pick the one that cost a dime."

Riding Pretty: The Motor Maids

By Margie Siegal

When Margie Siegal was seventeen years old, she had a boyfriend who had a 350 Ducati single. Although Margie says she wouldn't remember the boyfriend today if he walked up and shook her hand, she remembers the Ducati well.

Not coincidentally, it was also at seventeen that Margie realized that there was no need to put up with forgettable boyfriends to enjoy motorcycling. Eventually, she saved enough money to buy a 350 Honda twin. Margie is still riding today.

In the early 1980s, she celebrated her purchase of a new Moto Guzzi by going on a solo tour of California's Gold Country and keeping a diary of her trip. When she returned home, she had another brainstorm—she decided to turn the diary into a
magazine article. She didn't sell the article, but got the nicest rejection letters.

Some time later, she was introduced to Brian Halton, who was interested in starting a San Francisco motorcycling newspaper. After ten months of writing for free, the newspaper started to pay and Margie had learned to write. She is now a regular contributor to numerous magazines, including *Rider* and *Ironworks*.

"Riding Pretty" looks at some of the most famous women to ever ride Harleys—a history that continues today.

Gloria Struck celebrated her 78th birthday the first day of the 2003 Motor Maid National Convention in Chico, California. To get to the Motor Maids' 63rd annual meet, she rode her Harley-Davidson cross country from her home in New Jersey in company with her daughter Lori DeSilva and her son-in-law, each riding their own motorcycle with one of the DeSilva's teenage daughters on the passenger seat.

No longer painfully shy, Gloria is now a gregarious and infectiously happy woman, "See what motorcycling has done for me!" she crows.

Exactly 108 Motor Maids turned up for the 2003 convention, many accompanied by their husbands, children, and sweethearts. Half the Chico Holiday Inn parking lot was roped off for motorcycle parking. The lot was filled with bikes, mostly dresser Harleys and Hondas. A common comment was how surprised members were at the high turnout, given how rainy and awful weather in the East had been.

Most Motor Maids live East of the Mississippi, and Western convention turnouts had not been this high since the mid–1980s. The 2003 event marked a resurgence in Motor Maid participation in the Western states.

The Motor Maids were the idea of Linda Dugeau, a Providence, Rhode Island, enthusiast. She wrote to dealers and other motorcycle riders, suggesting the idea of a club for women who owned their own motorcycles. Dot Robinson, a well-known off-road racer from Detroit, heard of Linda's idea, liked it, and helped organize. The Motor Maids were started in 1940 with fifty-one members and Dot as the first president.

Most of the early Motor Maids were dealers, motorcycle industry figures, or relatives of dealers. Gloria Struck's mother was an Indian dealer in her own right. Dot Robinson ran the Detroit Harley-Davidson dealership with her husband Earl. Helen Kiss was not only the daughter of an Indian dealer, but a prominent rider. Hazel Duckworth's family made motorcycle chains.

In the 1940s, few women outside of the motorcycle industry rode. Although World War II had put money in the pockets of women war workers, new motorcycles were not available during the war, and were relatively expensive afterwards. In addition, motorcycling was not then a popular women's sport.

Betty Fauls, Dot's daughter, remembers riding to Motor Maid conventions on the back of Dot's motorcycle or in a sidecar. When she was fourteen, she got her own bike. "We ride to events—it is in our club rules. We do not trailer."

When the club began, most members rode tank-shift Harley and Indian dressers. In those days, motorcycles had to be kickstarted, and maintenance was more involved. "We had to adjust chains and oil them every several hundred miles," remembers Betty.

"I have never had trouble starting any motorcycle," states Gloria. "There is a ritual to starting each bike. If you know the ritual, even a small person like me—I'm five foot, one inch—can do it. I've seen big men not be able to start motorcycles because they didn't know how."

In the 1940s, between thirty and thirty-five women would turn up for a national convention, which soon became a yearly event. In between conventions, there were district rides (the Motor Maids are now organized into twenty-six districts, covering the United States and Canada), meets, and parades. The Motor Maids were first asked to stage a parade before the 1941 Ohio Charity Newsies race. Partly because of the many Motor Maid parades, the club developed a national uniform.

The first uniforms were a tailored jacket and pants that looked much like a military uniform. Some time after World War II, when the cost of tailored uniforms became prohibitive, the uniform evolved to what it is today: royal blue overblouse, white boots, white gloves, and a tie. Members wear the uniform at banquets, conventions, and parades.

In addition, members wear ribbons at conventions. Pink means a prospective member, and red means the first convention attended. A silver ribbon means twenty-five years as a Motor Maid and the golden ribbon means fifty years in the club.

The uniform has not changed for many years, and is now the subject of some controversy. "I like the uniforms," says Joy Maxwell, a member for three years. "They serve a traditional purpose. I think we are less Motor Maid–like without the uniforms. Some members are discussing an update, but I think we have to stick to our roots."

"I think we look very nice," states Gloria. "When we

parade, we look beautiful. It is very touching. It brings tears to my eyes."

Many members curtailed their involvement during the 1950s to have children, but kept in touch, and were back on their bikes when the kids were in their teens. Quite a few daughters of Motor Maids have joined the organization. In one case, grandma, mom, and daughter are all active members. "When I was little, I thought everybody's mother had a Harley," says Lori.

The Motor Maids provided a friendly, respectable organization for women riders during the 1950s and early 1960s when it was not respectable for anyone—man or woman—to ride. "Sometimes we were called names," remembers Gloria.

For many years, the membership was stable, but about 1992, Motor Maid numbers rocketed. Many more women were riding, and the Motor Maids were attractive to women new to the sport.

"I thought there was a stigma attached to a riding group," explains Joy. "Three years ago, I went to my first district meeting and was surprised. There was a wide variety of women. They were so very much *not* that way—the way I thought riding groups were. They were professional and well educated. They were all ages, although a lot were older."

One of the major reasons why women join the Motor Maids and stay in the organization is the support, encouragement, and mentoring provided by the older members. "I would not be able to ride without it," says Joy. "I had an accident and almost stopped riding. I was taken under the wing of the other members and I learned to enjoy curves. There is a lot of mental support.

"There is a lot of collective information. There are people who have been riding sixty years, and people riding three months. If you are a fly on the wall, you will learn something.

"I went to the Pennsylvania convention. It was my first long ride, and I packed way too much stuff. I ended up mailing a lot of it home. I learned how to pack for a long trip from the other members, and I learned how to tie it all down."

"Being a Motor Maid means having pride and self-confidence," declares Lori. "My mother [Gloria] made me ride to Daytona. We started when it was twenty-three degrees out. We made it, and I had a wonderful time."

Gloria has come a long way from being a quiet, withdrawn teenager. She credits motorcycling and the Motor Maids with taking her out of her shell. Now in her seventies, she is a vibrant, busy woman. "Maybe I'll slow down when I'm ninety." She owns two motorcycles and in 2001, flew one to Europe and rode it through seven countries.

Why has Gloria been a Motor Maid for all these years? "I am a motorcyclist. The Motor Maids is the elite of women's motorcycle clubs. We are well respected. We are very close, and look forwards to seeing each other each year. It's like a sisterhood."

"Why are Motor Maids so persevering and self confident? It is in the nature of the sport." Betty Fauls had just come back from a poker run, which started as the thermometer read thirty degrees. "It is not easy. We have to have determination and fortitude.

"Motor Maids ride."

My mother and brother ran the motorcycle shop after my father died. My brother made me learn to ride a motorcycle when I was sixteen. I was very quiet and withdrawn, and didn't ride again for another three years. Then he went into the service, and my mother kept the shop going during the war. She took a 1943 Indian Army Scout, a 30.50 cc twin, in trade. I thought I could ride it. I took the army manual, read it, and got on the bike. I started it—and went roaring across the street, just missing the gas pumps. When I came around the block, I knew how to ride.

—Gloria Tramontin Struck, fifty-seven-year Motor Maid member

Bally Harley-Davidson
pinball machine
promotional flyer,
1991.

Bad News

By Craig Vetter

Craig Vetter is a household name to anyone familiar with motorcycling.

Many cyclists have had motorcycles mounted with Vetter fairings; his Windjammer fairing concept from the 1970s helped inspire the touring motorcycle concept. By 1977, his Vetter Corporation boasted factories in Illinois and California that employed over five hundred people—second in size only to Harley-Davidson.

In 1969, Craig was hired by the BSA–Triumph group to update the BSA Rocket 3 design. His vision became the 1973 Triumph Hurricane, which was subsequently selected for inclusion in the Guggenheim Museum's "The Art of the Motorcycle" exhibit.

Today, every motorcycle manufacturer features at least one machine in its lineup that's derived from one of Craig's designs. In 1999, the American Motorcyclist Association inducted him into the Motorcycle Hall of Fame.

This essay travels back in time to the debut of Craig's Vetter fairings and a simple drag race that taught him to respect Milwaukee iron.

I knew him ever so briefly at Daytona in 1967, and then just by his nickname, "Bad News." He came in and out of my life in about one minute—the time it takes to stage and run a quarter-mile drag race. And I never forgot him.

Over the years, I would ask people from Daytona if they had ever heard of Bad News. Yep, invariably came the answer. Bad News was a legend in those parts. He had a shop south of Daytona where he made Harleys run fast—but not fast for long.

"That's why they called him 'Bad News'," folk said.

I first encountered Bad News on Sunday morning, March 18, 1967. The locals had directed us to this abandoned World War II airport runway just outside Daytona Beach, Florida, saying it was a safe place to camp. We tucked in and were soon all asleep under the palmettos on the sand. We had no idea we were sleeping on a drag strip.

My brother Bruce, and our friends Jim Voorheis and Duane Anderson had just ridden their bikes down from Champaign, Illinois. My business partner, Jim Miller, had driven down in his 1966 Chevy van, full of our new product to sell: Daytona would be the public debut of Vetter fairings.

I had just ridden in from L.A. on my brand-new 1967 Yamaha 350—the first YR1 in the United States!

What an adventure. Three weeks earlier, I had flown from Illinois to Los Angeles to pick up my new bike.

There it was waiting for me at Yamaha's Buena Park parking lot—a new YR1 in a crate. And fish oil. Japanese motorcycles in those days came with a peculiar odor that I assumed was some kind of fish-based preservative oil. I can still smell it.

The folks at Yamaha were kind enough to loan me a crowbar to get the crate open and I finished the job with the bike's tools. The anticipation was thrilling. By afternoon, I had my new Yamaha assembled, gassed up and ready to go. This was the biggest two-stroke made, and that meant that it was probably the fastest motorcycle you could buy.

I was moving up from my hot-rodded 305 YM1 Yamaha. Even with my home "five ported cylinders," sometimes I could not beat a good Suzuki X-6. It was well known that a good, lightweight rider on an X-6 would beat anything up to, say, 100mph. Thereafter, a good-running Triumph Bonneville would catch up and pass an X-6 as the Suzuki ran out of speed. Of course, a real TT Special was the ultimate, but you did not race TT Specials.

For comparison, here were some magazine quarter-mile published times of the era:

Triumph Bonneville: 14.2 seconds @ 88 mph (*Cycle World* January 1966)

Yamaha 350: 14.6 seconds @ 83.03 mph (*Cycle Guide* July 1967)

BSA Lightning: 14.92 seconds @ 92 mph (*Cycle Guide* May 1967)

Suzuki X-6: 15.9 seconds @ 80 mph (*Cycle Guide* February 1968)

Harleys? Not a chance of losing against a Harley. There was always some reason they were never running right.

After my new YR1 was ready, I zipped over to Long Beach where I met Joe Parkhust of *Cycle World,* who had just completed the magazine evaluation on a Vetter fairing I had sent to him earlier. Now I put that fairing on my 350 and took a break-in trip up the California coast, through Big Sur to San Francisco. I stopped for coffee in Carmel, hoping to see Joan Baez and wondered, "Who gets to live here?" Then I headed east with my sights set on Daytona.

When I arrived five days and 3,000 miles later, my Yamaha was broken in and running really good. This bike was fast! A quick run against my brother's tricked-out Yamaha 305 proved that the 350 was formidable. It wouldn't be hard to show off at Daytona.

Bruce had spent all of our available cash on bottle rockets in Tennessee. Now we were broke, but so what? We figured we would sell twenty or thirty Vetter fairings and have plenty of money to get home on.

We parked at the track during the day, showing my new fairing to anyone and everyone. At night, we shot off bottle rockets.

It didn't take us long to concoct the rules for a Bottle Rocket Fight. Never had a Bottle Rocket Fight? It just takes bottle rockets, Swisher Sweet cigars for igniting

Harley-Davidson-mounted Shriners with the "right stuff," circa 1960s.

them, open motorcycle helmets with shields, leather gloves, jacket, and some launch tubes. Fairing bracket pipes—intended for the Honda 160—made great launch tubes. Bottle Rocket Fighting is just made for motorcyclists.

The idea was to shoot rockets at each other in the dark from across the runway. A bottle rocket scream-ing in your general direction was hypnotizing because it didn't go straight. You couldn't move. A scream in the dark meant that it reached its target. Great fun! Fifty bucks worth of bottle rockets lasted most of the night and wore us out. We slept until we were awakened by the sound of thunder.

But it wasn't thunder. It was Harleys. Somewhere on those runways, Harleys were racing. We had to go check it out.

Following the sound to the southeast, we found a crowd of about a million black guys dressed in their finest Sunday church clothes. They were surrounded by their families and flashy Harleys. What a sight! They had marked off a quarter-mile section of the runway and were running them off, two at a time, with a real flagman and a checkered flag.

After a while, one of them asked me if I wanted to run. Silly question. Of course I wanted to run! Didn't I have the only broken-in Yamaha 350 in Florida? Maybe in all of America? Maybe the fastest motorcycle you could buy!

Besides, I had never seen a Harley I couldn't beat.

Run after run, I took them on, dusting off each challenger. Now I had the crowd's attention. These guys just didn't know about Japanese two-strokes. Money was changing hands. Yep, I was fast.

Then somebody asked if I would run Bad News.

"Of course. Why not? Bring him on . . ."

All engines stopped and the crowd got real quiet. After a bit, I heard the staccato of a Panhead fire up. Out from the mass of people came a junky black Harley ridden by a totally shaved, shiny brown guy in bib overalls, one shoulder strap hanging loose. He had no shirt underneath. As he approached, he bounced up and down on his seat, as if to warm it up. His eyes bulged. He looked like some kind of madman. He didn't say a word. He just bounced.

Now, great handfuls of money were held high as wagers were placed. The race was delayed by even more betting.

Finally, we staged, Bad News on my left.

The flagman gave us a little nod that he was about to drop the flag and I took no chances. When the flagman moved, I shot out of there, slipping my clutch exactly right. I was tucked down on the tank and shifting with my left hand, giving it my best. Perfect.

But it wasn't enough. I never had a chance. Bad News was ahead of me from the beginning and opening the gap! Nobody had ever beaten me with a Harley! But it was happening . . .

As he passed the quarter-mile marker ahead of me, Bad News stood up on his running boards and turned around to look back at me. I was in shock. I had never seen anything like this.

I just kept right on going. I knew it would not be a good idea to go back and face those who had lost money on me.

My brother tells the rest of the story: "Bad News returned to the crowd standing on his extended pipes. It was pure hysteria!"

Later, back at our camp, I could not understand how this could have happened. Weren't we at the forefront of a technological revolution of exotic, multi-cylinder, lightweight, high-rpm motorcycles? Weren't we the New Generation?

The fact is, there was a lot of life in that old Harley design, and guys like Bad News knew how to bring it out.

Today, almost forty years later, nothing has changed. It's still true: You can't beat the inches. Harleys always had inches.

We sold only two Vetter fairings that Speed Week—not the twenty or thirty we expected. But it was enough for us have a farewell grease-out at The House of Pancakes and make it back to Illinois.

Recently, I asked my friends who were there what they most remembered about Daytona in 1967. It wasn't the winner of the AMA race. It was the Bottle Rocket Fights and yes, Bad News.

Thirty-eight years later, I was finally able to track down Bad News once again. I had been asking around after him, even running an ad in a Florida newspaper. Someone finally pointed me in the right direction.

"Bad News" was actually "Pee Wee," who's real name in turn is Jewell Whigham. In my first and only conversation with him during a phone interview, Bad News told me he had been a mechanic at Palm Beach Harley working for Bruce Packard. "They called me 'Pee Wee' because I was so small on my first motorcycle," he said. "I ran with the 'colored guys' and drag raced."

One day, after he got beat, he went to his boss and said, "I can't get my ass beat working in a Harley shop. I gotta make this thing faster."

The owner agreed and told Pee Wee that he needed stroker wheels.

"What's 'stroker wheels'?" Pee Wee asked.

"Stroker wheels are the flywheels from an 80-cubic-inch Harley," he said.

Pee Wee soon found out that there were one or two Harley 80s around, and soon he had stroker wheels in his old Panhead, along with a cam and some trick push rods. In those days, there wasn't much else available to guys like Pee Wee.

Pee Wee was always fast, and soon he became known as the baddest MF on the east coast of Florida—thus, he says, the origin of the name, Bad News. He painted "Bad News" on his front fender and said that it would stay there until somebody beat him.

The sign stayed.

Along the way, Pee Wee learned to do tricks, like standing on the seat or on the pipes while the bike was moving. He could ride backwards. He could make it do figure-eights around him. He even learned how to get off, drag himself behind his bike, and get back on. Pee Wee became famous at the Palm Beach International Raceway. He made the 11 o'clock news one night, dragging himself

Pee Wee shows his stuff with his Harley-Davidson Big Twin trick-riding machine, circa 1970s. *Courtesy Craig Vetter*

behind his Harley. "If I hadn't seen it, I would never have believed it," said John Logsdon, one of Pee Wee's long-time friends.

One day, Pee Wee drove up to Byron, Georgia, to visit his girlfriend and ran out of money. Asking around, he discovered that there was a stock car track down the road. Pee Wee thought he would go over and offer to do some stunt riding after the races. His colored friends wouldn't go with him: they were worried about the white guys.

Pee Wee found the promoter and offered to do some stunt riding after the stock car race and he would do it for nothing if he could just pass his hat around afterwards.

"The last nigger we let fool around here got himself hurt," the promoter told him, but Pee Wee talked him into it. When the race was over the promoter announced over the loud speaker that if they just waited, "Some crazy nigger here from Florida is probably going to kill himself."

At that, Pee Wee roared out on his trumpet-piped Harley and proceeded to put on a show never imagined possible: He stood on the seat and went around the track. He stood on those extended exhaust pipes and did it again. He stood on the ground and held the bike in one hand and made it do figure-eights around him. And then he got on his knees and did it some more.

The crowd went wild. When Pee Wee was done, the promoter announced that he would be the first to put money in Mister Pee Wee's hat—a one hundred dollar bill—and told the crowd, "Nobody had ought to put in anything less than greenbacks." By the time Pee Wee left, he had $700! Best of all, he says, "I went from being a 'nigger' to 'Mister Pee Wee'."

Today, Bad News is still very much loved in his motorcycle community. Mr. Pee Wee is now seventy-one years old and has a little motorcycle shop in West Palm Beach, Florida. He no longer makes hot-rod Harleys, being content with washing and servicing. "Nobody pays me to make them go fast anymore. Harley will make you a 120-inch engine with a factory guarantee, and they are way too fast," he laments.

Today, that abandoned World War II airstrip has been redeveloped like much of Florida. It's now a fly-in community called Spruce Creek. Only one runway is left and it is surrounded by fine homes. I am told that actor John Travolta flies in and out in his private 727.

And today, the Harley Big Twin still rules.

My drag race with Bad News so many years ago taught me respect for Harleys. Until that day in 1967, I had never come across a fast one. I have seen the marvelous Japanese multi-everythinged engines come and go. I have watched Honda—followed by everyone else from Japan—up the ante with screaming, intricate, transverse fours. Somehow, they all have been exercises in futility.

Who could have imagined that Harley's Big Twin formula would outlive them all?

214

1924

1933

1933

Harley-Davidson
riders scrapbook,
circa 1920s–1930s.

Chapter 7

Kids,

Don't Try This at Home!

Color me lucky.

Of Mice and Motorcycle Stuntmen

By "Lucky" Lee Lott

"Lucky" Lee Lott began crashing motorcycles and automobiles at state and county fairs around the United States in 1935. In those days, the motorcycle was a relatively new kid on the block, and people thronged to Lee's shows to be wowed by his derring-do. By the 1950s, his Hell Drivers spectacle was famous in all corners of the continent.

Lee recounted his achievements in his rollicking 1994 memoir *The Legend of the Lucky Lee Lott Hell Drivers*, telling the two-fisted tales of his most famous stunts: The time he jumped a car into a lake, only to have it sink to the bottom and settle in three feet of muddy silt with him inside. The time he crashed a Ford Tri-Motor airplane into a house, only to have the plane keep flying out of control through the countryside and into a barn. The time he lost his hearing during a dynamite-fueled stunt. And the time in 1942 he set a world record by jumping 169 feet in an old Ford and permanently rearranged his back.

Before he died, Lee retired in Tampa, Florida, where he had a personal museum of old stunt cars and a scrapbook filled with memorabilia of the good old days crashing cycles and cars.

"The best laid schemes o' mice and men . . . ," the immortal words of poet Robert Burns were running through my head the time in 1942 when we were booked at the annual St. Louis Firemen's Benefit Show.

The committee hired the Lucky Lee Lott Hell Drivers to produce the thrill show division of the combined rodeo–circus–thrill show attraction. But all was not well. A booking agent had slipped a fly into the ointment by selling the same committee an English conception of a stunt show, billed as The Greatest Attraction of the British Empire. The St. Louis newspaper reported that the English motorcycle star was the highest paid stuntman in the realm.

The Greatest Attraction could do all sorts of tricks. He rode a motorcycle while standing on the seat, while seated backwards, while standing on one shoulder, and as the finale, he was to leap over ten men and crash through a flaming board wall at the same time.

The entourage arrived the day before the opening date and included The Greatest Attraction, three roustabouts, two wives (?), and six Norton motorcycles. My crew could see that there was no way that this conglomerate of nobodies was capable of fitting into the Firemen's quality of presentation. For the Greatest Attraction's leap over ten men, he wanted my crew to lay their bodies down; his few people couldn't be put in this hazard, they said, because they were British subjects.

Over ten of my men? No way.

The coup de grâce came when The Greatest Attraction wanted half-inch lumber for his flaming wall crash—and then wanted it planed down to a quarter-inch thick in the center. We always used one-inch lumber in our motorcycle walls. Quarter-inch lumber would burn through before the rider got to it.

Now, I've been around the block a couple times in the daredevil business and seen shows come and go, many making their exit stage left with a bruise on their noggin. In stunt driving, there are more Greatest Attractions than there are fleas on a dog, and the metaphor can be of a dual nature. I have met some of the dogs and shrugged off their parasites.

Well, the promoter of the show wasn't blind either. He paid off The Greatest Attraction and kicked him out of the arena.

The problem now facing us was that the program had already been printed extolling the deeds that the Britisher was to do. I knew one man who had worked for me on several occasions who could cut all the stuff on the printed program. We had the motorcycles with us already and materials for walls, so I got on the phone and called my old motorcycle stuntman Ron Childers to hustle on down for the opening the next night.

Ron was related to a couple of other performers who were with my show. He had shown up one day when I needed a truck driver to pull a Dodge tractor with a four-car auto transporter for one of my touring units. On the first or second day of the job, I discovered that he could ride a motorcycle like nobody's business.

I had been getting our show organized at a county fair racetrack and here comes this motorcycle with a guy standing on the seat with his arms stretched out like bird wings heading down the track at a good 40 mph. I saw it was Ron and in my mind wished him well because he was moving too fast for a tight turn that was coming up.

No problem. He made the turn alright with a little body English. So I watched him take another lap, this time riding on the crash bars. He was touring the track higher up on where there were deep ruts. Being in a bad position behind the handlebars and clasping the tank with his shins, he lost it. The ditch pitched him over the handlebars and smack dab into the outside hub rail, which he proceeded to take down with his shoulder.

I moved a little faster than usual and someone else called for the meat wagon. You see, there was no show going on, it was an open afternoon; we were to play that night.

The guys had a bucket of water handy that helped Ron come to. When he woke up, he didn't like the angle of his shoulder. I felt it. A slight case of dislocation, just like I had had a couple years earlier. In my case, I grabbed a post, jerked, and reset it. In Ron's case, I gave him a healthy handshake and he performed that night like a veteran. Oh, it was sore, but by this time Ron Childers was a showman.

He always itched for the chance to do a distance leap with a motorcycle. He was earning his money but wanted to do more. And the only reason he didn't get to do the distance leap—and I'm sure he could have—was that we didn't have an Indian Scout motorcycle, the only machine I ever used in leaping. The cantilever front spring is the saving grace on a leaping machine.

I digress once again. Back to St. Louis.

Ron Childers duly arrived, picked up where he would usually take over, and got the ball rolling. But the best laid plans . . .

On opening night, treachery was afoot. Ron was running through The Greatest Attraction's stunts with his usual class and it looked for all the world to see as if Ron was truly a great attraction. He did the numbers in the program that were worth doing or he did variations to fit his quality of stunt work.

Then came The Flaming Wall Crash.

The wall was set up and made of real one-inch lumber. It was packed with excelsior wood shavings to help the wall burn and then saturated with gasoline—or whatever else had been added to the jerry cans of gasoline! We never did find what had been added to the fuel! It burst into flames like a bomb! And we never did find out who did it—but we all could guess. . . .

Ron performed in his usual cool way. He came roaring down the track and made the jump without hesitation, but his motorcycle couldn't stand the heat and he rode the rest of the way across the arena on a fireball. He laid down the burning machine and dove for cover.

We let the firemen take over from there.

Evel Knievel X-2 electric toothbrush advertisement, 1975.

Bobby Becomes Evel

By Ace Collins

Robert Craig "Evel" Knievel is an all-American hero like no other. In the 1960s and 1970s, when the United States was dealing with Vietnam, the hippie movement, drugs, Watergate, and the sexual revolution, Evel Knievel was pursuing his own outrageous version of the American dream: Living dangerously by his wits, challenging the authority of gravity, and crafting P. T. Barnum–style spectacles. He was John Wayne on wheels, a daredevil Elvis, Bogart with a helmet, JFK with pointed sideburns—a true original.

Evel Knievel earned his sobriquet while stealing hubcaps in his hometown of Butte, Montana, when a victim hollered after him, "You're a little evil, Knievel." The moniker stuck and became a household name around the world.

This excerpt from Ace Collins' 1999 biography *Evel Knievel: An American Hero* tells the tale of how Bobby became Evel.

For all practical purposes the Knievel Honda dealership [in Moses Lake, Washington] had died. He just couldn't sell enough bikes to make ends meet. Bobby felt at least a part of the problem was the image of bikers. Most people thought of them as hoods. A part of the reason for this perception went back to Hollywood and the Marlon Brando movie *The Wild One*. Brando and his biker buddies had raped, pillaged, and terrorized a fictional California town. Even if it was just a movie, watching men on cycles become violent animals frightened many people. A large number assumed this behavior was typical of men who bought motorcycles. It was almost as if the motorcycle carried the disease that infected boys and made them terrors. Yet even though *The Wild One* seemed to embrace this concept, in truth Hollywood didn't create this image, it only built on it. Bobby was not only aware of this, he knew exactly where the bike had gotten its bad name.

It was the Hell's Angels, and other motorcycle gangs like them, who had blackened the reputations of almost all bikers. These men were so despised that most parents would have rather had their sons hang out with the Mafia than the Hell's Angels. In truth, for a period of time, organized crime and the biker gangs often worked together, so the mob and the Angels were on the very same road.

In the 1950s and 1960s, the Angels were a group of riders who represented blatant lawlessness. They were not unlike the guerrilla groups that terrorized many of the midwestern border states just after the Civil War. They were out of control and considered themselves not only above the law, but representing the final judgment on

everything. They did whatever they could get away with, they constantly pushed the limits, they dressed in black, and they always rode bikes.

Bobby could understand why the public image of these biker groups had led to his having to close his business. Certainly he wouldn't want his sons to have anything to do with gangs like the Angels. Even when he was all but starving to death, he wouldn't even deal with anyone from a gang at his dealership. He wouldn't sell them a bike or fix one for them. In most cases he wouldn't even speak to them. Now that he blamed groups like the Hell's Angels for not being able to feed his family, Knievel's bitterness toward the group grew even stronger. Some years later this hostility would spill over into violence.

As he closed his shop for the final time, Bobby was being driven by two things, the need for cash and the need to launch an honest career that would continue to provide for his family for years to come. He could no longer afford to get into a business only to have to move on to something else a few months later. With a daughter, Tracey, now joining his two sons, there were four mouths to feed at home. He had to find something he could stick with, an occupation that would pay his bills and buy him a future.

To make a few quick dollars, Bobby opted to put on a motorcycle show for the people of Moses Lake. Promoting the event himself, Knievel rented the venue, wrote the press releases for the local paper, went bar to bar trumpeting what he was going to do, set up the show, sold tickets, and served as his own master of ceremonies the day of the event. Even with all his work, and even though he was by now well known in the area and his motorcycle exploits were the stuff of local legends, he could only interest a few hundred people in watching him risk his life. Still, those few hundred did offer him a chance at the best paycheck he had seen in some time.

To more than a few who showed up to watch Bobby Knievel's first professional stunt show, the brash young biker reminded them of legendary St. Louis Cardinals' pitcher Dizzy Dean. Like the Hall of Famer baseball player, Knievel was loud and funny. He could charm the ladies and still speak man-to-man to the men. And like Old Diz, he was everywhere at once. Before he ever mounted his bike that day in Moses Lake, it seemed that he had personally visited with every man, woman, and child who had bought a ticket. In the process he had also convinced them that they were going to see one of the most spectacular stunts in the history of show business. People who had come out of curiosity, were genuinely excited by the time Knievel finished talking to them.

When showtime arrived, Bobby warmed the crowd up by doing a few wheelies, limited to only a few hundred feet due to the small size of the arena. He then turned off his motorcycle and spoke to the crowd. He asked each member of the audience to look behind him. There, in the middle of the arena, were two ramps placed more than twenty feet apart. In between the ramps was a very large box. After they had studied the box for a few moment, Knievel informed them that inside the box were more than 100 rattlesnakes. To assure the audience that he was not lying, he had several volunteers from the crowd come out of the stands and walk over to the box and look in. As the lid was opened, the witnesses were greeted by hissing and rattles. As they nervously peered into the crate they saw a mass of twisted, writhing, angry snakes, all looking for a way to escape through the one-inch boards that were between them and freedom. It was enough to give a grown man nightmares.

As the now pale and shaken witnesses climbed back to their seats, the audience began to whisper. What would happen if he missed? they wondered. If he landed short and hit the box, he would toss snakes in every direction. The crazy rider would probably be bitten a hundred times before he could get off the ground and run away. They just knew that he had to be insane to try this stunt. Yet none of them asked him to stop. None of them left to go home rather than watch this public suicide. They might have believed he was crazy and was going to kill himself, but they wanted to see it if he did.

After his audience had gotten used to the idea of Bobby jumping the box of poisonous vipers, he signaled for the final facet of his jump to be added to the mix. A man with two full-grown mountain lions appeared. As everyone watched, the man staked the two huge cats between the box and the take-off ramp.

Leaving the crowd to study the latest development, Bobby walked over to the animal trainer. He informed the man he wanted a lion on each side of the box. The man refused, explaining he believed Bobby would fall short of the landing ramp and kill himself. The trainer didn't want to have one of his cats killed when the biker crashed on top of it, so he was going to keep both of them at the front of the jump. He also wanted to be paid at that moment because he didn't think he could stomach asking a widow for the cash later.

After the debate between the jumper and the owner of the cats ended, Bobby strolled back to the crowd to tell them about the new setup.

"We were supposed to have one lion at each end of the ramp," witnesses remember the biker explaining the situation, "but the cats' owner doesn't think I can make a jump that long. He figures I will kill myself trying. That is fine with him, but he says he can't afford to lose one of the cats too. I understand that. I also understand why he wanted to be paid in advance. After all, what man in his right mind could expect to make a jump like this?"

As he would do so often over the next few years, Knievel had used a possible negative and tragic turn of events to his advantage. The lion owner balking at the original setup just made the jump seem much more dangerous. As he spoke to them, the rider could see the fear and nervousness written on everyone's face. A few minutes before, most in the crowd might have been thinking he would crash and kill himself, but after this turn of events, they now seemed sure that he would. It was exactly the reaction Bobby had wanted. They had to think he was going to die in order to really appreciate the performance.

After spending a few more minutes talking to the audience and building up the stunt to further heighten the audience's fear factor, a confident Knievel hopped back on his bike, kicked up a huge spray of dust and exited the arena. Outside the crowd's view, he racked off his cycle's engine several times, then gassing it to the max, raced back into the view, rushing just in front of the ramp at more than sixty miles an hour. Thinking that he was going to jump, the audience had risen as one and taken a huge collective breath. They had been unaware the rider would need a few practice runs to fully judge his speed and the condition of the loose dirt floor. They didn't know that he was going to make them wait for several moments before letting them watch his "leap to death."

After a couple more practice runs, Bobby decided it was finally showtime. As he left the arena for the final time, he must have felt the doubts crowd into his mind. He had never practiced this jump. He didn't know if his homemade ramps would hold. He didn't even know how much speed it would take to clear the open distance between the two ramps. He had no figures, no formulas, and no tests to prove that his guess at takeoff speed and angle of lift would be too much or not enough. He had built this stunt on gut-level instincts and guesswork. Now he had to wonder if this would be his first and last jump.

Twisting his handgrip throttle, Bobby closed his eyes and pictured himself flying from ramp to ramp. As he concentrated on a positive outcome, he considered every foot of the trip he was about to make. He made mental notes of when to shift and how much to accelerate. He also tried to imagine how his body would respond to coming down from the air and hitting the plywood landing ramp.

As he went over the jump step by step, it must have been hard to keep his own doubts and fears under control. He had already informed the crowd of all the things that could go wrong. He had told them that he would never make the distance if he missed a gear, had a valve stick or his carburetor hesitate, or a tire go flat. Even though he hadn't told them what would happen if he failed to hit the center of the takeoff ramp, he was aware of what would happen if he missed by as little as a few inches.

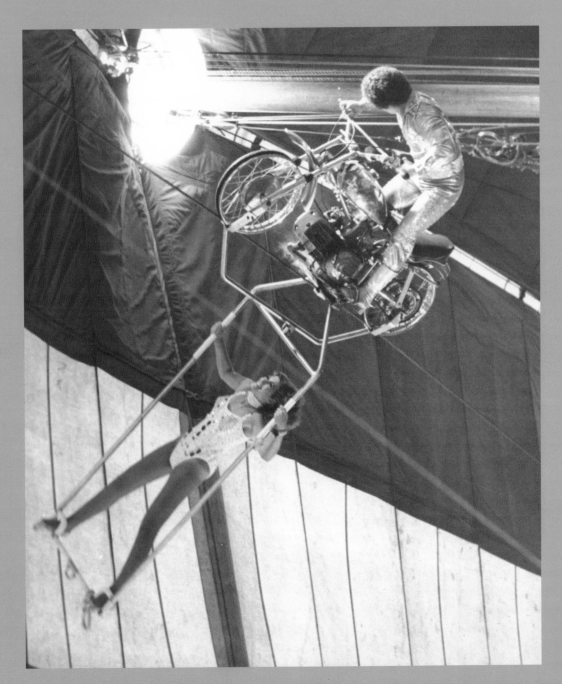

Circus high-wire acts starring Harley-Davidson Sprints, circa 1970s.

The takeoff angle would be totally wrong for landing. He would probably miss the landing ramp altogether. If he had waited any longer, he probably could have found a hundred more reasons why this was insane. However, he had promised he would make the jump, so there was no backing out or turning back.

Before doubts could wipe out his courage and any more fear could crowd his mind, Bobby gunned the engine and took off. This time his approach was smooth and flawless. There was no showboating, no spraying dirt or playing with the engine. As he approached the ramp he was dead serious and concentrating fully on what he knew he had to do.

The crowd was now as one. On their feet, many standing in the seats, they silently watched Bobby speed into the arena and head for his homemade takeoff ramp. He hit the board square and drove up the incline at almost a mile a minute, then, in an instant, he was airborne.

As he left the ramp, it seemed that time stopped for a moment. No one could hear the bike, the snarling cougars, the rattling snakes or the groaning of the old wooden grandstands. Everything was hushed, the wind seemed suddenly still, and Bobby and the bike were frozen in the air. Then, a millisecond later, the amazed patrons watched man and machine fly. He was over the lions and snakes and winging his way to the safety of the far ramp. The fans now thought the jump was a done deal. The rider knew better.

The instant he had taken off Bobby realized that he not had generated enough speed to make it as far as he needed to go. His back wheel was not going to hit the landing ramp. Still, in an attempt to lift the bike across the chasm with sheer willpower, the jumper pulled hard on the handlebars, trying to coax extra height from the bike. It was a futile effort. The back tire came down hard on the snake box at about the same moment the front tire hit the ramp.

Bobby should have been tossed like a rag doll over the motorcycle's handlebars. He should have flown from the bike and landed in the dirt arena surrounded by scores of angry snakes that his shortened landing had suddenly freed. Yet, rather than give up, Knievel hung on. Thanks to his tremendous upper body strength, he bounced the bike off the now shattering wooden crate and up onto the ramp. He then raced down the ramp, twisted to a spinning stop, placed his foot on the ground to hold the cycle upright, and lifted his arms triumphantly to the crowd.

At first too shocked to move, the audience finally realized that the stunt man had made it. Though there were scores of angry rattlesnakes slithering all over the arena, Knievel was safe. Cheering, screaming, and applauding, the fans raced to the edge of the fence to get near the crazy jumper. As he rode up to them, they reached out to Bobby like they would have a rock and roll singer or a movie star. At this moment in time, to almost all who had witnessed that first jump, this stunt man was the most important person in the world. After taking a victory lap, Knievel returned to his fans. Joining them in the grandstand, he signed autographs and told everyone how it felt to fly. Meanwhile, back in the arena, snake handlers tried to track down more than a hundred very hostile rattlers. Several of the snakes escaped; luckily, no one in the crowd was bitten.

Watching the adoration of those who caught his act in the small arena, Bobby felt he was on to something. He now fully believed he could make a motorcycle daredevil show into a big moneymaker. Yet he didn't want to do it alone. For starters there was simply too much risk in doing every stunt himself. Also, promoting, advertising, setting up and tearing down, servicing the bike, building the needed stunt equipment, and keeping it in good condition were simply too much work. He needed a hand-picked team with him, and he needed a sponsor to supply the bikes and advertising.

Trying to decide how to make his dream a reality was almost like determining which came first, the chicken or the egg. Without a sponsor and new bikes there could be no show. However, without riders who could do stunts, he probably couldn't interest a sponsor. Yet riders wouldn't quit their jobs and work for him without wanting to be paid, they couldn't be paid until they put on shows, and they couldn't put on shows without having the needed financing. Because he was broke, the situation seemed hopeless. Yet that didn't keep the ever-hopeful young man from making calls and visits trying to sell businesses on backing *Bobby Knievel and His Motorcycle Daredevils Thrill Show*.

In late 1965, Bob Blare, a distributor for Norton Motorcycles, stepped forward with an offer. He would give Knievel the needed bikes, but the deal came with a price. Blare wanted the daredevil to change the name of the show. He didn't want "Bobby Knievel and His Motorcycle Daredevils" on the marque, he wanted to resurrect Bobby's old Butte nickname, Evil.

Bobby had a problem with that. He didn't want to conjure up an image as a hood or as a Hell's Angels rider. He didn't want his own kids thinking of him as a bad guy either. Yet he understood why Blare thought the name made sense. By using Evil, the show had an aura that a name like Bobby simply couldn't provide. Besides, by tying Evil to Knievel, he would also have an easy name to remember. Bobby knew that name recognition and gimmicks were incredibly important in marketing and show business, yet even realizing this, he still felt uneasy about aligning himself with a name that conjured up images of black magic, history's demonic dictators, and the Devil himself.

As a beggar, Bobby didn't have a great deal of room to compromise. If this was what it took to put his show on the road, then he would have to do it. However, he did ask Blare to give him a little room to play. Knievel would drop Bobby and use the old nickname, but wanted to change the *i* to an *e*. By using Evel rather than Evil, he thought he could still represent himself as a potential good-guy hero. Norton and Blare agreed and ordered the bikes "Evel" needed.

If he was going to make a living with his thrill show, then Bobby would be forced to emulate the airplane barnstormers of the twenties. He was going to have to become a modern-day gypsy. He and his band of men were going to have to roam from town to town, live as cheaply as they could, put on performance after performance, then move on to the next town. They would have to drive at night, sleep in their trucks and cars, and work like field hands. If they stuck it out, they might be rewarded with better-paying bookings in larger venues. They also might die before they could save a dollar or perform a single show in an arena that seated more than a few hundred people. He had to have team members willing to accept this lifestyle and the risks that went with it.

With the sponsorship in place, Bobby turned to finding the members of his troop. He began and ended his search with riders he had known during his days of racing. Uncovering a few men who were hungry enough to give up the circuit for show business, he began 1966 by organizing a performance routine.

When he wasn't designing and working out his show routines, Bobby was on the phone and writing letters. Every spare moment he searched for bookings. He didn't have a track record or a well-known name, so in an effort to sell his unproven act, he resorted to trying to sound big-time. Acting like a modern day P. T. Barnum, he tailored his spiel to whatever it was each venue needed. Finally, as weeks went by with little interest being generated and no up front money being offered, Bobby agreed to perform for no guarantee and a percentage of the gate.

This deal should have been seen by some bookers as a promotional opportunity too good to be true. After all, Evel Knievel was giving them an opportunity to book a show where men might kill themselves doing really stupid things. This surely beat concerts, beauty pageants, and clown shows. However, few could understand the real potential they were being offered. Most still passed.

The California Date Festival in Indio was the first date Knievel signed. In February, the exposition offered Bobby something Evel Knievel's Motorcycle Daredevils dearly needed: exposure.

Bobby pulled out all the stops for the event. In comparison to his first professional outing in Moses Lake, Indio represented a major leap forward. The show had to make the most of it. Emulating many of the routines Knievel had once seen Joie Chitwood's auto troop perform, the new show promised to be spectacular in both its variety and its thrill quotient.

Evel was clad in white leather with red and blue trim. The outfit made him look like the biker version of Uncle Sam, and that was the point he was trying to get across. His name might have sounded like a son of Satan, but the performer wanted the people to know that he was a flag-waving patriot who loved his country and all-American clean living. During the performance he would speak out for the United States and against such things as the Hell's Angels and drug abuse. This combination of politics, patriotism, and preaching would soon evolve into as much a facet of each of his shows as the motorcycle stunts. These qualities would also pave the way for Knievel becoming a hero to a generation of American youths. For now, they served to set him apart from biker gangs and deadbeats.

Once he finished talking, slapped on his helmet, and mounted his bike, Knievel and his Daredevils were nonstop action. There was no doubt that this debut performance was unlike anything the crowd had ever witnessed. Besides the normal Knievel stunt of popping long wheelie runs, the biker hitched a kite up to a car and lifted himself into the air like a bird. As he rose to more than two-hundred feet off the ground, hanging onto the tiny bit of material and frame, the crowd strained to see the fearless man fly. While he soared he had their full attention, and when he finally came back to earth, his display of courage won a huge round of applause. Yet this was just an opening act.

After stunts of precision driving by the team and a unique display where Evel lay on the ground, braced a board over his body with his arms, and had his riders race up the board and do jumps off his body, it was time for the really big events.

Knievel's team lined up a series of a dozen plywood panels. Each board had been soaked in gasoline for a hour before the show, then braced and erected where it sat almost four feet off the ground. The boards were placed in a long row, each almost twenty feet from the next. When Evel gave the signal, the boards were lit. After a roaring blaze was leaping from each board, Knievel took off on his bike, hitting each of the fiery pieces of solid lumber with his shoulders and helmet. As the crowded silently stared, the rider struck one after the other at more than thirty miles an hour. Boom! Boom! Boom! With flames seemingly jumping off his body, Evel continued until all the boards had been smashed into at least two pieces and he and his bike were all that were left standing.

Most of the crowd thought the drive through fire signaled the end of the performance, but in truth, all that had preceded this moment had just been a warm-up. In the middle of the arena the troop drove two full-sized pickup trucks and parked them tailgate to tailgate. Then two ramps were placed at the front of each of the vehicles. As the stunt was set up, Knievel visited with the audience. He explained that no one would attempt this jump because it was simply too dangerous. Much like Moses Lake, his speech put each member of the crowd on the edge of their seats. As would be the case for almost all the jumps that followed, a poll would have probably revealed that half of the Indio fans wanted to see him wipe out, the other half was praying for him to make it.

Jumping on his bike, Knievel made his practice runs not only to add excitement to the stunt, but to check out the bike's mechanics. After assuring himself the cycle had been properly set up, he began his approach. Unlike at Moses Lake, this time his speed and lift were perfect. When he went into the air from the takeoff ramp, everyone could see that he would clear the trucks, now the only thing he had to do was land the bike.

It would have taken a slow-motion view to fully appreciate the pounding Evel took when he hit the far ramp. As the back wheel came down, his lower back compressed from the shock. Every muscle in his arms and legs strained just to hold on to the heavy Norton cycle and keep it upright. As sweat drenched his face, he landed the front wheel and roared down the incline and out onto the field. The crowd went crazy!

If Bobby had brought any souvenir caps or T-shirts, he would have sold out in minutes. Everyone wanted something from the man who could jump trucks. The Indio crowd hung around for hours just to get a chance to meet him and get his autograph. The adulation didn't stop there either. Word quickly spread up and down the West Coast and suddenly Knievel's phone was ringing. For a few days it appeared like the daredevil show really was going to be a gold mine.

Hemet, California, was the sight of the next show, but rain beat the troop to town. When the storms continued, the

I don't know why
I did what I did.
I did what I did
because
I'm Evel
Knievel
and I don't question it.

—Evel Knievel

performance was canceled. With no guarantee or insurance, suddenly the bright times promised by the results of the Indio show now appeared bleak. Out of cash, Bobby bounced checks trying to pay for food and lodging. He prayed the businesses and authorities wouldn't find out until he had secured another date and made the money to cover the back checks.

The Daredevils' third and biggest booking yet was in Barstow, California. On the days before the performance, Knievel had polished the act. Dropping a few bits that hadn't worked, he added a new stunt he believed would wow the crowd even more than his jumping over the trucks.

The leg-split jump was as spectacular as it was dangerous. It was a timing stunt, and if the timing was off by even a split second, then death was a very real possibility. What made the stunt even more perilous was that there was no way to really practice it. As close as the troop could get to a simulation was for a rider to push a bike up to fifty miles per hour, then Bobby would jump and spread his legs as the cycle passed a few feet to his side. The other members of the team would try to find an angle and guess if their leader's leap was high enough and if he had been able to time his jump where he would be at the peak of his leap just as the bike passed under him. In practice it had looked great. Everyone knew it would work. Still, the closer it came to performing the stunt, the less confident each member of the troop grew.

There was a great deal of wind in Barstow, and it picked up as the show went on. The windy conditions made for a great parasail ride. Bobby managed to fly the kite to a height beyond three hundred feet. As always, the audience was fascinated with the man and his courage. The crowd's positive reaction echoed the response that followed for each new routine.

The rest of the early part of the show went just like it had at Indio. There wasn't even a minor hitch. The cycle team performed as if they had been programmed by NASA. Each move was precise, each new facet of the act was a thing of ballet-like grace and jet-engine power. Then, as the crowd listened intently, it was time for the big finale.

As before, the motorcycle jump over two pickups would end the show, but before that Evel was going to do the spread-eagle leap over a powerful Norton cycle.

As he got himself ready for the stunt, a dryness filled Bobby's mouth. Athletes call the sensation cotton mouth. It seems to plague people before any big event. Dry mouth now had the man the crowd knew as Evel. However, he didn't stop to get a drink. He knew the only thing that would give him relief was getting through the stunt.

As the rider began to rack off the bike's pipes, Knievel took his position, attempted to loosen the joints in his body, and prepared for the death-defying leap. For the man in the spotlight, this feeling of laying it all on the line was what had been missing from high school and army track competition. During those days in the spotlight there had been no real glory in winning. Here, there was. This was a test of courage, guts, timing, skill, and fortitude. Yet in those earlier athletic competitions, losing didn't matter as much either. Now there was a real chance at something worse than disappointment if Bobby failed to finish on top.

Giving a wave to the cycle rider, Knievel crouched his body and readied for the jump. As the bike got closer, as

KING OF THE STUNTMEN EVEL KNIEVEL™

STUNT GAME

★ 3 ★ RAMP JUMP

EVEL KNIEVEL RACES AROUND TH

Evel Knievel Stunt Game, circa 1970s.

the speed reached almost a mile a minute, Bobby focused on the Norton's front tire. As the bike picked up more speed and grew closer, the crowd rose to its feet as one. No one, including the man in the middle of the arena, dared to breathe. Pushing off the ground with the balls of his feet, employing every muscle in his body to gain lift and temporarily defeat the grip of gravity, Bobby reached for the sky and started to spread his legs. Even as he did, he knew he had waited too long. As the Norton flew toward him, he involuntarily stared death in the face. There was nowhere to run, no way to escape. It was too late for the rider to turn the bike and too late for Bobby to roll out of the way. He was going to be at least a foot from the top of his jump, a full foot short, when their paths met.

The speeding bike's handlebars hit Knievel in the groin. His body spun in the air like a dishrag, the momentum of the collision between man and machine tossed Bobby more than fifteen feet above the ground. After completing a sickening twisting spiral, he seemed to hang in the air for a moment, then, as if a lead weight had been tied to his limp body, he fell to the dirt.

When he hit the ground, every one of his team thought he was dead. As they rushed to him, he didn't move. So sure were they that Bobby had been killed, they called for a blanket to cover him up. Unable to respond to anyone's questions, Knievel thought he was either dying or paralyzed. Yet as the numbness began to wear off, replaced by excruciating pain, he not only knew he was alive, but that he was seriously injured. The shocked crowd said little as the medical personnel worked over the fallen biker. Most figured that if he was still alive, he would die on the way to the hospital.

The fall had pushed Bobby's ribs into his lungs. Breathing was difficult at best. His lower body had been severely bruised from his knees to his waist. He was lucky to still have a groin at all. He had never known such severe pain. Like the fans, he too thought he was close to dying.

A major facet of the Evel Knievel legend began that day with his incredible brush with death. As the doctors began working on his body, they initiated a routine that would become just another facet of the showman's performance in places like Las Vegas, Chicago, and London. Evel would tear himself apart, and the physicians would put him together so he could do it all over again.

Though he quickly vowed to toss the spread-eagle jump out of his show and concentrate on other stunts, the public's fascination with Knievel's act would be based on death as much as life from this moment on. After Barstow a large percentage of his crowds would buy tickets just to be there the time he didn't make it. He sold seats because of the desire to witness the final Evel stunt.

When he was released from the Barstow hospital, Bobby was so busted up he could barely move. He couldn't even walk without help. He should have rested for at least six months before attempting to ride a motorcycle, much less jump anything, but he didn't have that luxury. He owed the hospital for his care and owed scores of other businesses for everything from his leather suits to the trucks and cars that took him from one show to the next. With only two shows under his belt, he had to perform. Besides, if he waited he knew his mind would suffer. If he spent too much time away from the stunts, then he knew that he could develop a real paralysis, this one steeped in fear. He might never get back on a motorcycle without wondering if death was stalking him at every corner. If he allowed that to happen, he would probably never jump again.

Just days after leaving his hospital bed, Knievel returned to Barstow to finish the show he started a month before. This time there was an overflow crowd waiting. Most were probably there to watch him kill himself. A few were there to welcome back a hero.

Bobby was so weak and his body so fragile, he was unable to walk without aid. When it came time for him to perform, he had to be lifted onto his bike. His ribs pressing heavily into his chest, every word he spoke an effort, Knievel nevertheless promised to do what he had said he would do. With pain etched on his face, he popped a few wheelies and rode out of sight. When he roared back before the crowd, he raced toward a ramp and somehow jumped two pickup trucks.

His troop and friends watched in agony as the landing pushed his body down hard onto the bike. As his fragile ribs absorbed the pounding, the man the crowd only knew as Evel, managed to hold onto the handlebars. Sliding to a stop, he painfully lifted his hands above his head.

As the audience chanted his name, Evel Knievel knew he had not only won the respect of the crowd, but legitimized his name. He had also paid a price, came back to the scene of his defeat, and won. Even in the midst of incredible pain, he had never felt so much exhilaration. Maybe a man had to get this close to death to fully appreciate the joy of living!

I could perform a wheelie until the oil ran out of the pan and the engine seized up.

—Evel Knievel

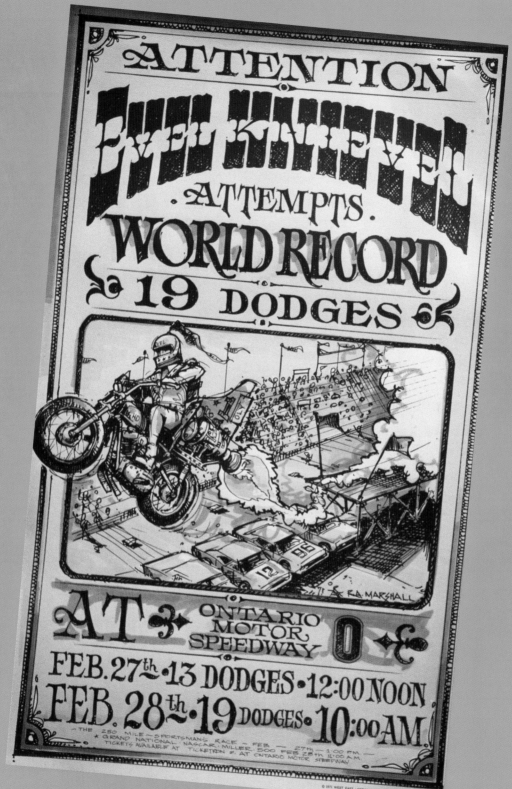

Evel Knievel
jump poster,
circa 1970s.

Evel Knievel Snake River lunchbox, circa 1970s.

Evel Ways

By Evel Knievel

It should come as no surprise that Evel Knievel went through many motorcycles in his long career. After all, the wheelies and jumps and, yes, crashes were almost as hard on the bikes as they were on the man.

These remembrances of motorcycles past come from the closest thing Knievel has done in terms of writing an autobiography. *Evel Ways: The Attitude of Evel Knievel* was published in 1999, and is filled with stories, quotes, photographs, and memorabilia.

When I was a kid, I had an old BSA Bantam 125 my dad bought for me. I was doing wheelies and other stunts at an early age, and also rode a Honda.

I rode a Norton 750 Commando when I started jumping, sponsored by Mike Berliner and his brother, Joe. Then I rode a Triumph but I couldn't get along with the distributor. It was a beautiful 650-cc bike, a T120 Bonneville.

Just before the Caesars Palace jump, I decided to cash in on some favors. I had loads of trouble with Johnson Motors out of California. They provided the Triumph motorcycle for me—one of the best motorcycles built—but did nothing in return for all the promoting I did for them. I threatened Pete Coleman, who was the president, that if he didn't put an attorney on the next plane to Las Vegas with a $20,000 check, the Triumph would miss so badly that it would make it the laughing stock of the motorcycle world. I told him I'd burn his cycle in front of Caesars Palace. Can you believe he accused me of blackmail?

But you better believe they sent that attorney and he had that check. I still have the motorcycle from that jump.

Then I rode the American Eagle. The American Eagle was imported from [Laverda of] Italy and introduced to me by Jack McCormack and Walt Fulton. When Jack was [part] of American Honda Motor Company, he coined the phrase, 'You meet the nicest people on a Honda.' He is solely responsible for the success of Honda in America.

Harley-Davidson sponsored me and paid me the money I needed to continue jumping. The Harley-Davidson XR-750 had so much torque that when I took off at 70 to 85 miles per hour the bike would twist in the air.

The people at Harley-Davidson were one of the finest families I ever did business with. They kept their word and stood by my side the eight years I worked with them. I was proud to be a part of the Harley-Davidson team.

Now I ride a custom bike built for me by California Motorcycle Company, a division of Indian Motorcycle Company of Gilroy, California. It's a limited-edition Evel Knievel Signature series with painted graphics and gold-plated accents that depict my famous jumps and crashes.

Chapter 8

Walls of
Death

Ladies and gentlemen, I am sure you can see by now watching the first three acts of the show that it would be next to

impossible

for any of our riders to obtain any kind of accident insurance. No insurance company will insure us because of the danger of the wall. So, we in turn have developed an insurance fund made up of two parts. One part: the rides contribute to the fund themselves. And the other part is you, the show-going public. If you have enjoyed the show, if you would like to help and contribute to the riders' fund, simply take a donation out of your pocket; we don't care how small or how large. It can be from a penny to a $10 bill. Take it out now and drop it over the side of the wall and onto the floor. The riders will pick it up. Remember, the money is put in a fund, and all summer long the fund builds. It is there when a rider goes down to pay his hospital bills and fix his machine. Let's hear some coins jingling and let's see some paper floating. The riders thank you for your generosity.

—Wall-of-Death rider Bill Cadieux's bally, from A. W. Stencell's
Seeing Is Believing: America's Sideshows, 2002

The Wall-of-Death

By David Gaylin

David Gaylin was first exposed to motorcycles while growing up on carnival midways that had been owned and operated by his family since the Depression. Art Spencer's Fighting Lions and Doug Hopkins were two of the Wall-of-Death operators that had once been part of their traveling show.

Yet David's parents did not approve of motorcycles, and upon reaching his eighteenth birthday, David moved out of his parent's house and bought his first motorcycle, a 1970 Triumph Bonneville. A motorcycle driver's license would come later.

After the Eastern U.S. Triumph distributor, the Triumph Corporation, closed in Baltimore, David acquired much of their internal documents and memos along with truckloads of brochures, manuals, and service bulletins, all of which would become the foundation for the book *Triumph Motorcycles in America*, coauthored with Lindsay Brooke. The archives also spawned a second book, *Triumph Motorcycle Restoration Guide* in 1997.

David plans further perpetrations, including an in-depth history of the Wall-of-Death.

The motorcycle thrill show known as the Wall-of-Death is a relic from another time. At the turn of the last century, water was not piped into most homes, let alone organized entertainment; there were no televisions, no videos, no computers, and no X-Boxes. Amusements, what little there were, required attendance in person. It was another universe.

This was the era of Vaudeville, theater houses, baseball, and bicycling. Bicycles were the rage on both sides of the Atlantic but bike racing fever really exploded in Europe first. Special tracks or velodromes were constructed, oval in shape, with steep banking at the ends to facilitate speed. The first motorcycles were created as one-off pacing machines or windbreaks for bicycle speed-record attempts in these velodromes.

It was quickly seen that at speed, inertia permitted bicycle riders to bank at fearful lean angles, and it wasn't long before trick-riders were performing before crowds in miniature versions of the velodromes. Called "Cycle-Whirls" or "Whirls-of-Death," these were basically baskets composed of vertical wooden slats spaced apart to permit viewing by the audience. The sides or walls were inclined at around 70 degrees and measured from fifteen to twenty-five feet in diameter. With the track sitting on the ground and minimally braced, the riders would build as much speed as possible before climbing onto the latticework, riding almost always in a counterclockwise direction. The inertia they generated allowed them to climb to the rim of the track, orbit with hands off the bars, and perform other stunts while coasting. Two, three, or more riders on the track racing simultaneously and diving beneath and above the other rider was actually as dangerous as it looked but a real crowd pleaser at Coney Island and traveling carnivals, the latter just beginning to make their appearance in the United States.

The next step was a Cycle-Whirl that was raised into the air after the bicyclists had begun making their circuits. Looking up 10 to 15 feet through the bottomless basket as the riders performed their stunts and risked injury or worse, crowds eagerly bought tickets. These aerial velodrome acts were very popular at the Theatre du Moulin Rouge and Folles Bergère in Paris. But at New York's Madison Square Garden, a performer by the name of Dan Canary actually rode up a long helical track to a bottomless basket suspended 60 feet off the ground. With any loss of pedal-power, inertia, or traction while trick-riding, Mr. Canary's "Circle-of-Death," as it was known, would have certainly fulfilled the promise of its name!

The most thrilling stunts were performed on tracks that had a narrow extension around the top that was perfectly vertical and allowed riders seemingly to defy gravity by circling completely perpendicular to the ground. By extending this vertical section upward, riders could now circle and perform their tricks in full view of everyone on the ground, accommodating larger audiences without a need to suspend the track. In 1903, after a five-year tour of Europe, Barnum & Bailey presented just such an act that they had discovered while there: Cyclo, The Kinetic Demon would race around the very top of the cylinder while others pedaled below!

Rise of the Motordrome

As motorcycles eclipsed the pedal cycle in popularity, it was only natural that they began to appear in carnival and circus acts. In England around 1910, the Tom Davis Trio were using Levis single-cylinder motorcycles in an elevated Cycle-Whirl track that was reinforced to withstand the extra weight and G-forces of motorized bikes. By that time, the motorcycle pandemic was sweeping the industrialized world. In the United States, motorcycle racing took many forms including hill climbs, horse or dirt track races, and match racing on bicycle velodromes. The cycle tracks quickly proved too small and narrow for motorcycle speeds and special wooden board tracks were designed that shared the same characteristics of steeply banked turns at each end and low, almost flat straightaways in between. But these motordromes, as they were called, were of heavier construction and larger in size, being four, three, and two laps to the mile (not to be confused with the larger, automobile board tracks that were built after World War I on which Harley-Davidson competed). Machines were specially designed for this type of racing, pared of all unnecessary weight, fitted with drop handlebars and lowered seats. Although other brands were competitive in this type of racing—such as Excelsior, NSU, Merkel and Thor—Indian motorcycles devoted the most resources to it and were the clear leaders.

Motorcycle board track racing was growing into a national passion and motordromes sprang up in many cities in the United States. A feature in *Billboard* magazine at the time, then an outdoor amusement trade publication, paints a vivid portrait: "Three years ago the Chicago amusement-loving public welcomed the first saucer track which was erected at Riverview Park, the largest of Chicago's amusement resorts. Then in a very short space of time, the news reacht [sic] the suburbs of the city and even to the small towns located probably twenty-five miles from the city. In every instance the 'bug' took firm hold of his victim. The motordrome bug makes the baseball fan a very mild variety of lunatic and his lungs are stronger than our most prominent alley-merchant." As indicated in the article, some of these race tracks were located on or near amusement park property.

In 1911, the popularity of the motorcycle board tracks inspired the creation of a smaller, circular drome 85 feet in diameter at Luna Park, an amusement area of Coney Island in Brooklyn, New York. For a fee, patrons would stand around the perimeter of the wooden saucer while riders made counterclockwise orbits with hands off the control bars, sitting side-saddle, standing on footboards, or draping their legs over the handlebars, all at what seemed to be breakneck speeds and frightful lean-angles. The attraction was the hit of the amusement park during its initial run. When the act became familiar and attendance fell, it was decided to take the miniature motordrome on tour, following the old Vaudevillian creed that you didn't need to find new tricks if you could find new audiences. However, the structure proved too difficult to move, and it is not known how many dates were actually played.

The following year at least three traveling carnivals were expressing the sincerest form of flattery with more portable versions of the Coney Island motordrome. *Billboard*

Corbeille de la Mort, the Basket of Death: Early French daredevil souvenir card, circa 1910s.

magazine reported, "many portable motordromes are being carried by some of the largest carnival companies, such as that of David Whittaker with Wortham & Allen, as well as that of Herbert A. Kline Shows and the Ferari-Patrick Carnival Company." But although the miniature board tracks could be dismantled and reassembled, "those lumberyards," as one referred to them, were still monsters to move from one location to another and required a large crew. Many Monday night openings were missed.

By 1913, there were as many as five manufacturers of portable motordromes in the United States including famous carousel maker C. W. Parker and J. Frank Hatch, a carnival owner who sold off his traveling show to concentrate on drome manufacture. Hatch also promoted his auto and motorcycle dromes complete with performing riders, and had as many as eight units booked simultaneously with various traveling carnivals. He was the biggest name in this form of entertainment at the time.

Makers' ads in *Billboard* magazine stressed portability and the certainty of making Monday night openings. While the portable autodromes measured up to 120 feet across, the motorcycle versions were 50 feet in diameter or less, and were becoming a better proposition than car tracks due to the smaller number of workers needed to move them. The smaller dimensions also permitted a canvas top, which meant performances in wet weather. Still, moisture on the track's surface—whether from humidity, a leaking engine, or a spilt beverage—would forever be a concern.

The Wall-of-Death

Although these motordrome structures had slanted walls like the earlier Cycle-Whirls, most had a narrow extension at the very top that was perfectly vertical and allowed riders to thunder around literally on the chests of the audience. The most crowd-thrilling and subsequently successful shows were those with performers who circled completely perpendicular to the ground while sitting side-saddle or with their hands off. With each drome operator trying to outdo the other, the appearance of an entire motordrome with perfectly vertical walls was a logical progression, and while J. Frank Hatch was busy arranging patents for his already obsolete slant-walled designs, several daring entrepreneurs were thrilling crowds with their vertical "silo-dromes."

It is unclear who was the first to create a vertical-walled drome. Carnival historian Joe McKennon recorded that in 1915, "a man named [Birdson] Greene had set up a structure resembling a large farm silo on a vacant lot in Buffalo, New York. In this structure men were supposed to ride motorcycles around on its straight up-and-down walls. Greene had already started selling tickets there in Buffalo for spectators to watch the practice rides and they booked this new silodrome with the Joseph T. Ferari Shows that season."

About the same time a man known as the "Human Silo" was performing in what appeared to be a rooftop water tank modified for portability. His promotional ads declared, "Riding a high-powered motorcycle at the rate of sixty miles an hour on a wall straight up and down, 16-feet high and 30-feet in diameter, performing a feat never before accomplished by a human being." Some evidence suggests that the Human Silo was Walter Kemp.

Yet another straight-wall motordrome was seen with the W. G. Wade Shows around the same time. This one differed in that it used a Harley-Davidson motorcycle and at least one female performer.

Regardless of who was first, the straight-wall motordrome would soon displace the earlier versions. The new silo-dromes were also smaller in diameter with even the largest combination dromes that could accommodate both motorcycle and car acts, being no wider than 40 feet across. The tighter girth created the appearance of greater height and danger. It also meant fewer panels were needed to complete the cylinder and thus easier moving. As Joe McKennon saw it, "such structures meant the end of the older, slant-walled drome." In reality, the arrival of the Wall-of-Death (a name borrowed from the old Whirl-of-Death bicycle acts) meant that the days of the slant-wall dromes were numbered, but not gone. Keeping in mind the scarcity of capital and that many in rural America had yet to even witness the earlier version, slant-wall acts continued to tour longer than they should have.

Cowboys on Indians

This same "shallow-pocketitis" of carnival operators also insured that when motordromes changed hands, as they frequently did, the bikes were included with the wooden arena. This factor accounts for the multitude of obsolete motorcycles being used well after better-suited machines became available (it also makes dating an image from the motorcycles difficult). Although Harley-Davidsons, Excelsiors, and at least one Henderson four-cylinder were used, Indian motorcycles seemed to be favored by drome riders, operators, and builders alike. The advertisements of J. Frank Hatch carried the offer of new motordromes with or without "Indian Riding Motorcycles." These generally were not the Model H racers but the less-expensive Powerplus twins stripped of all the unnecessaries and fitted with drop or racing handlebars.

The proliferation of carnival motordromes by 1920 when the Indian Scout model was launched created a ready-made niche market for the bike. No other American motorcycle manufacturer offered a similar model. The light weight, lower center of gravity, and short wheelbase made the 1920–1927 Indian Scout the preferred weapon on the Wall-of-Death. Incredibly, these first-generation Scouts with their total-loss oil systems, rigid frames, and leaf-spring front forks were still the predominant bike used in carnival dromes up until the attraction's disappearance in the 1980s.

Some have suggested that the 101 Model Scout was the machine most used but the longer wheelbase made it unwieldy in all but the larger, combination dromes. There are a few recorded instances of 101 Scouts being crudely altered or shortened for motordrome use but in most cases this was done when an earlier model couldn't be found. The definitive Wall-of-Death bike was a 1920–1927 Indian Scout model with a 37-ci engine. It was stripped of lighting and fenders, although some fitted a bobbed rear fender for safety. Seats were rigidly fixed, the handlebars abbreviated in length, and footboards were retained for the all-important standing stunts. "What" exhaust pipes were the components of choice and many operators also fitted a police siren for the act's finale. Oh, and over time, the bikes also had at least nine coats of paint as Wall-of-Death riders tried to keep them looking fresh!

A Golden Age

By 1920, there were more than 200 independently owned carnivals traveling across the United States, most by railroad as the state of roads between towns

The Motordrome near Playa del Rey, Cal.

COPYRIGHT 1910 BY A. B. DODGE, L. A.

Board-track motordrome racing souvenirs, circa 1910s.

Motordrome at Luna Park, Cleveland New City

9609. Columbus Motordrome, Columbus, Ohio.

and villages discouraged any other method of conveying equipment. At this time the small number of trucks and trailers were used chiefly for intra-city delivery work. The growth of the carnival industry was directly related to and dependent upon the railroads.

Mechanical rides, tents, and attractions, such as the Wall-of-Death, had to be disassembled, stacked by hand on wagons, and hauled to the train. If the trailer was not part of the attraction, it had to be unloaded into a boxcar or flat; if the wagon was dedicated, it still had to wait its turn to be loaded onto the train. After the ordeal of getting to the next town or fairground, a motordrome operator had to wait to be unloaded and then hauled by whatever form of drayage was available (truck, farm tractor, horse, and so on) to a predetermined location on the midway—in all types of weather. It was an incredibly brutal way of making a living, for officer and soldier alike!

Those equipment or show owners that didn't want to endure the expense and horrors of moving almost every week vied for contracts in an amusement park or seashore location. These opportunities where not plentiful in the United States and often meant surrendering a higher percentage of the winnings but the headaches encountered by the need of a large crew or having to kowtow to the railroad lines were nonexistent. By the 1920s, Coney Island, Chicago's Riverview Park, and Southern California's Venice Pier all had established motordromes as part of their lineup.

Semi-permanent locations permitted larger and sturdier structures to be used. These didn't shake or sway when motorcycles or midget cars were making their orbits as in the portable versions that in many instances would scare spectators off the rickety viewing platforms and back down to the ground. A Wall-of-Death that had its surface lapped together as a single unit without seams and was backed by steel or concrete instilled not only more confidence in the audience but the performers as well. In these structures, the only limit to the amount of bikes or cars that could be put on the wall at once time was its height. A Wall-of-Death act in Germany featured four BMW motorcycles circling in formation, one above the other. A concentrated mass of 2,000 lb. (multiplied by the G-forces) such as this rolling around inside a portable motordrome would have been dangerous to all concerned, even in the largest units.

A traveling U.S. carnival of any size in the 1920s had to have certain staple attractions in order to protect their contracts—a Ferris wheel, merry-go-round, Coney-Island Whip, a chair-o-plane or swing-type ride, and a Wall-of-Death. As competition between drome operators intensified, no feature or stunt was too outrageous. Motorcycle trick-riding in the dromes began to reach outlandish heights. Riders were thundering around the boards with hands off the bars, standing on the footboards or pegs, sitting side-saddle, and riding with legs over the tank (while facing up or down), legs over the handlebars, and perhaps the most difficult of all, completely backwards with legs over the rear wheel. Many drome riders would also take passengers—sometimes from the audience. A stunt called the Dips of Death meant shooting up to the very top of the wall, inches from the crowd, and then executing a sharp turn to dive back down to the bottom of the drome. Riders regularly included as part of their act snatching articles from the audience and returning them again while in flight. At least one operator would solicit a blindfold from the crowd and after tying it over his eyes would motor around inches from the top!

As perilous as the trick-riding could be even with the occasional tire puncture or power failure during an evening performance, the most deadly practice was sharing the wall with another rider (or driver, in the case of a car). Many injuries were the result of miscues between performers when climbing, crisscrossing, or descending the wall while most of the recorded fatalities took place when riders circled in opposite directions. Sloppy choreography or engine trouble often brought serious consequences as British performer Doug Murphy recorded in a letter to American rider George "Lucky" Thibeault. "Greek rider Cevtitas Arivas was killed in an opposite direction race, he always rode in the opposite direction to us, clockwise that is. He collided with two others." Murphy went on to mention American rider Earl Ketring, who was killed in the same way while performing on the Johnny J. Jones Exposition drome; the other rider would succumb ten days after crashing into Ketring.

But traveling in the same direction also had its hazards, as one of the more famous riders, "Speedy" Babbs, would relate in a letter to Thibeault. "One thing you must look out for is if you are on opposite sides of the wall and [at the] same speed, you get the impression you are just standing still, it has a hypnotic effect." Later when referring to performing with his younger brother, Howard, Babbs continued, "he got that hypnotic stare and felt like he was standing still and just overtook and hit me, broke his left arm and [two] bones right in the wrist. I didn't get skinned hardly any!"

Danger Girls

Woman riders on the Wall-of-Death seemed to be a particularly successful attraction, as they had been from the beginning in the bicycle-whirl acts. With names such as the Mile-a-Minute Girl, Speed Queen, or Danger Girl, some of the well-known early riders included Lillian La France, Marion Perry, and "Teddy" Walters. Female performers like Olive Hager and Marjorie Kemp would eventually headline their own motordromes featuring all-girl teams of riders. Many were trick-riders showing the same nerves of steel as their male counterparts.

One of the more famous of these was British rider Marjorie Dare, who was married to "Tornado" Smith. In their act, she would knit while sitting in a chair at the bottom of the drome, seemingly indifferent to her husband who was speeding his Indian around the wall only inches from her head. She would then jump in his sidecar and continue working on the sweater while the pair made the "rounds." For a finale, she would strap on a pair of special roller skates and allow her husband to take her in tow behind his motorcycle. When sufficient speed had been reached, she would release the tether and make a complete orbit on her own. It was widely printed that she held no drivers license because she was too nervous to take the test!

Woman riders always sold the tickets up until the Wall-of-Death faded from popularity. Today, the tradition is continued by riders like Samantha Morgan, who took lessons from Sonny Pelaquin and learned to trick-ride in the largest (and most difficult-to-master) motordrome touring the fair circuit in the Eastern United States during the early 1980s.

Lion motordome ticket from the International
Exposition in Chicago, 1933.

Compliant Lions

By the late 1920s, Wall-of-Death performances constituted the well-worn acts of trick-riding and multi-vehicle racing. The attraction had become familiar and the novelty was diminishing. It was during this time that someone (his or her identity is lost to the fog of time and carnie BS) saw the motordrome enclosure and elevated viewing platform as a natural arena for a lion act. The addition of man-eating lions within the drome while riders were circling above was also recognized as an irresistible attraction—the inference being that any mishap or machine malfunction would mean an easy meal for the King of the Jungle!

One of the first to add lions to his motordrome show was straight-wall pioneer Walter Kemp during the 1929 season. Kemp's Motor Maniac show used a larger, combination drome, meaning it could accommodate motorcycles, small cars (usually a midget racer), and a lion act. His presentation would include the standard regime of trick-riding and racing, but for his finale, a full-grown lion would be turned loose within to chase him while in flight, the animal's roars smothering the Indian motorcycle's rude report.

In reality, lions wanted no part of the noisy devices, and many a trainer's best efforts could not keep the big cats from panicking at first. As undesirable as a scared lion bounding around inside a motordrome was, the audiences' recognition of the animal's obvious fear was worse, attracting unwanted laughter and in some cases, jeers from the gallery above. In an effort to acclimate lions to the noise and motion, a car was modified to carry one as a passenger while circling up on the wall. Among the first to accomplish this was a British performer then in the United States going by the name of Fearless Egbert. He also used motorcycles and called his finale the "Race for Life." After many, many dangerous hours and hard work, the cats were trained to stay on special perches that slotted into the wall. As the motorcycles thundered above and below, the lions roared back, looking as though they would pounce at any moment. The act was finally perfected, and ticket sales would no longer be a problem for any motordrome featuring lions.

But to infer that these animals were tame and not a danger to the riders couldn't be further from the facts. Lions could be moody and have bad-hair days like their two-legged partners on the Wall-of-Death. In many cases, this was not realized until well into a show where a simple spill could confuse and anger a normally compliant lion. Walter Kemp's wife, Marjorie, seemed to be a favorite target. She was seriously mauled on at least four separate occasions, the first being so severe it was thought her arm would have to be amputated and the last attack, in 1940, infirmed her for more than a year!

When the animals got loose, the results were sometimes lethal for the "civilians." In 1933, a seven-year-old lion escaped from his enclosure in Wildwood, New Jersey, where he was employed in the lion-drome of Joe Dobish. The animal was at large for two hours during which time he attacked and killed a boardwalk concessionaire. Dobish was charged with manslaughter, and both of his performing lions were put down as a result.

Many of the motordrome operators became animal trainers and used the wooden arenas to stage lion acts in between motorcycle shows, maximizing the equipment's potential. Husband-and-wife duo Earl and Ethel Purtle were among the more famous, performing on the World of Mirth Shows. Earl trained lion cubs to ride on his motorcycle's fuel tank while Ethel gave rides to full-grown cats in a special sidecar outfit. Other lion-drome operators that achieved notoriety included Olive Hager, George Murray, Wallace Smithly, and Art Spencer, who it is said kept an old lion at great expense for no other purpose than to torture it daily in retribution for maiming his hand.

Lion-dromes became such a sought after sensation that officials of the 1933 Chicago World's Fair, "A Century of Progress," wanted to include one in their lineup of attractions. The contract was awarded to Walter Kemp, then the undisputed lion-drome leader. A special arena, 40 feet in diameter, was designed and a new car was built for Marjorie Kemp, who along with Sultan, her 500-pound pet, would be one of the show's features. In order to showcase the best trick-riding possible, Kemp extended an invitation to other carnival motordrome riders around the country and assembled an all-star team of performers, including Texan Red Crawford, motorglobe rider Virginia Dawn, Dottie Barclay, "Teddy" Walters, and William "Speedy" Palmer. Along with the best riders in the United States, Kemp and his trainer Chubby Guilfoyle had ten lions on hand and performed animal acts in between the motor shows. It was the Wall-of-Death high watermark, and there would never be anything like it again!

Loud Pipes Save Lives!

Yet not everyone thought the Wall-of-Death so wonderful. The pre-show demonstrations, or "ballys" as they were called, were staged in front of the dromes on elevated platforms—usually the wagons or trailers used for transport. These shows were naturally crafted to attract as much attention as possible. Motorcycles with little or no baffling were kept out front and when fired up and repeatedly blipped, did much to alienate operators of other shows, games, and even rides in the immediate vicinity. In the 1920s when the attraction had become familiar and a slower sell, motordrome owners started using rollers under the demonstration bikes that allowed short teases of stunting and trick-riding, which only lengthened the pre-show. Many times, this bally would run much longer than the paid performance! The addition of electrically amplified loud speakers as well as the unpleasant odors attendant to a pride of lions made the Wall-of-Death a midway pariah.

It became standard practice to assign the motordrome's location to the carnival's "back end," well away from the two-headed baby show and the corn dog trailer. One carnival owner went as far as to declare "he wasn't going to book anymore dromes on his show, as they make too much noise and detract from the neighboring attractions." The resolution was short-lived!

All Good Things . . .

The Second World War brought a halt to all fun fairs and Wall-of-Death shows in Europe. Although not as severe, the effects of the war were felt in America as well. Gasoline rationing hit the carnival industry like a sledgehammer. Most traveling shows by then had weaned themselves from the railroads and were moving over the road by truck. Fuel

Daredevil Jimmy Reed circles the Wall of Death aboard his customized Harley-Davidson, 1954.
Courtesy Samantha Morgan

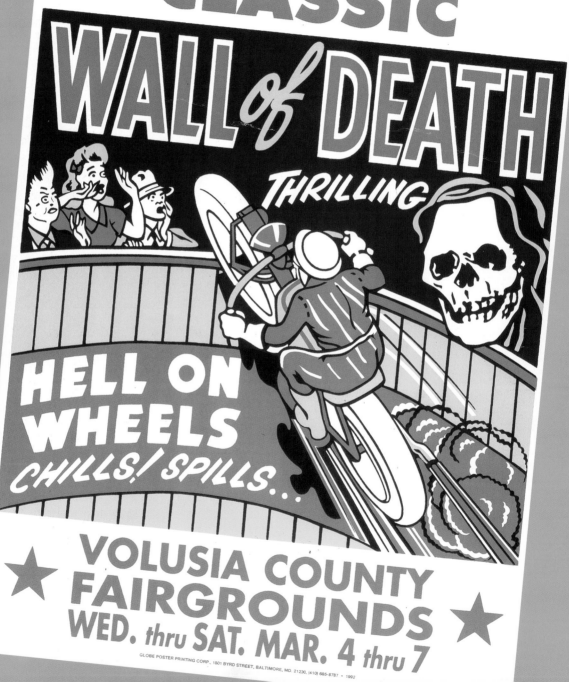

Wall of Death posters, circa 1980s.

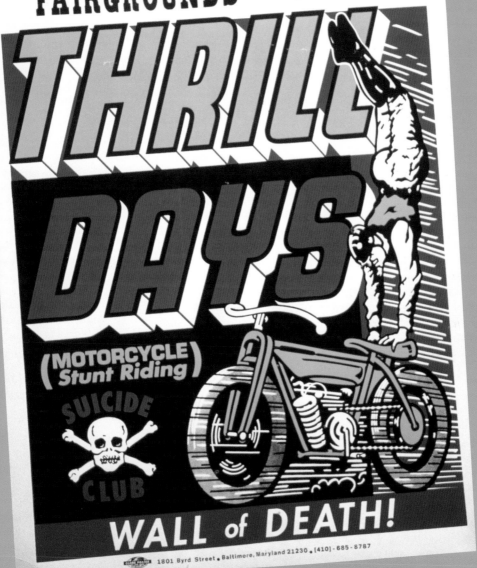

restrictions also dissuaded Joe Public from driving to out-of-town carnival lots or fairgrounds. In 1942, Earl Purtle was ordered to stop performances of his motordrome show by the Office of Defense Transportation, claiming he was in violation of regulations. He would soldier on with a lion act but would not use motorcycles or cars again for another six years. Curiously, many other drome operators were allowed to continue. Later that year, Walter Kemp was killed in an airplane crash while giving lessons to would-be pilots in Florida. And during the 1944 D-Day invasion, carnivals closed for almost two weeks. As Joe McKennon recorded, "The average citizen was in no mood to visit a carnival midway as his sons and brothers fought their way ashore at Normandy and forced a blood-stained corridor across Northern Europe."

After the war years, like everything else in America, the outdoor amusement industry boomed and the number of motordromes was never greater. However, most of them did not include lions as part of their show and those that did found the added expenses that included hundreds of pounds of horse meat each week overburdening for all but the most lucrative carnival routes. One by one, the lion-drome operators sold off the animals to zoos and by the early 1960s they were no more.

The Wall-of-Death in its feline-free form continued to be a viable carnival attraction, however. Independent drome owners had some luck leaving the well-trodden routes of the bigger shows and booked with smaller outfits. Many citizens attending the remote county, or "pumpkin," fairs as they were known had yet to experi-

ence the motorcycle shows and eagerly climbed the rickety steps to peer into the pit of death.

But even as early as the 1950s, the American public's entertainment threshold was increasing and all forms of outdoor entertainment would feel the arrival of the television set, from which they would never recover. More thrilling amusement rides were also being introduced and the fierce competition for fair contracts meant that even smaller carnivals had to acquire the equipment. As carnival historian Bob Goldsack opined, "The general public was less and less interested in freaks, unborn and similar types of shows. Fair committees and patrons were looking for newer and more thrilling riding devices, requiring large expenditures by the show." The days of the show-owned motordrome were over.

Like all carnival sideshows, the number of Wall-of-Death operators steadily declined until only a handful remained by the 1970s. Sadly, many of the drome structures were abandoned to rot on their transport trailers as they languished in carnival winter quarters. The clapped-out motorcycles that didn't turn into rusty boat anchors were sold to or cannibalized by drome operators still working. Some of these diehards included the Pelaquin family, "Speedy" McNish, Joe Boudreau, Les King, Jack Hatcher, and Doug Hopkins, the latter using one of the smallest structures, only 20 feet in diameter.

Some of these motordromes are still in use today by a small few who keep the tradition alive. Rhett Giordano can be seen trick-riding at many Harley-Davidson rallies across the United States, including Bike Week in Daytona, Myrtle Beach, Sturgis, and AMA Vintage Days at Mid-Ohio. Don Daniels Jr. continues a more authentic tradition by booking his Wall-of-Death at major fairs in the Eastern United States as well as many motorcycle events.

In Europe, where the number of traveling carnivals were less prolific and the average stand of the fun fair much longer in duration, the Wall-of-Death seemed to enjoy more life. Today, the brilliant colored arenas of Ken Fox and Allan Ford are still dazzling crowds in the United Kingdom while the Varanne family and other operators perform on the continent.

Daredevil Hepburn

As to the question of who was the most famous motordrome rider, the answer may depend on how you define legitimate fame. Many drome operators were characters, to speak politely, yet self-promotion was a valid part of their business. Just about all claimed to be the originator of a technique or particular type of performance. Louis "Speedy" Babbs was a Kentucky-born rider who emigrated to the West Coast; he was also a shameless self-promoter. He held many "occupations," including tightrope walker, Wall-of-Death performer, and motorglobe rider. He even staged a bullfight while riding a motorcycle as a publicity stunt. Babbs loved the spotlight more than anything, and managed to arrange at least four separate profiles of himself in national motorcycle magazines as well as a biography in Joe Scalzo's *Evel Knievel and Other Daredevils*. He

is remembered today mainly as a result of this exposure.

In England, George William "Tornado" Smith was clearly the best known but again, mostly through his own machinations. In many respects, he was similar to his American counterpart Walter Kemp: Smith was an accomplished trick-rider, worked extensively with lions, and even married a "Marjorie." Like Babbs, he was addicted to the narcotic of notoriety, and arranged numerous personal features in British periodicals. He stopped riding in 1965 and moved to South Africa where he died six years later. A biography of his life was published in 1998 but this time through no scheme of his own.

Ironically, the rider that may have achieved the most fame was one who downplayed his carnival motordrome days and was known for his subsequent association with Harley-Davidson. During World War I, Ralph "Daredevil" Hepburn was an Indian motorcycle trick-rider in slant-wall dromes with the Evans Shows and C. A. Wortham Shows, then the largest traveling carnival in the United States. In 1919, Hepburn became a member of the Harley-Davidson factory racing team known as the "Wrecking Crew," along with Jim Davis, Fred Ludlow, Otto Walker, and Ray Weishaar. As a professional motorcycle racer, Hepburn regularly performed before crowds of 25,000 or more and became a national hero before the era of radio and television. Riding for Harley-Davidson, he won the Ascot 200-mile National in 1919 and the Dodge City 300 in 1921. Hepburn would return to the "Wigwam" when he joined the Indian factory team and won the 300-mile National in 1922. Three years later, he began an auto racing career that included fifteen starts at the Indianapolis 500 and four top-five finishes. He is most remembered at the Brickyard for a crash that took his life there while qualifying in 1948.

If there was such a thing as a Golden Age of the Wall-of-Death, it must be the period from 1925 to 1940. It was during this era that motordrome trick-riding reached its highest levels due in no small part to the arrival of the versatile and tractable Indian Scout motorcycle, which was almost unanimously adapted as the machine of choice. When lions were added to the equation, culminating in the appearance at the 1933 Chicago World's Fair, the shows were nothing short of spectacular even by today's standards. The arenas built during the 1930s for Walter Kemp, Earl Purtle, Olive Hager, and many others were by far the most beautiful. The Art Deco trim, neon lighting, and elaborately painted show fronts would not be seen again on the same scale. It truly was another universe!

Wall of Death poster, circa 1990s. *Courtesy Samantha Morgan*

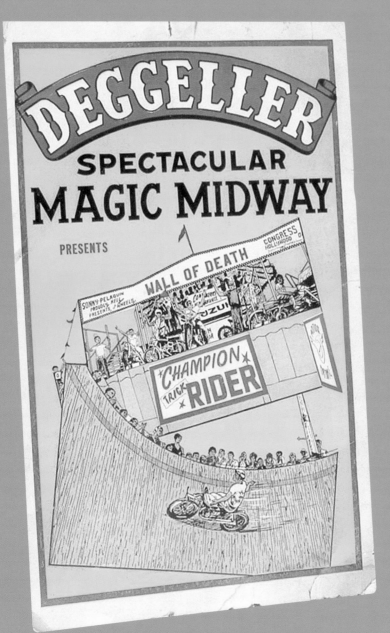

Wall of Death
poster, circa 1990s.
*Courtesy Samantha
Morgan*

Riding the Wall of Death

By "Tornado" Smith

George William Smith was best known by his sideshow moniker "Tornado," a name that came from riding around and around the cyclone track within the Wall of Death. Tornado Smith was England's greatest Death Wall rider, a pioneer on the boards with both motorcycles and automobiles on the British Isles.

He penned this essay on the trials and tribulations of riding the Wall of Death for the English weekly magazine *The Modern Boy* in 1937. As the magazine promised, "After nine years of riding the Wall some sixty times a day, Tornado still comes up smiling."

How would you like to roar around a perpendicular wall on a motor-cycle and in a car at 60 m.p.h. for a living?

That has been my thrilling job for nearly nine years, doing an average of sixty seven-minute shows a day!

Many of you, I expect, have watched me "doing my stuff" on the Wall of Death at the Olympia Fun fair, at Christmas, or at the Kursaal, Southend-on-Sea, or have seen other "Wall of Death" riders in action at other pleasure beaches or fairs.

For those who have not, picture a circular, wooden wall, about twenty feet high. Inside, at the foot is a four-foot ramp, sloped at an angle of forty-five degrees., Around the top of the Wall is a gallery for spectators. This is guarded by a steel hawser, or safety cable, to prevent—in case of a skid, a broken chain, petrol failure, a choked motor, a jammed back wheel, or a miscalculation—my motor-bike or my car, whichever I'm riding, roaring over the top.

All those mishaps I've mentioned have fallen to my lot at one time and another, but so far—touch wood!—I've escaped without breaking a single bone in my body!

Mounting my 7.9 Indian Scout motor-cycle, which weighs 300 lb., I career round this ramp at the foot of the Wall, gaining speed. Then, with a quick wrench of the handlebars, I roar up and around the Wall itself, circling higher and higher until I am careering round only a few inches below that cable.

How is it done? Well. It is the speed chiefly which keeps the machine upright, at right angles to the Wall, and makes it possible to defy the pull of gravity. So long as I maintain a speed of, at least, 50 m.p.h., the centrifugal force is stronger than the pull of gravity, and I don't drop.

Any good standard machine is capable of riding the Wall. But to stand up to the severe strain of stunting, it *must* possess certain essential features, namely, rigidness of frame, a low saddle and a low set of handlebars, and a smooth-running engine capable of first-class acceleration.

The Indian Scout machine I use is not specially constructed for the job. It is simply a standard model, stripped for lightness and to avoid a bad mix-up, in case of accident.

Three amateur motor-cycle enthusiasts once challenged this statement, after trying unsuccessfully to ride the Wall on their own machines. These were a 346 c.c. Royal Enfield, a 550 c.c. Triumph, and a 349 c.c. James.

My answer was to borrow each machine in turn and ride it around the Wall!

When you first start to practice riding the Wall, you begin by careering round the 45-degree ramp at the foot, until you feel confident enough to have a "crack" at the actual Wall itself!

When you do, it's a pretty frightening sensation, too! It is rather like ascending in an express elevator. The Wall seems to rush towards you and vanish beneath you. You cannot see very far ahead, for, of course, you are circling constantly. On your right is a circle of blurred faces; on your left the bottom of the pit is apparently rotating at a dizzy speed. It needs a terrific effort to hold your head up!

Speedway riders, T.T. cracks, enthusiastic amateur motor-cyclists have all tried and failed to ride the Wall. So it seems that Wall riders are born rather than made. One I trained, however, did attain "wall standard" after practicing daily for a fortnight. But all-round proficiency and stunting ability did not come for a year.

Riding the Wall without holding the handlebars, lifting your legs over the tank when roaring around, turning completely in the saddle with your back to the handle-bars, and my famous "dips of death," during which I roar up and down the Wall, wrenching the handlebars at the last moment to prevent a "crash" at the bottom or a leap over the lip at the top, can only be accomplished after many months of intensive practice and many a spill. They need, as you can imagine, cool and unerring judgment in execution.

The Austin 7 stripped chassis I drive around the Wall is a standard model, with a standard carburettor, an ordinary back axle, and a standard three-speed gear-box. Extra springs and over-size spokes on the wheels are the only "extras." The latter obviate wheel spin when getting away from the floor.

I selected the Austin from twenty different makes of British and foreign cars. When I had chosen three "probables" from this twenty, I widened the ramp at the foot of the Wall to take the width of the cars with a few inches to spare.

Then I practised with each car in turn, racing them round and round the ramp to discover any weak spots. Finally, I decided the Austin was the most satisfactory in performance and most suitable for my particular purpose, took the car up on the actual Wall—and hoped for the best.

The best I could do on that first occasion was to get the Seven three feet above the ramp. But I got her down again—more by luck than judgment, I think—on all four wheels.

Skidding, slithering, wobbling, and flopping, expecting every moment to be my last, I persevered for weeks, until I won the proud title of the only man ever to drive a car around a "Wall of Death"—a feat which I now do sixty or more times a day!

Taking a side-car outfit up the Wall isn't the sort of thing you can do at the first attempt. I had to put in no end of practice before I attempted the stunt in public. But once I got the "feel" of the outfit everything was plain sailing.

Although, as I said before, I've been riding the Wall for nearly seven years now, I still treat my job with respect. I know only too well that it might prove fatal to do otherwise. A moment's inattention, the slightest carelessness in carrying out my tricks, and—well, I'd probably finish in a nasty heap at the bottom of the Wall!

The Modern-Day Mile-a-Minute Girl

By Samantha Morgan

Samantha Morgan rides the Wall of Death for a living. Known by her nom de guerre as "S. Morgan Storm" with the American Motor Drome, she tours the United States from Daytona to Sturgis to the sunset horizon with her show.

Samantha is also a passionate historian of the motor drome. Through her travels, she has collected a vast archive of photographs, posters, and stories of the men and women who built, rode, and made a living with the thrill arenas. It's a history that's all too easily lost along with the carnival sawdust.

But Samantha not only collects and chronicles Wall of Death history, she lives it. This memoir tells of her love affair with the wall.

I saw my first motor drome at a carnival in Miami, Florida, when I was fourteen years old. At that time, dromes had already almost disappeared in this country, so it wasn't unusual that I had no idea what I was walking up those stairs to see. The moment I looked down into the barrel and saw that guy riding a bike on the side of the 90-degree wall, I knew what I wanted to do with my life!

Back then, the shows ran continuous performances, and if you missed part of one show you could stay and catch the next—or the rest! I stayed up on top of the barrel all day, threw in all my money, and clapped until my hands hurt. When I came down, I asked the crew if girls could do it too. After the usual daredevil guy comments had been made, Sonny Pelaquin—the "Mad Penguin," owner, trick rider, and the man who was to become my mentor and beloved friend/dad for the rest of his life—kindly explained that, yes, girls could learn, but he had a full crew and did not need any more help right then. It was the last weekend of the fair, so he let me hang around; taking tickets, cleaning up, and getting to know the show and the guys. When it was time for teardown, I proved I could work like a guy by helping them load the building. I was employed at the horse racetrack at the time, and was a tall, strong kid who knew how to work. I also had no trouble at all lying that I was 18!

The show left town, but not before I found out where they were going. I packed my guitar and my belongings on my motorcycle (my first bike, which I had owned for just two weeks), and headed for a shopping center in Jacksonville, Florida, their next spot. I blew a tire on the way, riding on the flat for about 20 miles on the shoulder of the road. Soon, the whole Deggeller Shows carnival, as well as the drome, was going past me. When one of the drome guys saw me rolling slow on the side of the road, he stopped, loaded up my bike, and brought me along.

Sonny had definitely said, "No" in Miami, but it was the slow time of their season, and I guess he now felt sorry for me, because he let me stay on. I helped them set up, sold tickets, and so on, all the while nagging Sonny to teach me to ride. It worked, and even though we were only doing three shows a day, I started my training.

The moment you walk inside and enter the "pit" of the drome, you get a whole different perspective than you do from "upstairs." You can really see how steep the 90 degree wall is, and Sonny's starting tracks (the ramp leading to the wall) were almost as steep as the wall itself. The track angle is a personal preference (there are no books on how to build a drome), and Sonny's family built them this way to eliminate washouts more quickly so as not to waste valuable training time—and it works! The first time I saw the show from the inside, I realized just how close everything is—and how fast everything happens in there!

The Pelaquins only trained during shows, as I do to this day. That way, no one ever gets hurt for nothing. And if someone doesn't have the mental discipline to block out the crowd and other external input, you find out in the beginning. Again, no wasting training or needless injury for someone who shouldn't be there in the first place.

Uncontrolled emotions can take a rider down as sure as a blown tire or a broken chain. Sonny always said there was a "force field" in the doorway—as you pass through into the pit, you leave all the bad stuff in your brain on the outside. It was one of the most important lessons I ever learned in my life. Once you're riding, the wall takes care of the rest.

While training, I had major butterflies every time I backed up to the track to take my turn. It was exciting yet scary—*good* scary! It was the most awesome thing I had ever experienced in my life! And years later, I still feel the same way.

I had more than my share of spills (not being a natural), but I wanted it so much that I was willing to work and do whatever it took. I used to lie in the drome, looking at the walls and dreaming of trickriding someday. Because of the physics and the Gs, it takes a while to learn, and you stay low until you have the control to go up, so training falls usually lead mostly to scraped elbows and knees. I learned on a little 70 Indian and Harley peashooters without much power, which is safer until your strength develops and you have more control. We pull up to approximately 3Gs inside—the higher and faster, the more Gs—and so the longer you ride, the stronger you get.

I struggled for a while until one day Sonny came in to guest ride, and I closely watched the way he went up. It was like a breaker switch flipped on, and after that I had it; my days of hitting the floor going low and slow were over. From then on, any spills came from up higher and faster and were way more serious.

I became a trickrider through a luck of the draw: I had no place to go home to, so I stayed with the show. The drome became my home ("drome sweet drome"), and luckily, Sonny was out on the road all year long. The guys came and went—home to their families for the holidays, and so on—and that was how I became a trickrider . . . because I was there.

Sonny Pelaquin came from a lion motor drome family. They had lion acts with big cats that rode in sidecars and on bikes with the riders, as well as the more conventional type of cat acts. Sonny's brother, Joe, wanted to be a lion trainer, and rumor has it that Clyde Beatty got his start with drome cats. Sonny's mom and dad, Viola and Joe Pelaquin Sr., rode together until the birth of their first son, after which Joe Sr. was on his own until his family grew. They had five boys and one girl. Four of the boys followed their dad's bootsteps into the drome business. Joe Sr. was a strict, safety-minded taskmaster with a dry sense of humor who ran a tight drome and a safe show. Most of the family shows were that way back then. The Pelaquins also were globe riders, as were many of the other families.

Sonny was much like his dad, but with more of an obvious sense of humor. He was just as strict and safety minded, and if he caught us doing the things daredevil kids tend to do—going over the red line at the top of the wall, taking each other up, showing off, or being generally unsafe—he gave you the day off. And *he* told you when you were ready to come back to work!

Sonny kept us safe always. We rode two years in Canada on one of the biggest carnival routes in the world.

Ballyhoo: Sonny Pelaquin stands before his motordrome while Porky (seated on the cycle) gives the bally, circa 1970s. *Courtesy Samantha Morgan*

California Hellriders duet: Samantha Morgan and Don Daniels Sr. ride high on the Wall, 1987. *Courtesy Samantha Morgan*

We did four shows an hour for sixteen hours a day for two years—and had no accidents! This was unheard of, and is a record Sonny was proud of his whole life.

Motorcycles are only machines, and we do things to them at tolerances they were never designed to take. You are supposed to check your machine continuously to avoid accidents, and Sonny went behind us checking everything constantly, unbeknownst to us. If he found something we missed, he waited until the show had started, came inside the pit, interrupted the show, pointed to whichever bike had the problem, and then left. Now, you had to make the repair in front of the crowd. These were lessons we never forgot, which kept us safe—and still save me.

A cracked frame needs to be found before you go up and take the spill, so Sonny painted the frames white. When you wipe your bike down (like you're supposed always to do) a crack appears as a line you can see. This is just one example of the ways he took care of us. I wish I had realized how wise he was back then.

I don't know how we managed to ride that much in those two years. Our shows were twelve minutes long with three minutes in between letting the crowd in and out. We were riding an old restored lion drome which held 300 people, so we were really rockin'. No need for a stage show here! I nodded in a chair for two of the three "between minutes," then it was back to work.

I was trickriding with Russ Noel, Sonny's much younger cousin, who had helped teach me to ride. We did a double trickride because no one person could do it all. I had never before, nor have I ever since, seen a double trickride. I sure wish Sonny could have prevented the

Sonny Pelaquin's motordrome on the Deggeller Shows midway, circa 1970s. *Courtesy Samantha Morgan*

bloody saddle sores we all had! Nevertheless, riding was always well worth anything we had to endure.

Once you hit the wall, all pain goes away as the Gs kick in and you arrive in that place that only exists up there. There is nothing that compares with wall riding—although jumping out of an airplane comes close! It's like doing aerobics and lifting weights at the same time. You get really strong and fit, but not big and bulky. With your heart pumping and the Gs on your body (especially trickriding, where you move around on the bike), it's an amazing sport in all ways! A place where the mind and body come together, and for a hyper, scattered kid it was a dream come true. Nothing can touch you up there, or take it away . . . it all comes from within, and you get back so much for what you put in! It also stays with you after you land. You get to take it away with you!

Setting up and tearing down the drome also takes its toll. Most people don't ever start training because they can't handle that part of the job. It's heavy and dirty and exhausting, and is part of the dues one has to pay before starting to learn to ride. Jay Allen of Broken Spoke Saloon and the late, great Indian Larry both carried walls before they had their first lesson. Most potential riders usually leave after carrying their first wall. It's a great screening tool, and a necessary evil: if the building doesn't go up, no one rides.

More commonly known as a "wall of death," the correct names for these shows are "motor dromes" or "thrill arenas." Motor drome barrel riding started in this country at the turn of the twentieth century, shortly after the dawn of motorcycles. Motordrome boardtrack racetracks (of three-quarters or one mile, etc.) were shut down in the mid-1920s due to public outcry because of so many accidents and many of the public's favorite riders losing their lives. That was when the portable motordrome barrel-type buildings appeared in carnivals with a vengeance. The first ones were more like bowls than walls, but it wasn't long before these early daredevils pushed the envelope to the 90-degree wall, which is what we still ride today.

Dromes were the spectaculars of the carnival shows from the 1920s through the 1950s, when they started disappearing. The families were getting out of the business, the older guys retiring and not so many having kids that continued in the business. It is not an easy life on the road, and many wanted families with more conventional lifestyles. As other folks took over these shows, it was the beginning of the end. It takes a special breed to live and work on the road, risking your life every day. Without the care and cohesion of a family-type group, things started to change, and the shows began to unravel. The drome riders came to be known as rowdies who fought and partied all the time. Many rode drunk; some even fought and ran each other off the walls! The carnivals were hesitant at first, and flat refused to have these shows on their midways after a while. It was the beginning of the end. Back then, and even today still, a drome crew is the epitome of dysfunction.

Sonny stayed in the business longer than anyone (except me, now). He was able to change, and his crew changed with him. No more drinking and riding. We had to dress neat, look presentable, and behave like showmen. If not, the carnival office would shut you down, and your livelihood was done. I was lucky. Being a lightweight, I never could drink and ride, but I grew up with a beer cooler always out back of the drome. Thanks to Sonny Pelaquin, we are still around today. He passed a few years ago, but his voice is still in my head, and his spirit always with me. Thanks for my life, Penguin!

There were many great riders back in the day. In the United States: Sonny and his family, George Murray, Skinny Stevens, Flash White, Lefty Johnson (who now lives in Alaska), Jimmy and Marjorie Hawthorne (who travel as musicians these days), the great "La Vonnie" (she was not even five feet tall, came from a circus family, and was one of the greatest lady riders ever), and the large Kemp family. Also Speedy Babbs (dromes and globes always), Speedy McNish, his wife Josephine, and his son Ronnie (who we lost in Vietnam). More recently, Tim Allen, Rodney "Hot Rod" Housley (both of whom Sonny trained), Terry Johnson and his partner Mark (who tragically died in a truck accident), and many more. There are just too many to mention them all.

In Europe, the Varanne family is from France; Alan Ford's wall and the Calladine family's show are from England; Pitt's Todeswand and the Motorellos from Germany; and there are more in other countries around the world.

Sadly, in the United States, dromes are going the way of the dinosaurs. But like the birds and crocodiles, there are still a few of us left. Though I have ridden eleven walls in my life so far, we have only three walls left in the United States at the present time: the California Hellriders, the American Motor Drome, and one other. The American Motor Drome is the first new barrel to be built in more than fifty years.

Sonny Pelaquin left a legacy of showmanship and a passionate love for a show and sport; if not for him, I believe motordromes would already be gone. He laughed when he rode and thankfully, gave me that gift. I am forever grateful for the opportunity this great man and those awesome daredevils who started it all have given me, and I hope to ride until the end of my life.

There is still limited public knowledge about these shows. The photography then was not what it is today, and there were only primitive television and news sources back then to spread the word. Sadly, most of the original show performances have been lost. Those folks did things on the wall that no one would imagine, or will ever see again—like the lions!

There are many people telling drome history stories now, but most of them were not there, nor really know or care. The egos in this business are causing history to be perverted according to them. Only a few riders are left who can really tell it like it was, and they are not the ones being filmed and interviewed. It's so sad that the real deals are being replaced with tales told by those who have more access to the media than the truth. I promised Sonny the world would know who and what came before in the motordromes, and that end is one of the reasons I feel it is so important to get the stories right. My goal is to give proper and true credit to those great people who actually risked their lives entertaining the public.

When we ride, there are always those folks who come up and say, "You know, when I was a little kid, my dad (or whomever) took me to see one of these things. Even though I don't really remember what I saw, I do remember I was scared to death! It was the greatest thing I ever saw! And now I'm bringing my kids to see it!" The smiles these folks give us, and the memories they take away, are a testimony to the talent and daring of all those many riders who came before and to the few who remain—still riding high on the wall!

Chapter 9

Bobbers
and
Choppers

I think the **Hell's Angels** are responsible for a lot of the current designs and workmanship on modern motorcycles. When you look at current custom Softail motorcycles (not the full dressers) you see a lot of our design innovations. **Our chopper motorcycles inspired even kids' bicycles,** like the Schwinn Sting Ray with its **banana seat** and **gooseneck handlebars.** It was only a matter of time before everybody on top would cash in on selling custom motorcycle parts. **Custom motorcycles and bike-riding gear has become a bigger business than ever.** Thank the Hell's Angels for that.

—Sonny Barger, *Hell's Angel*, 2000

Riding Easy

By Michael Dregni

The Wild One shocked the world with its noir images of the outlaw biker, indelible stereotypes that motorcyclists still haven't outrun. But it was another movie released a decade later that unveiled a new image of the biker—an image of a modern-day cowboy, free to ride wherever his iron steed would take him. That film was *Easy Rider*.

As with *The Wild One*, there was also a story behind the inspiration and making of *Easy Rider*. And befitting the times in the mid-1960s and the movie's message of antidisestablishmentarianism, it was certainly a bizarre tale.

They were Don Quixote and Sancho Panza for the twentieth century. A dynamic duo like Batman and Robin. Outlaws of quality like Butch Cassidy and the Sundance Kid. Or maybe they were Laurel and Hardy. In the end, they were themselves, Captain America and Billy, and through a simple, low-budget, shot-on-the-run movie called *Easy Rider*, they created a legend.

Captain America and Billy were good bad guys. Anti-heroes on the run, they rode on the wrong side of an Establishment that did not understand them and their times. They were part motorcycle outlaw in the style of *The Wild One* and part modern American cowboy looking for a home on the range. They were something new, and they became cultural icons. Captain America and Billy rode their chopped Harleys off the movie screen of *Easy Rider* to inspire generations of motorcyclists on their "great American freedom machines," as Harley-Davidson advertisements would jump on the bandwagon and label them.

The first of many ironies was that in *Easy Rider*, the greatest on-the-road, wind-in-the-hair, hippie-biker movie ever made, the motorcycles were built from former Los Angeles Police Department cruisers. Peter Fonda, a.k.a. Captain America, bought four Harley-Davidson Panheads—a 1950, two '51s, and a '52—at an LAPD auction for $500 apiece. These lackeys of the Establishment were about to become the wheels to fuel the anti-Establishment's wildest dream.

The idea for *Easy Rider* came to Fonda in a marijuana-fueled vision. It was 1967, the Summer of Love, and he was trapped at a movie exhibitors' convention in Toronto, flogging the latest biker flick that he was starring in,

The Wild Angels, facing an endless, Kafka-esque sentence of tedious press interviews. Then, the chief of the Motion Picture Association of America stood up to harangue the audience, denouncing Fonda and his film, saying, "We should stop making movies about motorcycles, sex, and drugs, and make more motion pictures like *Doctor Doolittle*."

Fonda finally escaped. He made it back to his red-flocked room at the Lakeshore Motel, only to be greeted by piles of promotional 8x10 glossies that required his autograph. Unable to face the promotion routine, he drank a couple bottles of Heineken and smoked a joint. As the marijuana settled his mind, he gazed at one of the photographs, which showed him and co-star Bruce Dern on a chopper.

The vision came to him.

"I understood immediately just what kind of motorcycle, sex, and drugs movie I should make next," he wrote thirty years later in his autobiography, *Don't Tell Dad*. The movie, which he originally planned to title *The Loners*, would be the modern Western: Two cool cats would take off on their choppers in search of America. They had just made a big drug score and were riding across the country to retire in Florida, when a couple of duck poachers in a pickup truck gun them down because they didn't like the way they looked.

Fonda was on a roll. It was 4:30 A.M., and he telephoned his best friend and biggest enemy, Dennis Hopper, got him out of bed, and told him the story. Hopper was ready to go.

Then Fonda told the idea to his wife. Her response was straightforward enough: "That's the corniest story I've ever heard."

Golden days: With his chopped Harley-Davidson aimed to the horizon, a rider saddles up, circa 1960s.

The second irony was that Hollywood—or at least the semi-underground, low-rent, youth-exploitation side of the movie industry—was ready to ride with Fonda's dream. With the help of novelist and screenwriter Terry Southern, Fonda and Hopper put together an audiotape of Hopper describing the storyline, and they set out to pitch it. A deal fell through with American International Pictures, the champion of biker flicks up to that time. But Fonda was not to be stopped. He was turned on to two producers, Bert Schneider and Bob Rafelson, who had struck gold with the faux-Beatles TV "rock group" The Monkees. The producers dug the concept. There and then, they wrote out a check for $40,000 to start things rolling. As Fonda noted in his autobiography, "Monkee money made *Easy Rider*."

Fonda then took a portion of the grubstake to the LAPD auction and bought the four Panheads. With the help of some buddies, the cycles were rebuilt in a manner far from Milwaukee's or the police department's concept. "I'd designed the extended and mildly raked front forks, helmet, sissy bar, and the tank," Fonda wrote, "but the forty-two degree rake that was suggested by [black activist and sometimes-motorcycle customizer] Cliff Vaughs was some piece of work."

As soon as his cycle was ready, Fonda took to the road to get the hang of riding a chopper. "I began riding the L.A. freeway system," remembered Fonda. "I was stopped every night by the police. They measured my handlebars, measured the height of the headlight, checked the taillights, the registration. They didn't touch the throttle."

Choppers were a new scene, but after the Captain America motorcycle rolled across movie screens around the world, they would become the rage. In garages every-where, ersatz Captain Americas were soon hurriedly chopping their cycles, raking the forks, throwing away perfectly good but out-of-fashion parts, and painting American flags on any surface large enough to hold the stars and stripes.

The third irony was that filming and production of the ultimate anti-Establishment road movie approached the workings of a fascist state.

"Dennis started with a bang," Fonda remembered. In lieu of a pep talk, Hopper led off the first day of filming in New Orleans with a Mussolini-esque rant to tell everyone that this was *his* movie and they all better follow orders.

They began filming by shooting from the hip in the best cowboy tradition, a technique that was ideal for the making of this modern Western. Fonda and Hopper knew what they wanted to capture on film but they eschewed the convention of a script, although there were numerous attempts to write one with the help of Southern. Instead, they just started the cameras rolling.

They filmed in New Orleans during Mardi Gras, before the motorcycles were ready. They wanted to capture an LSD trip on film, so they shot Captain America, Billy, and a bevy of girl groupies in a cemetery waxing poetic on things that made metaphysical sense to them at the time.

After several rounds of fights between Hopper and most of the rest of the crew, the people who hadn't quit returned to Los Angeles. Fonda and Hopper fired up the cycles, and they began filming as they rode across the United States.

Easy Rider was true *cinema verité*. They planned some scenes ahead of time, got set up, and then let things unfold as the camera shot their improvisations. One campfire conversation was inspired half by marijuana and half by their feel for the moment:

The Lawyer (Jack Nicholson): "They're not scared of you. They're scared of what you represent to them."

Billy (Dennis Hopper): "Hey man, all we represent to them, man, is someone who needs a haircut."

The Lawyer: "Oh no, what you represent to them is freedom."

Billy: "What the hell's wrong with freedom? Man, that's what it's all about."

The Lawyer: "Oh yeah, that's right, that's what it's all about all right. But talking about it and doing it, that's two different things. I mean, it's real hard to be free when you are bought and sold in the marketplace. But don't ever tell anybody that they're not free because then they gonna get real busy killing and maiming to prove to you that they are. Oh yeah, they gonna talk to you and talk to you and talk to you about individual freedom, but when they see a free individual, it's gonna scare 'em."

Other times, serendipity was the director. On one occasion, the crew arrived at a restaurant in Morganza, Louisiana, to film a scene where locals harass the bikers—only to run into a group of true locals that actually did harass them. Fonda remembered their taunts: "I kin smell 'em!" one local said about the grungy bikers, who just happened to be the director and producer of the film, "Kin yew smell 'em? I kin smell 'em!" Fonda and Hopper enlisted them in the movie, and they repeated everything they had just said, this time with the camera rolling. One of the locals turned out to be a deputy sheriff, pleased to play a role in a real Hollywood movie.

The final—and ongoing—irony is that the movie made big money, money that is still contested between many of the principals in the production of the film. The movie cost $501,000 to make, and according to Hopper, "We made all of our money back the first week. In one theater."

The time was right for *Easy Rider* when it finally rode onto the movie screen, and it was no irony that the film made it big. As Hopper recollected later, "Nobody had ever seen themselves portrayed in a movie. At every love-in across the country people were smoking grass and dropping LSD, while audiences were still watching Doris Day and Rock Hudson."

From the start, Fonda and Hopper knew they had a good thing, and they demanded a share of the profits, 11 percentage points each of the take. And somewhere along the road, this film about down-and-out drifters made Fonda and Hopper millionaires.

It also inspired ongoing legal wrangling between the movie's principals as to who owns the legend. Fonda, Hopper, and Southern have battled for decades now over who authored the script—such as it was. In 1995, Hopper sued Fonda for a larger cut of movie profits. Not happy with the 33 percent of the proceeds he has earned, Hopper wanted 41 percent of the $40 million to $70 million that the movie was estimated to have made since its debut. The legal battles continued.

But the story of *Easy Rider* did not end when Captain America and Billy were gunned down by rednecks in a pickup truck along a nameless stretch of road somewhere in the middle of America. Like the gas that fueled Captain America's chopper, the movie fueled an image of the motorcycle as the Great American Freedom Machine that lives on today as strong as ever.

Decalcomania: Ed "Big Daddy" Roth decal artwork, circa 1970s.

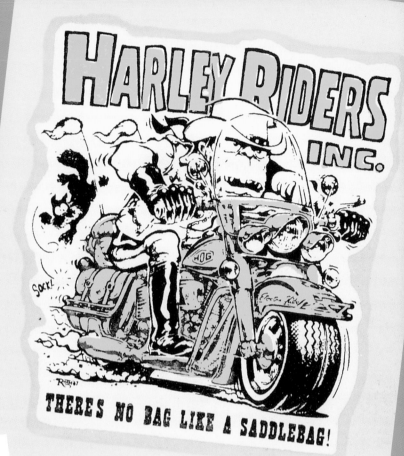

"No Motorcycles Allowed"

By Arlen Ness with Timothy Remus

Arlen Ness is *the* name in custom motorcycles. From humble beginnings painting gas tanks in the evening hours after his day job, Arlen has become the best-known Harley artist wherever customs are spoken of around the globe. Whether it's the bend of a set of bars, the sculpted line of a tank, or the style and color of his paintwork, he has something special, an eye for customizing motorcycles that many others try to emulate but few can equal.

Arlen is also a gracious man. He's friendly and approachable on the streets of Daytona Beach or Sturgis, ready to share ideas or check out your own ride.

Surprisingly, for the man who would make his name with cycles, Arlen grew up in a household with the strict rule "No Motorcycles Allowed," as he relates here.

Though it seems hard to believe, I grew up without any motorcycles. It was my father who established the "No Motorcycles" rule, which meant that most of my early vehicles were cars instead of cycles.

The one exception was a certain Cushman scooter that I brought home during my early high school years. I don't think I was ever off that scooter. I didn't have a permit yet, so I had to stay close to home. I rode it around the block hundreds and hundreds of times each day. I must have worn a groove in the concrete in front of the house I rode that scooter around so much.

It had a body and a two-speed transmission. The shifter was keyed to its shaft and I was always shearing that key. Of course we didn't have the right key, so we would cut a small washer in half with the hacksaw and use that for a key. That would work for about a day's riding and then the key would shear again and the whole thing started over.

Before I was old enough to get a permit to ride the scooter legally, my dad made me sell it and he never would let me buy a real motorcycle.

Later, in high school, I started buying cars and fixing those up. I had a '51 Merc that was pretty cool. Then I sold that and bought a T-Bucket. I put a Caddy engine in the T-bucket and painted it orange.

This was the mid-sixties, and on weekends I did a lot of cruising in the T-bucket. East 14th Street was the place to be, you spent your time going from drive-in to drive-in. The motorcycle guys hung out at The Quarter Pound and I drove by it all the time just to see the bikes. At the time I didn't know a Harley from a BSA, but the ones I liked had that low-slung look. Those turned out to be Harleys, of course, and I wanted one. Heck, I wanted one all the

way back in high school but I could never have one. When I got married, Bev said she would never be married to a guy who rode a motorcycle. In those days a lot of the guys who rode were outlaws and she just didn't want me riding with them.

At this time, I was driving a truck delivering furniture. Each week I would save a few bucks out of my paycheck—I kept that money stashed in the back of my wallet in case a good deal came up on a bike. There was this cement factory in Oakland that I drove by sometimes when I was doing deliveries and there were always a couple of pretty nice Harleys parked there. Sometimes I went out of my way just to drive by and have another look at those bikes. One day there was a for-sale sign on one of the Harleys at the cement plant. The bike was 300 bucks and that's about how much I had saved in the back of my wallet.

I still didn't know anything about them at all, but an old friend from high school had a Harley. He went with me to look over the bike and said it was OK, so I did the deal. This Knucklehead had a suicide clutch and I didn't really know how to ride yet so my friend rode it to his house for me. He lived a mile from my house and I had to ride it the rest of the way home. I bet I killed it a thousand times between his place and mine. Finally, I pulled it up at my house and rapped the pipes, Bev opened the door, saw me on the bike and slammed the door.

I did learn to ride it, and then I met other guys with bikes and rode with them. At the time I bought that first bike I already knew how to paint, so I put on a peanut tank and painted the Knucklehead right away. I put on some different bars too, but there really wasn't much stuff available in those days.

"the bike builders encyclopedia"

Choppers magazine

MAY 1969 75¢

a Roth publication

SMITTY'S CHICAGOLAND SPORTSTER!

j.c. mcfadden tells all about RAM TUNING the intake and exhaust manifolds.

Once I painted the Knucklehead, other guys asked me to paint their bikes. I painted motorcycles part time for almost two years and pretty soon I had a lot of paint work, but I was still driving the truck delivering furniture during the day. I painted after my regular job and on Sundays and still couldn't get all the work done. I eventually decided I didn't have enough time to do the painting so I quit driving furniture and started working as a carpenter. That way I had more free time because we worked four and a half days a week with days off whenever it rained. I did that for about six months.

Finally, I quit the carpenter's job and began just working at home full time. It was a big deal to do this because I already had a wife and two kids. Then the problem was my place became a hangout. Whenever one of the guys had a day off he came over with a six pack. So I didn't make any money that way because I didn't get any work done. That's why I rented the store, the little one on East 14th Street in San Leandro. It was open from 6 to 11 p.m., and people could see me there, so I wasn't bothered at home and got more work done that way. Then I started making parts. The ramhorn handlebars, for example, were one of my own products and they sold very well. Eventually we added tires and learned more about business at the same time.

In those days I didn't have enough money to just go out and buy another bike to customize. So I kept working on the Knucklehead. The third time I built that bike I made a sissy bar and a set of up-swept pipes. The rear fender came from an automotive continental kit and I put on a 21-inch front wheel. That was just coming into style at the time. The Avon was hard to get, so if you had a 21, you had a pretty cool bike.

Later, when I learned more about motors, I added the supercharger and grafted a Sportster transmission onto the back of the Big Twin engine. Nobody was doing work like that at the time. Eventually I got together enough money to buy a wrecked Sportster, which I fixed up and sold, and then I could start buying and selling a few bikes.

But I always kept the Knuckle and I'm really glad now that I did, because not very many guys still own their first Harley.

Choppers Magazine, circa 1960s.

The HIMSL fiberglas trike body, $149.95

This strong polyster body is sent to you ready for paint & upholstery. Fits most three wheeler frames. Send at least 50% deposit & the rest C.O.D. All bodies sent freight collect.

HIMSL'S
Show Creations & Custom Pai
939 LANDINI LANE, CONCORD, CALIF. 94520

Chopper-builder
advertisements,
circa 1960s–1970s.

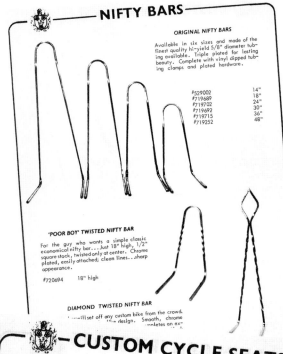

NIFTY BARS

ORIGINAL NIFTY BARS

Available in six sizes and made of the finest quality hi-yield 5/8" diameter tubing available. Triple plated for lasting beauty. Complete with vinyl dipped tubing clamps and plated hardware.

#529002	14"
#719689	18"
#719702	24"
#719692	30"
#719715	36"
#719252	48"

'POOR BOY' TWISTED NIFTY BAR

For the guy who wants a simple classic economical nifty bar...Just 18" high, 1/2" square stock, twisted only at center. Chrome plated, easily attached; clean lines...sharp appearance.

#720694   18" high

DIAMOND TWISTED NIFTY BAR

...will set off any custom bike from the crowd. ...the design.   Smooth, chrome ...pletes an ex-

CUSTOM CYCLE SEATS

DIAMOND STUDDED SEAT

Deep, luxurious pleats with contrasting silver colored buttons. Universal front bracket included. Black naugahyde cover, molded foam padding.

713724

HONDA 350 MARK 2

Newest addition to the Honda Series. 1 backrest, self supporting, comes comple with hardware, black naugahyde cove molded foam padding, hiback also finishe on the back side.

#543758	Black
#543761	Brown

WIDOWMAKER MARK I

For any hardtail or rigid bike. Self supporting hiback, universal bolt locations in the nose and rear of seat. Black naugahyde, matching buttons, molded foam padding.

#543266

CUSTOM COMBINATION SEAT

A banana seat teamed with a 30", fully padded sissy bar. Deep 3-D pleats, black vinyl cover - aluminum base.

#713656

STINGER MARK 2

Deep, sculptured comfort, for rider and passenger. Fits all rigid and hardtail bikes. Guaranteed to keep its shape. Black naugahyde

#543253

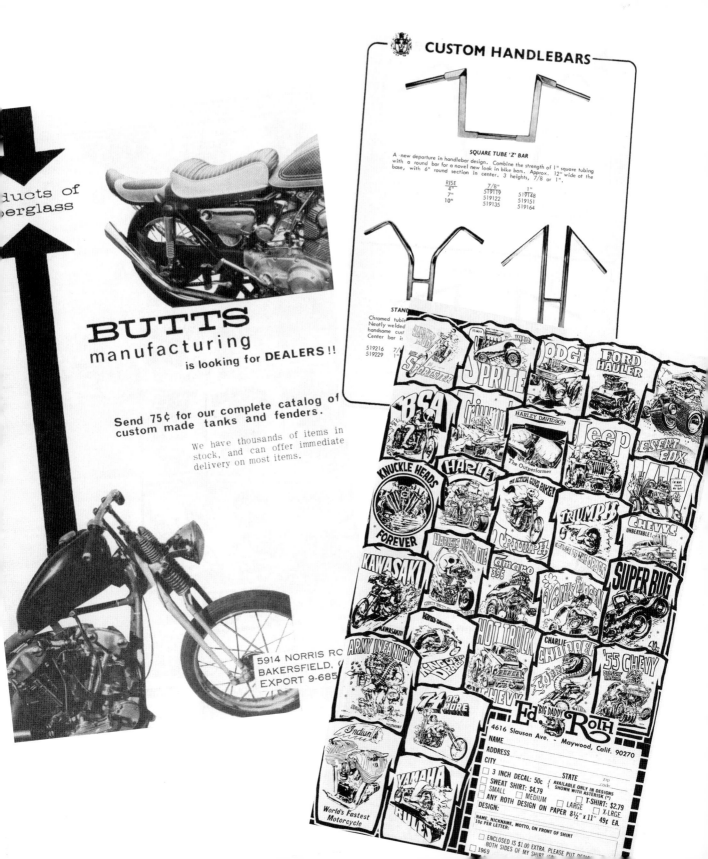

Choppers Then and Now

By Alan Mayes

Alan Mayes was a conservative participant in the first chopper craze of the 1960s. He gave his new BSA a lime-green metal-flake paint job and gave up its front fender to the cause. Due to horror stories about broken slugs, the 8-inch AEE slugs that he bought were thankfully never installed.

Today, Alan is managing editor of *The Horse Back Street Choppers* magazine and a regular contributor to *IronWorks*. His personal stable of bikes currently includes a Harley Ironhead Sportster chopper project, a Buell chopper, a Norton Commando, and a couple of newer European bikes.

In this essay, he looks back at choppers of the past, examines current stylings, and muses over what may come in the future.

Who Knew?

How could we have known that what was once considered avant-garde thirty-plus years ago would become mainstream? I'm talking about choppers, of course—the motorized darlings that are the object of affection for America's latest love affair with self-propelled conveyances.

Back in the late 1960s and early 1970s, choppers enjoyed their first wave of popularity. But things were much different then. In those days, reasons for building choppers had a rebellious root. Foremost seemed to be non-conformity. While Joe Average was learning to "meet the nicest people on a Honda," Benny Badass was trying to convince those same folks that he was *not* one of those nice people. Benny did that by making his bike as radical and different as he could. Changes included radically raking the front end, then extending the front forks at least two inches longer than anyone else had done. Hang a sissy bar out back and spray on some metalflake paint, and *voilà*, two-wheeled individuality was born.

The vision of choppers was etched into young heads through movies like *Easy Rider*, *Wild Angels*, and others. With the exception of *Easy Rider*, those formula B-flicks usually showed gangs of wild bikers terrorizing the countryside on their noisy—and usually dirty—choppers. They were the epitome of non-conformity, causing grandmas and children alike to shake in their shoes. Magazines like *Street Chopper*, *Custom Chopper*, *Easyriders*, *Chopper Guide*, and many others sprang up to feed the frenzy. That few of those original titles survive today is testament to the fickle nature of the motorcycling public.

Fast forward thirty-five years and choppers are in vogue again. Or at least motorcycles that are *called* choppers are. Even such straight-laced entities as the Discovery Channel are now associated with the bikes. In fact, credit the Discovery Channel for much of the chopper's move to Main Street. Their two series—*American Chopper* and *Biker Build-Off*—have enjoyed phenomenal acceptance and have helped to propel names like Indian Larry, Billy Lane, Paul Teutel (junior and senior), and Jesse James to national attention. Even those who have never ridden a motorcycle, or even shown any interest in them, know who these guys are.

Most of the people reading this book are probably somewhat motorcycle savvy, but it's interesting to note the differences in acceptance of chopper-style motorcycles among the average person on the street today as compared to many years ago. This was brought to my attention recently in Ft. Worth, Texas, as I was test riding one of American IronHorse's new models.

I was attending the dealer intro of their new models and was offered a bike to use during my stay in Ft. Worth. I chose one of their less-chopper-styled models, the Slammer. The Slammer is a low-slung machine without the usual chopper accoutrements of a long front end or stretched frame. Even though I was riding a $32,000 flame-painted hot rod of a motorcycle, I was invisible to the general public.

Another journalist I compared notes with had picked one of American IronHorse's Texas Chopper models. Even though it was painted a blend-in shade of blue, he reported that every time he stopped somewhere, people swarmed over the bike. Little kids waved at him at stoplights. My bike and I were ignored. He and his were stars.

There are a couple of funny things about today's chopper craze. One is that most hardcore traditional chopper guys are not involved in it. There are a few notable exceptions to that, but for the most part, long-time chopper riders are pretty much ignoring the current chopper craze, or at least shaking their heads at it. Unless they make their livings building bikes, that is. Hey, a guy needs to make a living and most feel they'd better grab the apples while they are ripe.

The second point is really much to blame for the first. The motorcycles being built today and called choppers are not choppers in the strictest sense. They are new bikes assembled in a chopper *style*. Nothing was chopped; hence, they are not technically choppers. Sorry, French fries that are baked in the oven are not French fries, either. They're baked French-cut potatoes, potatoes that *look* like French fries.

And therein lies the rub. Old school chopper guys don't build new bikes from all-new components, buying a frame here, an engine there, fenders and gas tank from another catalog. Such bikes are custom bikes, but not choppers. Real choppers are made from existing motorcycles that have been . . . that's right, chopped!

Early choppers were fashioned by heavily modifying stock, existing motorcycles. Frames were raked in the garage by cutting behind the neck and fabricating new pieces to fill in the gap. Forks were extended by making new tubes and fitting them to the existing triple trees. Sometimes they were made with solid front tubes and no suspension. I didn't say the old days were smarter; I'm just explaining the differences!

There were many other things done back in the old days that are thankfully not being repeated these days by savvy builders. One of those was the use of slugs to extend forks. One of the cheap ways to make a front end longer was to add slugs to the top legs of a telescopic fork. Basically, these were just machined metal pieces, offered in various lengths, which screwed onto the top of the fork tube, lengthening it by the given amount. Want to extend the front end by ten inches? Screw in a set of ten-inch slugs. Slugs were offered by companies such as Tom and Rose McMullen's AEE Choppers for everything from Harley-Davidsons to BSAs, Triumphs, Honda 450s, and just about any other bike you can think of. They were extremely unsafe, especially in lengths that exceeded the distance between the upper and lower triple clamps. Stories were rampant about someone riding his bike along at a fair clip, only to have the slug break, usually at the base of the threads. The results could be fatal.

The aforementioned one-piece tubes were famous for failure, too. See, the styles one could get by with on smooth California freeways might prove to be unwise designs on a frost-heave pot-holed chunk of Michigan or New Jersey byway. Long, bouncy front ends have been known to snap in two, or at least fold in half, when the front tire fell into a chuckhole.

While we're on the subject of front ends, a couple of styles popular in the early days were springers and girders. Aside from their aesthetic beauty, springers were popular because they were plentiful. Remember, 1930s and 1940s Harleys and Indians were only twenty-five to forty years old then, the equivalent of a 1965 to 1980 bike today, not all that old. They were also fairly easy to make or to modify for someone with some mechanical and welding skills.

The same holds true with girders. The early chopper magazines had many advertisements for girder and springer front forks built in someone's backyard or garage "factory." Though some girders and springers of the day, such as the ones built by Durfee and by Smith Brothers & Fetrow, were well engineered and built with quality and safety in mind (and are sought out today by traditional chopper builders), some others were less than safe. Reports of broken welds and riders catapulted over handlebars were not uncommon.

What was extremely different about building a chopper back then was that there was only a minimum number of aftermarket parts to work with, at least as compared to today's huge market. And that's how the term "chopper" really got its origin. Guys had to *chop* their stock bikes to get the look they wanted. Originally, there were no custom frame manufacturers, so the idea of stretching and raking a frame meant the ol' hacksaw and welder were employed. Around the end of the 1960s and beginning of the 1970s, some companies started to build custom frames that utilized the look chopper builders were after. Such names as Santee, Paughco, Amen, and a few others come to mind. Santee and Paughco are still in business and still building frames. The name Amen is alive, but with a different direction of building mostly high-dollar, very low-slung customs.

In 1968, bobbed fenders were just that, stock fenders that had been cut shorter—bobbed. Although there are chopper purists still doing that, the more common origin of a so-called bobbed fender now is a catalog. New fender, pre-bobbed, made in Taiwan.

Early choppers often wore a combination of parts that may have come from several different motorcycles. A frame from one bike—say, a 1940s Harley Knucklehead—may have been mated to an engine from another, like a late 1950s Panhead. A springer off a 1938 bike may have been extended fourteen inches in the garage. A ribbed fender from the neighbor's Triumph was then shortened and painted to match the tank off of Uncle Louie's Mustang. A chopper was born.

Yes, boys and girls, there actually was a motorcycle called the Mustang. And many of those humble little bikes donated their gas tanks to the first chopper craze. They were so popular that Paughco and some others still make reproduction versions. In fact, I have one of those new Mustang tanks in my garage right now, waiting for my next project to begin.

But enough of the past. What about "choppers" of today? There are actually a couple of different schools of thought on choppers today. For want of better terms, we'll call them Old School and New School although I hate those names because they are confusing—or confused. I don't know which. Maybe I'm the one that's confused.

New School first. Into this group I would throw all the bikes that are choppers in name only. Lump the boys from Orange County Choppers, the dozens of small builders around the country turning out new chopper-styled bikes,

CUSTOM SPRINGERS

DIAMOND MODEL SPRINGER

Solid steel bars set in diamond fashion form this distinctly unique springer. All parts are solid steel, wear points have bronze oilite bearings. Finished in triple chrome plate. 8 to 16" lengths, others on special order only.

#756008	8" Extended
#756011	10" Extended
#756024	13" Extended
#756037	16" Extended
*#756040	19" Extended
*#756053	22" Extended

*Special Order Only

TWISTED MODEL SPRINGER

Same basic features as the model at left except front bars are twisted. Gives a highlight effect. Triple chrome plated. NOTE: Handlebar riser not included. (see page 149) 8" to 16" lengths, others on special order.

#756150	8" Extended
#756163	10" Extended
#756176	13" Extended
#756189	16" Extended
*#756192	19" Extended
*#756202	22" Extended

*Special Order Only

ALLOW 4 WEEKS FOR 19" OR 22" SPRINGERS

SPRINGER AXLE

5/8" steel axle, approx. 7 1/2" long, threaded on both ends, includes 2 hex n... Axle and nuts plated to resist rust.

DELUXE SPRINGER AXLE

For custom spool wheel. Inclu... steel axle approx. 7 3/4", 2 stee... and 2 chromed spike nuts. Over... about 13 1/2".

SPORTSTYL PADS, SEATS

TRIANGLE PAD

Unusual, steeple shaped pad. 18 1/2" high, black vinyl, rolled welt. Features 3 dimensional diamond pleat-2 1/2' thick. (No hardware). Made to fit with Diamond Twisted Nifty Bar.

#719511   Black Pad Only

SPORTSTYL SISSY BAR PADS

Sportstyl Sissy Bar Pads will fit all Sissy Bars and Nifty Bars. Made of the best weather-resistant plastic vinyl, plywood backs, all seams concealed. Complete with mounting bolts and brackets.

#719359	Plain Black
#719346	Pleated Black
#719333	Pleated White
#719320	Red Metal Flake Pleated
#719317	Blue Metal Flake Pleated

NIFTY BAR SLIP-ON COVER

Black vinyl slip-on cover slips down over Nifty Bar. Comes in 5 different sizes, fits all 14" 18", 24", 30", 36" Nifty Bars.

#504700	Black Pleated 14"
#719249	Black Pleated 18"
#719236	Black Pleated 24"
#719223	Black Pleated 30"
#719210	Black Pleated 36"

and the "production" chopper builders (an oxymoron if there ever was one) like American IronHorse, Big Dog, and Swift.

These bikes are in almost every example brand-new bikes built from brand-new components in a style reminiscent of true choppers. That is, they have long front ends and raked frames, usually stretched in the backbone and downtube. The majority of these bikes are built from catalog parts, starting with a catalog frame carrying a Manufacturer's Statement of Origin (MSO). To that the assembler will have usually added a catalog tank, either from the frame manufacturer or another company. From another source will come a front end. Wheels and engine will usually come from other various sources. In the case of the individual builder or small shop, these bikes will have to be registered as "special build" or "assembly" or something similar, depending on the state the bike is registered in.

Another twist on this formula exists. It is possible to buy a chopper kit bike from companies like Bikers' Choice and Drag Specialties that includes everything but the gasoline needed to build a rideable, running "chopper." Some kits even include the oil and brake fluid. All you do is bolt it together and paint it.

The factory-built bikes like American IronHorse, Big Dog, and several others will actually have an MSO that carries the manufacturer's name and will be registered as that brand of bike. As I've stated before, these motorcycles are not choppers in the strictest sense of the term. They are, however, what the motorcycle newcomers and Discovery Channel watchers think of when someone mentions the term "chopper."

Old School choppers are a different animal altogether. These are bikes being built in much the same way

bikes were built thirty to forty years ago. The builders of these bikes gather parts from swap meets, junk yards, buddies' garages, eBay (a huge, global swap meet), their own donor bikes, and local dealers' back rooms. Then they fabricate mounts, cut here, weld there, and make things work together that don't usually belong together. The result is often a bike that is very distinctive and unlike any other.

These bikes create two different reactions in those who first see them. They cause gearheads with an eye for creativity to smile. They cause the fans of new school bikes to turn away, looking for something more shiny and expensive.

That brings us to another differentiator in the New School–Old School discussion. Though it seems extreme, one of the New School Orange County Choppers bikes recently sold through Sam's Club (yes, *that* Sam's Club) for $137,000. To be fair, that price included a weekend for two in New York City, so let's say $130,000 for the bike. Yeah, one bike. American IronHorse's factory choppers run in the $30,000 range, give or take five grand, depending on options.

I know a small custom builder in the Midwest who recently built a beautiful Old School bike by gathering parts from the various aforementioned sources. It has a new engine that he built himself from purchased components, a swap meet frame, and various parts from old bikes, tractors, and cars. He plans to sell the bike for $36,000. He confided to me that he has $6,500 invested in it.

There is another group of builders that is somewhat in between the Old School and New School. Let's call it Middle School—or maybe Reform School. The most famous of these among the current movie-star-popular builders are Billy Lane and Jesse James. Either of these fairly young builders has the ability to personally fabricate almost any component on one of their motorcycle creations, and they often do. Both know their way around a planishing hammer, an English wheel, and any other fabricating utensil you can name. They can build flashy, New School bikes with the best of them, winning build-offs, and wooing fans begging to be deemed worthy to buy one of their customs. But for themselves, for their own use, they usually go with an Old School style of bike. The late Indian Larry fit this niche as well.

There are really so many different types of motorcycles, such varied tastes, and so many opposing opinions, that it is difficult to try to define what makes something Old School or New School or any other category. Smarter men and women than I have tried to do so with limited success. Considering it from that point of view, I don't know why my opinions would be any better received.

Forget I said anything.

The Lawyer: "Well, you boys don't look like you're from this part of the country. **You're lucky** I'm here to see that you don't get into anything. Well, they got this here scissor-happy 'Beautify America' thing going on around here. They're trying to make everybody look like Yul Brynner."

Chapter 10

On the Road

Speed!

It had a good smell and a pretty sound. You taste it . . . **hear it sing** while you watched things streak by and felt the **heart-tripping chill** of it sometimes on close shaves to your bones. Then the deep breath and you were with-it. Really living it up. And life was swift and **worth the risk.**

—Edward De Roo, *Go, Man, Go!* 1959

Motorcycles as a Way of Life

By Jean Davidson

Jean Davidson hails from the family whose name graces the gas tank. The granddaughter of Harley-Davidson cofounder Walter Davidson, she's naturally an avid fan of motorcycles. Which should come as no surprise.

Justly proud of her family and its Motor Company, Jean researched details of the history and wrote *Growing Up Harley-Davidson: Memoirs of a Motorcycle Dynasty*. The book uncovered many new aspects of the story behind the world's most famous motorcycle.

That memoir was followed by *Jean Davidson's Harley-Davidson Family Album*, an illustrated scrapbook of family, company, and motorcycle lore.

The following excerpt comes from *Growing Up Harley-Davidson*, telling of Jean's own first ride. No need to question what brand of motorcycle she rode.

My earliest memories are not of birds chirping outside my nursery window or my mother cooing to me in my crib. No, my earliest memories are of the roar of a Harley-Davidson V-twin motorcycle engine as my dad rode to and from work. My dad was Gordon McLay Davidson, and work for him was the Harley-Davidson Motor Company. We are part of the Davidson family; my dad was the eldest son of Harley-Davidson founder Walter Davidson, the firm's first president.

When I was very young, my dad would put me behind him on the seat of his Harley-Davidson and say, "Hang on!" I was too small to see around him so I would just lay my head against his back and feel the vibrations through his leather jacket. Even at such a young age, I loved the sound of that engine and the excitement that I felt on a Harley-Davidson. As far back as I remember, motorcycles have been a way of life for my family. I grew up on a motorcycle, as did my father, my grandfather, and my cousins.

I first rode a Harley-Davidson when I was three, but that doesn't quite count as I rode in the seat of a sidecar while my dad drove. I wasn't much older when my dad would place me behind him on the seat of his Harley-Davidson and say, "Hang on!" as we took off. My earliest memories are of the roar of a Harley-Davidson V-twin motorcycle engine.

When I was twelve years old in 1949, Dad came home to the lake on a large Harley 74. It was a big, beautiful motorcycle and I begged him to let me try riding it. He laughed and said, "No," because my feet barely touched the ground when I straddled it.

That didn't stop me. I kept pestering him, and finally he said, "OK, but don't cry if you get hurt." My mother heard this and naturally did not like the idea at all. In my mind, that made it even more exciting.

Dad showed me which hand controlled the gas and where the brake was. I got on and thought, "This is easy." I turned the throttle all the way open and at what felt like full speed, I rode that beautiful new Harley right into the lake. Mom screamed while Dad laughed and said, "I told you so."

I burned my leg on the exhaust, but worst of all, my pride was hurt. I immediately made a vow that I would try this venture again as soon as I was a little older.

When I was fifteen years old in 1952, I wanted to go to Milwaukee to visit a boyfriend. I did not have a driver's license, so I decided to ride the twenty-five miles on a new Harley-Davidson 74 that my father had left at the lake. I had been practicing in the front yard since my fateful ride into the lake, so I was full of confidence that I would do just fine on the roads. My only concern was that if I tipped over I knew I was not strong enough to pick up the bike.

It was a grand ride. I was wearing a swimming suit and tennis shoes. I enjoyed the look of other motorists as I zoomed by; I presumed they were not used to seeing a young girl on a motorcycle and was all the more proud for it. When I rolled in the driveway of his house, I gunned the engine to let him know I had arrived. I will never forget the look of shock on his mother's face when she looked out to see this skinny girl in a swimming suit sitting on a big Harley in her driveway and smiling to beat the band.

She came running out and queried me, "What were you thinking? You don't weigh more than ninety pounds! What were you planning to do if the police caught you or you tipped over that big motorcycle?"

I was so proud of my accomplishment that I couldn't understand why she thought it was a foolish thing to do. As usual, I had no answers; I just thought it would be fun and so went right ahead and did it.

Most of my life was spent doing whatever sounded like fun. Water-skiing by moonlight sounded exciting so a group of us kids pushed my father's Chris-Craft out onto the lake as quietly as we could and then started the engine. What fun we had, whipping around on the lake and taking turns driving and skiing. The big concern was if one of us would fall down, the boat would not be able to find us in the dark of the night. But of course that just added to the excitement.

After I discovered that kissing boys was a fine thing, my interest in boys changed. Yet in my teens when a boy asked me out on a date, many times the first question out of his mouth was, "Can you get me a motorcycle?" I was often hurt because I wanted him to be only interested in me. Anyway, what did he think? I could just call up my dad and Dad would give him a motorcycle. No matter how silly it sounded, it happened over and over again.

My answer to this dilemma was to not tell people my last name; I even went so far as saying my name was Smith. I wanted to be sure these boys liked me for who I was and not for what they thought I might get them.

One time, I became good friends with a young man from the other side of town. We shared many good times, and finally I decided it would not make any difference in our relationship if I took him home and he saw how my family lived. He saw the big motorcycle in the garage and the house with all the help and our relationship ended because he felt out of place.

Later in life, I heard my future mother-in-law telling her friends her son was marrying a Davidson. She wasn't saying that her son was marrying a wonderful girl, which maybe she thought, but the most important thing to her was that I was a Davidson.

Still to this day I do not openly tell people, "I am a Davidson from Harley-Davidson." I want people to like and accept me for my own unique qualities.

Proud Silent Gray Fellow riders, circa 1920s.

The Old Bike in the Barn, or, How My Wife's Classic Harley Got Off on the Wrong Foot

By Allan Girdler

Allan Girdler is full of stories. And full of more than one story about a bike found in a barn.

Everyone knows at least one good "bike in a barn" tale—the kind of barn find of which all motorcyclists dream. Whether it's an old Harley-Davidson, Indian, or anything in between, there's always that hint of lust that lingers after the story's done.

In this story, Allan tells of a twist on the classic tale—a different sort of Harley-Davidson that works in a different sort of way.

Just because the Old Bike in the Barn is one of those urban legends, like the $10 Cadillac and the alligator in the sewer, doesn't mean it can't happen.

Not only are there old bikes in barns, they can be found by real people, you and me for instance, while the other legends always happen to people from whoever's telling the tale.

Agreed? OK, because first, this is a true story, reported by a man who actually did retrieve an old motorcycle from a barn, plus second, the happy ending isn't gonna be what the reader expects.

Once upon several years ago my friend Paul remarked to my wife and I that his aunt and uncle had a ranch in western Nevada. On that ranch was a barn and in the barn was an old Harley-Davidson.

Husband and wife leaned forward and chorused, "Tell us more."

The story then became believable. The old motorcycle was relatively old, in that it was a 1964 model, as is old but not antique, nor very valuable. It was a Sprint, a single-cylinder 250cc model made in Italy when Harley-Davidson owned a company there and was trying to compete in the small motorcycle market.

Sprints were good machines, unappreciated mostly because they weren't the big twins traditional Harley buyers wanted and because the bikes were labeled Harley-Davidson, which discouraged non-Harley buyers.

In this instance, Paul's cousin had used the Sprint to commute to college and when she graduated she rode the bike into her folks' barn and left it; shabby, neglected, intact, and operational.

The special circumstances here begin with wife Nancy not having begun riding until she was in her 20s. She'd always sort of envied my having begun in my teens, and been even more envious that my first Harley was older than me.

The Sprint in the barn, remember, was made in 1964.

Nancy was born in 1965.

Further, while we had his-and-her Sportsters, mine orange with white trim, hers white with orange trim, and we both had Honda enduro bikes, we hadn't reach spousal equity because I was a Harley up on her, in the form of a 1970 XR-750, a TT racer assembled from used parts and licensed for the street. I got to show the bike, and show off and go racing, all of which looked like fun, which of course it is, and looked like something she'd like to do.

Thus, we trucked to the ranch, dragged the Sprint out from behind the piles of tack and broken furniture and hosed it down.

Not bad, at first glance. The ten-plus years had been in dry air, so while the tires and other rubber parts were gone there wasn't much rust and everything that should revolve or rotate, did.

As usually happens, the big pieces were present, and the little pieces, a knob not here, a switch or button not there, were gone. (This is a good thing, in that little parts cost less than big parts, and a bad thing in that connecting rods are always on the market but a badge or shield or the reflector for the taillight used just that one year, can be tough to find.)

We trucked the Sprint home and I cleaned and freed everything within reach; no point in taking everything apart until you have some idea of where it's supposed to be.

Tires and tubes were easy. The brakes worked, and although the battery was terminally (sorry) dead, Aermacchi was used to the vagaries of Italian electrics and there was a secret switch, so when (not if) the battery was dead, the juice from the generator was routed direct to the points and coil, giving the extra voltage needed to fire the engine.

This narrative is moving faster than the actual project did. We parked the Sprint in the back of our barn and when I had a spare hour or so, I'd haul it out and fiddle.

There's a good company supplying Sprint bits so I ordered all the missing parts I could see weren't there, so to speak.

No doubt the bodywork needed to be straight and painted, the seat had to be recovered and so forth.

You'll understand I was fooling myself here, eh? There was spark, the carb was cleaned, the engine was freed and so was the clutch, there seemed to be compression, that is, I could push the kick lever through slow and easy and feel the sequence of strokes.

Yes! Why not?!

And it worked. Couple kicks through with choke on and switch off, then vigorous application of the right boot and it ran! OK, not exactly as smooth as a sewing machine but it did run, and would pull me up and down the driveway and around the farm, after one initial revelation.

Um, this part is confession. I had forgotten that between the time of my first Harley, a 1934 VL, and the Sprint of 1964, there had been a series of ergonomic revolutions.

That VL had hand shift and foot clutch, just like a car, in large degree because the springs needed back then were too stiff for hand power, or maybe it was because that's the way they'd always done it.

Smaller motorcycles, the Harley hummers, the post-war Indians, the newly imported English motorcycles and then the Japanese, used foot shift and hand clutch.

They used them any way they pleased, as in some had the shift lever on the right, some on the left. Some had neutral at the bottom of the pattern, some put N between 1 and 2. This maker might have first gear up, the rest down, while the factory in the next country had first gear down and the rest up.

Nor was that all. It was traditional for racing motorcycles to have first gear at the top as you could push down with more authority than you could toe up.

And there was marketing. When Harley-Davidson introduced the two-stroke singles and then the contemporary Model K, the gearshifts were by foot, on the right side because that's where the rivals, imported and domestic, had their levers.

Several years later, when the FL series acquired foot shift and hand clutch, the levers were on the left: Less linkage was required, although I suspect the big reason was that arch-rival Indian had always had the (hand) shift on the right, while Harley's was on the left so no true H-D rider would move over.

Why all this? Because there was a generational gap here. I grew up with the revolution, as in hand to foot and foot to hand, then right side shifts for BSA and Triumph, left side for Hondas until the companies got smart and the world's governments got dictatorial and it was decreed and agreed that all motorcycles would have their gearshifts on the left, with first gear down, then neutral and then the other speeds, literally shifting up.

I wonder who he was?

I wish I had a
machine like that.

I could make better time
than I can on my bicycle.

Perhaps
I'll get one
some day.

—Victor Appleton, *Tom Swift and His Motor Cycle*, 1910

Happy Harley-Davidson riders, circa 1920–1950s.

Sounds confusing? It's really not. Consider when you had a truck with stick and a car with automatic. When you drive both every day, you not only do so without bother, you don't even need to think about it. Like breathing, it's something your mind takes care of without bothering your consciousness with the details.

So when I headed down the road, I'd clicked into second and realized it and clicked up into first, oh yeah, of course.

But when Nancy came out to ride her new old Harley, she threw a leg over and looked happy, I mean, the Sprint was as light as her enduro bike and as low as her Sportster.

"Okay," I said not thinking about it, "Take it easy, and don't forget the shift is on the right and first is up."

"What?" (She had of course no inkling of this because I hadn't thought it was worth talking about until now.)

"Oh, yeah, shift is on the right."

"Why?"

"I dunno. . . . Because it is."

"That's ridiculous, and I don't know how."

"Sure you do, just toe up for first and down for the rest of the gears."

"Up for first? But first is always down."

And for her of course it always had been, with the bikes when she took the Motorcycle Safety Foundation Course, and with her enduro bike and my Sportster and her Sportster and the Dyna Glide in the demo fleet at Daytona's Bike Week.

If there was a drawback to being younger than a 1964 Harley-Davidson, we had found it.

Displaying no confidence at all, most unusual for her, Nancy dutifully clicked up, revved the engine, eased out the clutch and rode down to the edge of the orchard, around the farm and back home.

She was not a happy biker.

"Whuddaya think?"

"What do I think? I don't know what I think. All I could think was, am I going to mess up the shifting."

She retrieved her leg, if that's how to describe the reverse of throwing a leg over, and went back to her chores. I put the Sprint back in our barn.

That's where it was for the next month, and the month after that, until one day I remarked she seemed to have lost interest.

She had, she said, and in keeping with her generous nature she suggested that if we sold the Sprint and her enduro bike, which she hadn't ridden since she crashed out of Barstow-to-Vegas, we (catch the plural here) could make the down payment on the remains of an XR-750 a pal had seen neglected in a repair shop near Vancouver.

And that's how the script worked out. The second XR has been rescued and restored, the enduro went to a good home, the Sprint is sort of back in the barn except the new owner knows what he's got and needs only time.

Nancy meanwhile is riding her Sportster, the only motorcycle she really wants to ride until she finishes graduate school and is presented (can't resist, sorry) with a Dyna Glide.

She's earned it.

A skittish **motor-bike** with a **touch of blood** in it is better than all the riding animals on earth, because of its logical extension of our faculties, and the hint, the provocation, to excess conferred by its honeyed untired smoothness.

—T. E. Lawrence, a.k.a. Lawrence of Arabia

"MOTOR - AMERICANA"

a c a SPIRIT 76

ROAD RACING EXTRAVAGANZA
WILLOW SPRINGS RACEWAY in ROSAMOND

SATURDAY, JULY 2

Field meet for dirt and street bikes. Trophies in all classes. Sign-up closes 10:30 a.m. Also on Saturday, grand prix scrambles. Trophies in all classes. Black-top, dirt and sand.
Saturday night discotheque dance at start-finish line. Midnight Saturday economy run. Full lighting equipment required. Trophies in all classes.

SUNDAY,

Grand prix and p
race. Entries clos
Admission $2.00
Inquiries 145-B W
ton, California
714) 847-7629.

Motorcycle race posters,
circa 1950s–1970s.

Route 31 or 68 to

KENTON, O.
FAIRGROUNDS

MOTORCYCLE
RACES

PROFESSIONAL

4 STAR

FLAT TRACK

FREE PARKING

A.M.A. SANCTIONED
and N.W.O.M.A.

ADULT ADMISSION $3.00
POKER RUN 11 A.M.—MILLSTREAM, FINDLAY TO RACE MEET

NINE EVENTS

SUNDAY
T.T. 12:00

RACES
2:30 P.M.

JULY 15, 1973

Sponsored by KENTON LIGHTNING RIDERS MOTORCYCLE CLUB, Inc.

Springfield Commercial Printing, Inc., Springfield, Ohio

NATIONAL ROAD RACES
RIVERSIDE INTERNATIONAL RACEWAY
DEC. 11

PRACTICE STARTS A
1st EVENT 12
GRAND PRIX & PRODUC

aca

Motorcycles return to Carlsbad raceway's new road race course. This is the final national championship race of the year. Top riders plus the popular "production" class.

american cycle association
national championship
CARLSBAD RACEWAY 1965

ALL ACA CLASSES
INCLUDING THE 100cc CLASS.
ALSO TWO RACES FOR THE
"PRODUCTION" CLASS. PRACTICE
BEGINS AT 9:30. ENTRIES CLOSE
AT 11:30.

NOV. 28 th **12:30 pm**

Entries and inquiries: 145-B West Whiting, Fullerton, Calif.

Motorcycle racing posters, circa 1960s–1970s.

The Riders of the Mile-A-Minute Wheels

By Ralph Marlow

In the early days of motorcycling, the Big Five Motorcycle Boys were the fictional heroes of many an American youth. In a long-running series of novels penned by author Ralph Marlow, the boys rolled across America—and into the daydreams of teens wishing they too owned a Harley-Davidson or one of the other newfangled machines on the market.

The Big Five Motorcycle Boys was far form the sole series of motorcycle-oriented books available for hungry readers in the pioneering days of cycling. The Motor Boys series authored by Clarence Young may have been the first in the mid-1900s. This was followed by Andrew Carey Lincoln's Motorcycle Chums series about 1910. And the titles kept on coming. Most of these books were Horatio Alger-styled rags-to-riches themes: With perseverance, honesty, and a reliable-running motorcycle, the heroes could accomplish anything!

This excerpt is from the first chapter of *The Big Five Motorcycle Boys in Tennessee Wilds*, or *The Secret of Walnut Ridge*, published by Marlow in 1914. The writing is quaint and characteristic of motorcycling in the day.

"**B**etter bring your motorcycle in under the trees, Hanky Panky, with the rest off our machines."

"Sure, Rod, I mean to do the same, after I get rested up a bit. That last run up-hill and down, was a swift one, believe me."

"But say, did any of you notice me turning a flapjack on the way; or taking one of my old-time headers; tell me that?"

"No, Rooster, you've struck your gait, all right, it seems, and away down in old Tennessee at that, where the going ain't such great shakes to boast of."

"Thank you, Josh; I'm doing my level best. But Elmer warned us before we started on this trip to the South, that we'd likely have some hard bumps to knock up against."

"It was a ride on velvet, though, coming down through the Blue Grass country of Kentucky, near Lexington; own up to that, suh!" said the boy who seemed to be the Elmer in question; and whose voice had the indescribable musical quality that so frequently marks the native born son of Dixieland.

"That's all right, Elmer, but we've sure paid up for it, after climbing all sorts of hills, and polishing through bad roads ever since. My arms are sore with holding my machine in the middle of the track, and that's as true as my name's Josh Whitcomb."

There were five of the wanderers, all boys of about the same age; and as a rule sturdy of build, as though accustomed to outdoor sports that go to bring the hue of health to the cheeks.

Besides Josh Whitcomb, who seemed to be a rather impatient sort of a chap, there was Roderic Bradley, to whom the rest looked up to as a natural born leader; Elmer Overton, the Southern lad already mentioned; the

one called "Rooster" by his chums, and whose real name was Christopher Boggs; and last of all, a nervous fellow going under the queer nick-name of "Hanky Panky," when at home he was registered on the roll of the high school as Henry Jucklin.

One of his favorite pastimes was the practice of the Black Arts; for Henry aspired to be a magician, and already, in the estimation of his admiring chums, he could vie with the famous wizard, Hermann, in sleight of hand, freeing himself from ropes that had been wrapped around him and knotted; and all such things calculated to bewilder the average mind.

When he dazzled some of his mates with his expositions of transforming a handkerchief into a pocket-knife; or restoring one that he had apparently burned right before the eyes of the owner, he was accustomed to using certain phrases in which the words "hanky panky" occurred, and by degrees the boys had corrupted his former nick-name of Hank into this queer "handle."

These five lads belonged in the thriving town of Garland, situated not far from the center of the State of Ohio. Those who read the preceding volume of this series, and have thus already made their acquaintance, will recognize old friends in the owners of the up-to-date motorcycles that had been brought to a stop in this wild region of Tennessee.

For the benefit of any new readers it may be only fair to relate how these lads came to possess such costly toys, worth possibly a couple of hundred dollars each.

During a flood, when the river that ran past their home town was on a boom, they had discovered the wreck of a house floating down the swift current, and upon this was a man, frantically waving his arms, and calling for help.

The boys had succeeded in rescuing the one who was in deadly danger, and who proved to be a rich old recluse named Amos Tucker, who, soured with the world for some reason or other, had lived almost alone.

Perhaps his nearness to death may have aroused the old man, and caused him to look at things in a different light; for to the great astonishment and delight of Rod and his four chums, there had come a notice one day that if they called at the freight station of the railroad they might each of them take away a splendid motorcycle that had arrived from the factory, charges all prepaid.

Of course they quickly suspected who had sent these wonderful presents, and upon interviewing the rich old man in his new home found that sure enough he had discovered how it was a dream with the boys to some fine day own such a machine for spinning over country roads; and in order to partly pay back the debt he felt he owed them, he had sent for the five latest models in motorcycles.

Nor was this all, for in the bank he had deposited to the order of Rod Bradley the magnificent sum of a thousand dollars, which was to be drawn upon from time to time, as their expenses for the care and maintenance of their machines, or a desire to take trips abroad, warranted.

When good fortune starts coming it often pours, and so it happened that Rod and his friends had been chiefly instrumental in following a pair of precious rogues who had broken into, and robbed the Garland bank, only a couple of weeks previous; and not only securing their arrest, but returning the stolen securities and cash intact.

For doing this they received a reward of five thousand dollars, which was split evenly with a farmer named Bi-jah Spruggins, who had rendered them great assistance in making the round-up.

So it may be readily seen that their treasury was full and overflowing, and that when Rod proposed they accompany their chum, Elmer Overton, who was bent on taking a flying trip down through Ohio and Kentucky, to his old home not a great distance from Chattanooga in southern Tennessee, every one of the others agreed to the plan, without a dissenting murmur; indeed, they were fairly wild about it, even Rooster, who was the poorest rider of the lot.

Possibly a word of explanation may not come in amiss regarding that strange cognomen that had been fastened upon the Boggs boy. Whenever Christopher felt in a happy frame of mind, or his team had accomplished something worth while, he invariably slapped his hands against his thighs, to make a sound like a rooster that has flown up on the upper rail of a fence flapping its wings, and then he would proceed to give the finest imitation of a crow ever heard. Under the circumstances it was a foregone conclusion that his schoolmates would quickly forget he ever had such a name as Christopher; and from that day until the end of the chapter he must answer to the suggestive one of "Rooster."

They had not attempted anything like great speed while on the trip. Indeed, save when passing over those fine roads in the celebrated Blue Grass country in Central Kentucky such a thing would have been practically impossible; for as a rule they passed over very poor thoroughfares, where it seemed next to a miracle that the clumsy rider, Rooster, had not come to grief more than once.

Up to now they had managed to strike a town or village when night came on, and so found accommodations at

Proud Harley-Davidson rider, 1930.

a tavern. But this promised to be an experience of a different character; for Josh had discovered something wrong with his machine, that would necessitate immediate attention; and when Rod proposed that they camp out for a change, every fellow eagerly agreed.

They had come prepared for such an undertaking in-so-far as having the means for gratifying their desire for food went, though without tent or blankets. But then the weather was warm, and they could keep their camp- fire going, if they felt disposed.

And so Rod had halted them near a little stream that gurgled along the side of the road, and which promised to supply water for their coffee. Each one had something securely hidden away in his bundle that, when brought to light, seemed to promise a fairly decent supper.

"Here's the coffee-pot, and inside of it a package of the best Java we could buy in old Cincinnati as we came through!" called out Josh, as he started to undo his package.

"And this frying-pan looks like it just wanted to get busy right away with these slices of fine juicy ham!" echoed Rooster.

Each of the others announced the finding of certain articles of food, which were placed near where the fire had already been kindled by Rod.

Soon the scene was a bustling one, with each of the boys trying to do what they could to hasten the cooking of supper—all but Josh, who was kneeling alongside his motorcycle and apparently starting to get to work remedying the fault that had been giving him anxiety.

Chapter 11

Living Harley

From my mother I learned to write **prompt thank-you notes** for a variety of occasions; from Mrs. King's ballroom dancing school I learned **a proper curtsy** and, believe it or not, what to do if presented with nine eating utensils at the same place setting, presumably at the home of the hosts to whom I had just curtsied.

From motorcycles I learned practically everything else.

—Melissa Holbrook Pierson, *The Perfect Vehicle: What It Is About Motorcycles*, 1997

Rolling Thunder

By Michael Perry

Michael Perry has been a farmer, cowboy, registered nurse, firefighter, backpacker, and reporter. As a writer, his work has appeared in numerous publications, including *Esquire, the New York Times Magazine, Salon,* and *Cowboy Magazine*, and his essays and humor are frequently heard on both Wisconsin and Minnesota public radio.

He is the author of several books, including *Population: 485: Meeting Your Neighbors One Siren at a Time; Big Rigs, Elvis & The Grand Dragon Wayne*; and *Why They Killed Big Boy & Other Stories*.

This essay comes from his *Off Main Street: Barnstormers, Prophets & Gatemouth's Gator*. It chronicles a small group of Vietnam veterans who in 1988 rode their motorcycles through Washington, D.C., to protest the U.S. government's abandonment of prisoners of war and soldiers missing in action. Since then, the protest—known as Rolling Thunder, in reference to the sound of the bikes and the massive bombing campaign carried out during the Vietnam War—has grown to include more than 270,000 participants.

Midnight at the Wall. We enter on an incline, descend past the first thin sliver of names, then edge silently downward to the darkened vertex, the incline running deeper and the sliver widening until the names stretch beyond the reach of a tall man. A smattering of candles flutter along the footpath and set the polished Bangalore marble to gleaming like sheets of black ice. But if you lean in close and turn your head, as if listening for the names, you'll see the candlelight caught in a film of fingerprints. The satin marble face—cool and smooth as lacquer—invites touch. Few people are drawn to the Wall without being drawn to touch it, and the prints are trace elements of this instinctive ritual.

But then your fingertips come to rest on a sandpapery row of etched letters. The letters form a name. You think of the mother then, cradling the baby, speaking that name. Then you conjure a young man's face to match. The image is necessarily incomplete, necessarily ghostly. And then you find yourself wondering what you might have been doing that day in '59, or '68, or '75 when—still young—he fell. The power of the Wall is in those names—a silent roll call grit-blasted into the stone to remind us that we are not honoring an abstraction, we are honoring 58,214 comrades; each with a life, each with a death. Each with a name.

But there are names missing. And so early the next morning, after four hours of sleep, here I am on the tail of an Eighty-fifth Anniversary Edition Harley-Davidson driven by a sharpshooting ex-marine everyone calls Murdoch, wind slapping at my ears, rolling up Interstate 66 toward Washington, D.C. The sun is risen and the land is green, but it's early, and the cold air stiffens my knuckles. A staggered double line of dancing headlights trails us in the mirror. And running right behind them, looming like the mother ship, is a big black Class 8 Volvo semi tractor. Most of the guys in this motorcade had a hand in building that Volvo as part of UAW Local 2069, and they've brought it with them to help honor the names you don't see on the Wall, the prisoners of war and missing-in-action soldiers who never came home.

By 7:45 a.m. we pull into a fifty-eight-acre parking lot outside the Pentagon. There are already several thousand bikes in line. It'll be a noisy day. Then I think of the names on the Wall, and the names not on the Wall, and I think, well, it oughta be noisy.

The bikes—Harleys, mostly—roll in for hours, in fits and starts at first, but then in a steady, rumbling stream. By 11 a.m., the overpass leading to the parking lot is swarmed with spectators; like a gaggle of flightless birds, they perch chockablock on the railing, flock the sidewalks, and spill down the grassy slope overlooking the swelling sea of cycles below. The bikes are packed cheek by jowl, clicking and cooling, canted on their kickstands in ranks roughly ten abreast. Riders milling around on foot lend the scene a sort of constant motion. They check out each other's bikes, snap pictures, reunite with friends. There are a lot of bare arms, a lot of tattoos. A group of eight riders who look like a bad stretch of highway are holding hands and leading each other in prayer. Artie Muller, Rolling Thunder's founder, stands alone in the center of a clear spot, surrounded by lights, cameras and satellite gear, all rigged up in a C-SPAN headset, answering questions none of us can hear. It's overcast now, but warmer. The bikes keep coming.

At high noon a cluster of red, white and blue balloons rises into the air and the parking lot begins to rumble. Beneath me, the seat shudders as Murdoch fires up the Harley. One row over, a long, tall biker with skin to match his leathers pogos up and down on the kick starter of his chopper, a rough hunk of work that looks more like a plumbing project than a motorcycle. He runs out of breath and a buddy strides over to help him. The buddy is heavier, and when he brings his full weight down on the kick bar, the bike backfires, then chugs to life. For a while, while we wait to get moving, the exhaust becomes a little overpowering, but everyone is too keyed up to care.

When we finally swing out toward Arlington Memorial Bridge, and I catch my first glimpse of the spectators, I feel a thrill. And when Murdoch snaps off a salute to a solitary middle-aged Ranger standing at ramrod attention, the thrill turns to tightness in my throat. I get that feeling all along the route.

We swing right at the Lincoln Memorial, rumble up Independence Avenue, hang a left around the Capitol and cruise the home stretch down Constitution Avenue. I remember the trip in glimpses: the family, curbside, holding a homemade sign: *Where Is Private Jack Smith?* Clenched fists, raised alongside peace signs. Murdoch exchanging "Hooah!s" with grinning marines. Kids with flags. A man in fatigues, with a quiet face, just watching. Murdoch rapping the engine, and the echoes splattering back from the government buildings. The smell of overheating engines, hot clutches.

And then it's over. National Park Service police on horses direct us onto the grass of the Mall. Murdoch and I leave the bike, double back and catch a ride on the back of the Volvo. Then we end up sitting in the grass beneath a tree. I remark on the irony of so many Vietnam vets being here, on the very ground where their actions were so vehemently opposed. The protested have become the protesters. He agrees, but points out that many of the original protesters show up to support Rolling Thunder. "They realize the soldiers did what they were told," he says. "They were called, and they went."

In this age of declining postmodern irony, it is fashionable to dismiss such loyalty as gullible foolishness or blind jingoism. But to do so is to deny a cold truth: Vietnam may have been a mistake, but the loyalty of the troops misused there still underpins our very existence. The time will come when it is required again, and if you have grown used to freedom, you better pray someone is still willing to risk theirs for yours. Like it or not, deny it or dismiss it, eventually you need someone willing to do a little dirty work in defense of the ivory tower and the well-groomed suburb. Murdoch and I talk a long time, then walk to the Wall. The bikes are still rolling across the Memorial Bridge.

On Monday, a few of us returned to the Wall for a memorial service. The speakers on the dais were joined by an empty chair draped with a pair of fatigues, a helmet, and a set of boots. It was a reverent coda to the previous day's thunderous remembrance.

When I got back home, I tried to describe the thunder of 270,000 motorcycles, the passion in the peace signs and fists and salutes, and the desolate power of the names, and the empty boots. Mostly people were polite, but their eyes took on that wary glaze we reserve for street preachers and proselytizing relatives, and I had just the faintest taste of what it must have been like to return from the jungle in '68 and search for a sympathetic ear.

When you face the Wall at midnight, the Washington Monument is all lit up at your back, standing clean as a butcher's bone and solid as a compass pointing the way to Glory. It is a monument to look up to, a monument to remind you of all this country ever hoped to be. The Wall, on the other hand, is cut darkly into the earth. To see the Wall, you have to hunker down and peer into the marble until you find your own face looking out, strung with names.

PS: In *All Quiet on the Western Front*, Kropp proposed that wars be resolved by having the leaders dress in swimming trunks and beat each other with clubs. It does not happen, and we find ourselves back on the overpass, waving at our neighbors as they depart on our behalf.

It felt so good to be out on the open highway that he wondered why he hadn't split before. He glanced over at Treb and their eyes met for a second. It was like communication without words. They were a team, no doubt about it. The two strong Harley engines were beating like one. The sound made a rhythm that played in your head like a sweet dream.

—Robert "Bob Bitchin" Linkin, *A Brotherhood of Outlaws*, 1981

Early Harley-Davidson advertising posters. *Courtesy Harley-Davidson*

The Outlaw Impulse

By Darwin Holmstrom

Darwin Holmstrom has worshipped at the Church of Motorcycology since the anterior fontanel at the top of his infant skull began to harden. He rode his first minibike at the age of six and got his first dirtbike at eleven. He took his first long-distance trip ten years later, to the motorcycle rally in Sturgis, South Dakota, back before the advent of the Evolution engine. Since then, he has toured nearly every state in the continental United States, along with a handful of Canadian provinces. He has logged well over 500,000 motorcycle miles and is a member of the Iron Butt society. A debilitating road-racing crash at Brainerd International Raceway's infamous Turn One ended his budding career as the world's slowest motorcycle road racer and taught him to appreciate forward-mounted foot controls.

Darwin has authored, coauthored, and contributed to a number of motorcycle books, including *The Complete Idiot's Guide to Motorcycles*, *Honda Gold Wing*, *BMW Motorcycles*, *Harley-Davidson Century*, and *Billy Lane Chop Fiction*. His most recent book and his first non-motorcycle title, *Muscle: America's Legendary Performance Cars*, is a history of muscle cars coauthored with Randy Leffingwell. His work has appeared in numerous motorcycle magazines, including *V-Twin*, *Motorcycle Cruiser,* and *Motorcycle Consumer News*. He served as the Midwestern editor of *Motorcyclist* magazine from 1997 until 2001, during which time he pounded several long-term Buell test bikes into dust. He lives in a heavily armed compound in central Minnesota with his wife and dogs.

Since Hunter S. Thompson wrote his seminal book on outlaw motorcycle culture, *Hell's Angels: A Strange and Terrible Saga*, the entire world has been turned inside out. Today, sex and drugs, and anything else that hints at pleasures of the flesh, are taboo subjects, while war and rigid adherence to the status quo are considered the highest goals toward which a human can aspire. What was once deemed obscene is now noble.

Where does the motorcycling culture fit into all this? Like society at large, the motorcycling world has been flopped on its watery head. When Thompson wrote *Hell's Angels*, Harley-Davidson motorcycles were archaic remnants of an earlier time, well on their way to becoming jokes to the broader motorcycling community. Riding a Harley was not sport; it was a political statement. Harley riders knew their machines were fat, slow, unreliable, over-priced, and what the hell were you going to do about it? Trying to debate functionality with many Harley riders was as likely to find you picking your teeth out of your own lower intestinal tract as it was to instigate meaningful discourse. If you wanted to meet nice people, you associated with Honda riders, not Harley riders.

Then things changed. We got Richard Nixon and Watergate; we got Ronald Reagan, AIDS, and the war on drugs. And we got the Harley-Davidson Evolution engine. It still looked like a Harley engine, sounded like a Harley engine, shook like a Harley engine, and even smelled like a Harley engine. But it was a completely different animal. No longer did you need to have the ability to overhaul the top end alongside the road in the dead of night with nothing but an adjustable wrench and a Zippo lighter. Suddenly any mechanically inept fool with a good line

of credit could park his bad ass aboard the quintessential outlaw machine.

This changed everything. People were becoming more conservative; they were forced to lead more rigidly conforming lifestyles. Yet the basic human instinct to rebel against conformity remained intact, if buried deep within our collective psyche. In the mid-1980s, finding expression for that urge grew increasingly difficult. It was no longer socially acceptable to go out and have promiscuous sex for fear of contracting some horrible disease, or to go out and indulge in the drug of your choice for fear of having annoying friends and family members do an intervention and admit you to some mind-numbing rehab clinic. Along came Harley-Davidson at just the right moment, with a machine that carried the stench of outlaw, minus the real baggage of life outside societal norms, and minus the need for any prerequisite mechanical aptitude. Outlaw lite.

Fast forward fifteen years. We are in the initial spasms of a new millennium. Hedonism is making a cautious comeback attempt, but by and large we are a nation of aging boomers too old for serious debauchery and Reagan babies who do not even know the meaning of serious debauchery. Your average biker is about as much a rebel as Ward Cleaver. He goes to work on time, pays his taxes, and seldom fornicates outside the sanctity of marriage. He even drives at the speed limit, often while hogging the left lane. Though he enjoys his Budweiser and may, on occasion, still burn a fatty when his old high-school buddies come to visit, his only real vice is using the cell phone while driving.

Yet each weekend he dons a leather vest sporting the "Harley Owner's Group" patch, applies his henna tattoos,

starts calling his domestic partner "the ol' lady," drops the g's from his gerunds, and roars off on his Harley, parading along at 5 miles per hour under the legal limit from tavern to tavern with his peers. This man has likely earned, at the very least, a degree from a technical college. He may even be an accomplished professional, though the lawyer and doctor bikers are nearly as mythological as the few remaining one-percenters who populated Thompson's book. More likely he hangs Sheetrock, drives a Metro Transit bus, or manages a restaurant. He may even be a she, since many more women ride today than did in 1967, when *Hell's Angels* was first published. And for all his (or her) attempts to portray an outlaw image while aboard his Harley, at best he portrays a caricature of an outlaw biker. His riding is not sport; it is a pantomime performance of his outlaw biker ideal.

This may seem silly, but it is understandable. For most of us, the option of continuing to live the real outlaw lifestyle was not there. Our bodies gave out, we became impoverished, we landed in prison. Billy and Wyatt died at the end of *Easy Rider* for a reason. Had they lived, they likely would have ended up in some dismal trailer court in Fontana, penniless and bikeless—if they were lucky. In an even more likely scenario, they would have ended up in a hideous southern prison, serving life sentences for passing bad checks under some draconian three-strikes-and-you're-out law. Or else they would have become fat old men, pontificating in various 12-step groups. They would have long since ceased being the beautiful biker poets depicted in the movie. No, it was better they went out in a blaze of glory at the hands of redneck duck hunters in some nameless Louisiana swamp. Sometimes it really is best to "ride hard, die young, and leave a good-looking corpse."

But for most of us, our corpses would not have been good-looking enough to warrant an early death. We soldiered on, accepting the ever-increasing limitations placed on us by a more conservative society. We abandoned the sex, drugs, and rock and roll of our youth and accepted the yoke of responsibility, sacrificing our free-wheeling ways in the name of comfort and security. Still, somewhere deep inside, we feel that old outlaw itch, an itch most of us are unwilling to scratch with reckless abandon. Harley-Davidson provides us with a socially acceptable poultice to help alleviate that itch.

Left: Billy Lane leads the pack to Tybee Island, Georgia. *Photograph © Russ Bryant*

Harley-Davidson lineup, circa 1920s.

Harley-Davidson family scrapbook,
circa 1910s–1920s.

Night Riding

By Biker Billy

Best known by his Biker Billy nom de plume, Bill Hufnagle is as prolific as an author as he is logging miles on his Harley-Davidson.

Billy is the author of two cookbooks—*Biker Billy's Hog Wild on a Harley Cookbook: 200 Fiercely Flavorful Recipes to Kick-Start Your Cooking From Harley Riders Across the USA and Biker Billy Cooks With Fire: Robust Recipes from America's Most Outrageous Television Chef*. He also pens a column appearing monthly in numerous local motorcycle magazines.

This essay sums up the glory of riding a Harley with all the eloquence of a V-twin's own roar.

The moon, just past its zenith, hung like a giant eye in the ether. Full and bright in the pale night sky, it wore the wispy clouds like a shawl against the moisture-laden air. Viewed from the corner of my eye as I dove into a curve, it for an instant took on the shape of an enormous squid. Tendrils stretched out to capture me as the bike and I swam in the waters of the warm summer night. With a sharp downshift and a growling crack of the throttle I narrowly escaped into the shadow of the mountain. No easy meal to be had of this biker.

Off into the sultry night I roared, my headlight playing amongst the shadows along the edge of the road. Just like the moon sometimes turns into a creature of the night, the shadows are at once merely darknesses yet to be penetrated by my headlight and mysterious forms threatening to leap into the path of my front wheel. While I know the illusions the moon casts upon my ride are always just stellar fantasies, the shadows are another thing entirely. At least once each time I answer the call of the night ride, a shadow sprouts eyes, takes on solid form, and darts across my path in the endless dance of life and death.

It is late and I have this ribbon of asphalt all to my-self—that is, except for that one creature, which tonight is a possum that scurries along the relative safety of the shoulder and never dares to tempt the front wheel. I am thankful for its choice to not dance with me this time. On this late summer night, I am content with the company of the moon; perhaps its fullness and the resultant tidal pull are what invited me to ride. But then, I don't need much

of an invitation to ride in the wee hours of the night. Always a night owl, I have ridden while the world sleeps since the beginning.

The night is my friend, my confidant, and my solace when the daytime world crowds me with work and stress. The road is my favorite drug. What a rush to consume mile after mile of intoxicating asphalt, both invigorating and soothing; I am addicted. By night the road is also a wild animal. Tonight it is a snake draped across the landscape, its smooth surface punctuated by bright yellow dots. As I race along its back, following the pattern of its skin, I am aware that at any moment it could whip around and bite me. It is in that edge of risk and that need to see where the road-snake heads that the attraction lies. At night the scenery is reduced to an almost black-and-white shadow play, which serves to bring the road into beautiful Technicolor focus.

But the night ride is so much more than drug or beast. It is a pathway through time, a portal into my memory and a touchstone in my life. Many a crossroad or complex juncture of existence has been sorted out on night rides. In the darkness of indecision, my headlight has led me to see the solutions and has illuminated the decisions I needed to make. The road and the moon are always there when I need them.

Yet the night ride is not always a medicinal. Sometimes it is just candy, a treat after a long day of toil, boredom, and heat. The rich summer air is like water rushing across my skin, like swimming—only better. It cleanses the senses and refreshes the lungs. The vibrations of the

Harley-Davidson family scrapbook,
circa 1910s–1950s.

motor massages my sore muscles, the gentle manipulation of the handlebars works the kinks out of my shoulders and neck. The sweet perfume of honeysuckle sugarcoats the donut of rich green and brown earth smells that surrounds me. It is a calorie-free delight.

Other times it is passion and foreplay, arousing the senses so completely. While a night ride sometimes takes you off into the ether of deep thought, other times it centers you in your physical reality. It stimulates your nerve endings and connects the Chakras of your body so that your spiritual energy flows freely. Then the road takes on the voluptuous curves of the earth mother and becomes a virtual outline of an ancient fertility goddess. Long ago, buried in our genetic memory, there is a caveman who—inspired by the force of life—carved a primitive sculpture shaped like a Venus. If he had wheels, surely they would have carried him home to his cave where he would slide under the sabertooth-tiger-skin covers, do what came naturally, and become our collective ancestor. Sometimes one good ride begets another.

Just like your bike needs to have its pipes blown clean from time to time by a full-throttle dash towards the horizon, your mind has the same need. At those times when your brain is fried, your creativity blocked, and your thought processes stymied, you need a good long night ride. It truly is a miracle cure. A few dozen miles along a peaceful country road at a comfortable pace will take only a short piece of time, yet it can be more relaxing than a two-week vacation. There is no stress of travel arrangements and scheduling. There's no backlog of work awaiting you on your return. And talk about bargains—even at today's outrageous gas prices, a tank full of premium is dirt cheap compared to a trip to the islands. It is just what the doctor ordered.

Night rides always work for me; whatever ails me is sure to come into its proper perspective. While the moon watched me ride just out of its reach tonight and the possum decided not to tempt the fate of my front wheel, I found the cure for my writer's block and this essay magically appeared on my computer.

The real cycle you're working on is a cycle called yourself.

—Robert M. Pirsig, *Zen and the Art of Motorcycle Maintenance*, 1974

Joe Namath

oving, brawling and bustin' it up!

Joseph E. Levine presents An Avco Embassy Film starring

JOE NAMATH & ANN-MARGRET
as C.C.Ryder   as his girl   in

C.C.AND COMPANY

AN AVCO EMBASSY EXHIBITORS' SHOWMANSHIP M

The roar of their pipes their battle cry...the ope road their killing groun

THE Savage Seven

THE DEADLIEST OF ALL THAT VIOLENT BREED...THEY'LL TURN YOUR TOWN INTO AN ARENA OF TERROR AND SHAME

7

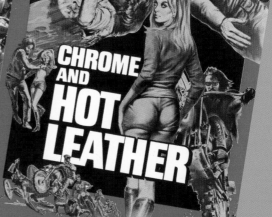

DON'T MUCK AROUND WITH A GREEN BERET'S MAMA!

He'll take his chopper and ram it down your throat!

CHROME AND HOT LEATHER

AN AMERICAN INTERNATIONAL RELEASE

Harley-Davidson family scrapbook, circa 1920s.

We want to make good time, but for us now this is measured with emphasis on

"good"

rather than "time" and when you make that shift in emphasis the whole approach changes. Twisting hilly roads are long in terms of seconds but are much more enjoyable on a cycle where you bank into turns and don't get swung from side to side in any compartment. Roads with little traffic are more enjoyable, as well as safer. Roads free of drive-ins and billboards are better, roads where groves and meadows and orchards and lawns come almost to the shoulder, where kids wave to you when you ride by, where people look from their porches to see who it is, where when you stop to ask directions or information the answer tends to be longer than you want rather than short, where people ask where you're from and how long you've been riding.

—Robert M. Pirsig, *Zen and the Art of Motorcycle Maintenance,* 1974

Mitch Bergeron rides the desert. Photograph © Russ Bryant

We say that the world's **magnificence** has been enriched by a **new beauty:** the beauty of speed. . . . **Time and Space died yesterday.**

We already live in the absolute, because **we have created eternal, omnipresent speed.**

—Filippo Marinetti, Futurist philosopher, 1909

Impatient to ride, circa 1930s.

Sitting pretty on his Harley-Davidson V-twin, a proud rider strikes a cool pose, circa 1920s.